A Soul's Guide to
Abundance, Health And Happiness

Jody Howard

© 2006 Jody Howard
All Rights Reserved

Dedications

This book is dedicated with eternal love and gratitude to four of my earth angels:

*My best friend and husband Johnny, who patiently listened to me and lovingly supported me as I wrote this book, and who has always encouraged me to express my true self
and follow my dreams.*

My beloved sons Josh and Jason, the greatest blessings in my life, who have always stood by me, believed in me, supported me, and gave me the courage, desire and reason to get through the darkest times of my life.

My dear friend and soul mate Jill, who was my sounding board, backbone, spiritual buddy, mental stimulator, mentor, biggest supporter, and most dedicated fan throughout the writing and completion of this book.

Gratitudes

*I extend my deepest thanks
to all my angels and guides
for their eternal and unconditional love,
immense patience, gentle guidance,
constant reassurance, and continuous protection.
Even if I were to thank them
every second of every day
it would not be often enough to express
the depth of my gratitude.*

*I am also extremely thankful to have three
very special soul mates and Earth Angels
to enhance and share my life with. Vicki, with her soft, gentle,
compassionate and nurturing energy,
Pearl, with her strong determination, courage and
playfully optimistic energy, and
Ofelia with her devoted, loving, hard working and tender energy.
Their love and friendship help me tremendously.*

*I also thank Melissa, Mary Ellen
and all the talented staff involved at Dixie Press
for their support and efficient work
on getting this book to print.*

Contents

Foreword   i

Part I
Your Spirituality

Chapter 1	Your True Self	3
Chapter 2	Spiritual Contracts	7
Chapter 3	Your Future	13
Chapter 4	A Closer Look at Death	17
Chapter 5	A Closer Look at Birth	21
Chapter 6	Your Past	25
Chapter 7	Cell Memory	29
Chapter 8	Past Lives	33
Chapter 9	Remembering Your Past Lives	39
Chapter 10	Communicating With Your Soul	43
Chapter 11	The Many Voices of Your Soul	47
Chapter 12	Oneness With God	57
Chapter 13	Channeling With Your Guides	63
Chapter 14	Methods of Channeling	69
Chapter 15	Surrendering to God	87

Part II
Your Mind

Chapter 16	Positive Thoughts	97
Chapter 17	Positive Affirmations	103

Chapter 18	Dreams and Sleep	109
Chapter 19	Meditation	125
Chapter 20	Live in the Moment	133
Chapter 21	Be Creative	141
Chapter 22	Be Playful	145

Part III
Your Emotions

Chapter 23	Love Yourself	153
Chapter 24	Be Love	159
Chapter 25	Let Go of the Past	165
Chapter 26	Everything is Perfect	173
Chapter 27	Be Thankful	179
Chapter 28	Forgiveness	183

Part IV
Your Body

Chapter 29	Energy	189
Chapter 30	Chakras, Meridians & Auras	195
Chapter 31	Checking Your Chakras	209
Chapter 32	Energy Influences	213
Chapter 33	Increasing & Protecting Your Energy	225
Chapter 34	Rocks and Crystals	239
Chapter 35	Essential Oils, Aroma Therapy, Rock and Flower Essences	247
Chapter 36	Vitamins and Minerals	275
Chapter 37	Herbs and Homeopathy	277
Chapter 38	Diet & Exercise	281
Chapter 39	Pamper Yourself	297
Chapter 40	Energy Healers	303

Suggested Reading Material	307

Foreward

*Unto you a gift is borne;
a gift of love and Light.
Live it, breathe it, share it.*

This is a time of an amazing new dawning, or recollection, of personal growth and expanded wisdom that reaches beyond technology, logic and matter. This expanded growth and wisdom unveils the secret to life itself, and to the greatest power in the universe... our inner wisdom and understanding.

Since the beginning of time we have had the ability to possess and connect to an unlimited supply of universal truth and wisdom, yet through the evolution of mankind and technology we slowly distanced ourselves from it more and more. Although technology has improved the quality of our lives, we are missing an important link to who we are and why we are here on earth if we don't look within ourselves for knowledge as well.

Our gut instincts have become suppressed as we seek the comfort of logical answers. We have grown more dependent on fact and reason than on our natural feelings. Personal power comes from within and intensifies when we develop and utilize our natural gifts. If we shut off the connection to our inner power we can not live a completely satisfying life. We will not be totally connected to our true self because there will always be a missing link. The power is still within each and every one of us and only needs to be realized, acknowledged, and acted upon to allow it to flow freely in our lives once again.

We all have unique gifts, talents, specialties, power and wisdom. When we consciously work toward rekindling and igniting our personal power we discover who we are and why we are here on earth. The first step is to simply awaken this reality within ourselves. As you begin to awaken your natural gifts, your life and the lives of your loved ones will be greatly enhanced. This awareness not only fulfills you completely, but it will begin to influence and affect everyone in your life. As you change and grow, your entire energy level begins to intensity. As more and more people begin to raise their energy levels, it affects the entire planet, creating a higher frequency energy vibration rich with peace, love, abundance, purpose, compassion and spirituality.

There are many levels to your existence. These levels include the spiritual, emotional, mental, physical, conscious, subconscious and energetic you. This book provides you with techniques for growth and healing in each of these areas. With growth and healing in all areas of your *being*, the birth of a new you will emerge. This exciting and phenomenal experience sheds a Light of understanding 'Who am I?' and answers the question, 'What is my purpose in life?' Thus, your true self is born and your life path becomes clear and precise.

As a healer, it is my passion to not only heal others, but to teach them how to heal themselves and their loved ones. When I started my own journey of self exploration I began reading book after book. Some books were wonderful, some repeated what I'd already learned, and others held only a small amount of new information. It was very frustrating, time consuming and expensive to read so many books. After reading over fifty different books, I began to understand that my life path included providing others with one book that would introduce readers to everything I had already learned.

When I call myself a healer it doesn't mean I am more powerful or qualified to heal you. There is no one more powerful or qualified to heal yourself than you. Being a healer does not mean you are perfectly healed and require no healing. Even healers need healing. Each and every one of us are healers, regardless of whether or not we choose a life path of healing. We all have an inborn knowledge of how to keep ourselves healthy, in fact our bodies do it without us even being aware of it most of the time. It is my desire to help you

Foreward

access and extract this knowledge from within yourself and put it into your consciousness.

Through the information and exercises in this book you will begin to heal yourself and open up those hidden secrets and that inner knowledge. As you begin to remember your own gifts, talents, and wisdom, life will become more fulfilling and you will want to be a teacher for others in their own awakening.

Self healing is a wonderful gift that dramatically enhances every aspect of your life and it is part of our growth spiritually, mentally, emotionally and physically. We must continually and constantly be healing ourselves if we are to continue growing. You will find that as soon as you think you have mastered one healing issue, a new one will pop up right in front of you. My advice is that you never think of your self-healing work as finished, for if you think this to be true, you have stopped growing and evolving. Healing is a life long process by which any amount significantly enhances your life. There is no goal other than to continue to grow and heal.

I purposely broke this book down into smaller sections. You can read it traditionally from front to back or read one chapter at a time. Reading one chapter a day allows more time for the information to be absorbed. Many of the chapters conclude with exercises designed to help you practice and incorporate the information into your daily life. Taking time to participate in the exercises will speed up the process. Read it all the way though or take it piece by piece. The most important thing is to apply what you learn. Remember that knowledge is only truly useful if it is acted upon. *Knowing it and doing it are two separate things.*

As you read through the pages of this book try to begin thinking outside your body, mind and emotions as you know them now. Allow yourself time to absorb the material, participate in the exercises, and put its content into action within your own life. Don't hurry through the changes and don't get frustrated if you forget the lesson or fall back into your old habits. It has taken years to create those habits and they won't go away just because you know the difference. Live your life with a conscious mind and be happy for every good change and growth you see within yourself. A little bit goes a long way.

A Soul's Guide to Abundance, Health And Happiness

This book contains a lot of information that may be new to you and your current way of looking at life and yourself. The contents have encompassed a wide variety of topics, each of which I only touch briefly upon. Take what feels right to you and be open-minded to the rest. In my own self-discovery I found certain topics jumped out at me as soon as I read them. I felt a *knowing* that it was a part of my own inner wisdom. When it's right, you will feel it with all your heart. If it doesn't feel right, consider it and then move on. We all have inner knowledge and we all have lessons to learn. Sometimes we're recalling wisdom deep within and other times we are acquiring new information. That is why it is so important to work together and help each other.

If you find a topic that seems to ring a bell or sparks your curiosity to learn more, I have included a section in the back of this book to give you suggested reading material. Each of the authors listed in this section have books that specialize in one particular topic.

Life is meant to be exciting, abundant and fulfilling. Each of us deserves to feel this way with each new day. I now invite you to begin a wonderful journey of self remembrance and self enhancement.

Part I

Your Spirituality

Remember who you are,
Admire the true self within.

Life's journeys take you far,
As your new life will begin.

Suppress your own control,
Surrender each task to God.

Please listen to your soul,
Even though it may seem odd.

True happiness is there,
The secret to life is found.

No longer you'll despair,
For peace and love will abound.

Chapter 1

Your True Self

*Your body is a temple;
your soul the inner sanctuary.*

When I first started writing this book I intended for this section to be later in the book, not because it lacked importance but because I was putting more emphasis on energy and how you can use it to heal yourself. It wasn't until I began writing that I realized everything begins and ends with spirituality.

I'm not talking about your religious preference, for that is entirely different from your spirituality. It doesn't matter what religion you choose to follow or if you even choose a religion. What is important is that you are connected to God spiritually and completely. Only then can you find the meaning to life and discover your true self.

The spiritual side of you is the real you, your true self, where you came from and where you are going. Once you meet your true self, we can talk about all the modalities associated with healing your emotional, mental, and physical body and create a life as fulfilling and abundant as possible for you.

As you connect with your spirituality you begin to understand your true self and the person you are intended to be. When you discover your true self beneath that shell of a body and mind, you will know complete and utter peace, understanding, fulfillment and joy. No longer will you feel hopeless, helpless, depressed, stagnant, lonely or abandoned. God is the essence of all that is and He is the life force within your soul. Without Him and your spirituality we could not go any further with this book and what I hope to teach you about inner healing.

Before you came into this world, you were a soul. At that time, you and your Creator made plans for your life on earth. Those plans were for spiritual growth and learning objectives to be worked on in this lifetime. To think that you merely exist here on earth with no specific job other than basic survival is not true and can make you feel unimportant and make your life seem meaningless.

Realizing that you already have specific plans for yourself gives your life purpose and brings meaning to everything you experience. The truth is, you are extremely important and you have a job to do that reaches far beyond your physical body and mind. Your true essence is of your soul. It is through your soul, not your mind and body, that your life should revolve. Your beautiful soul that is unlike any other, is the real you... your true self. Remembering the life lessons and life path you planned for your soul will help you find your true self and begin living each moment with purpose, importance and direction.

We all have our own unique purpose for this life and our soul desperately longs to fulfill it. Discovering your own intended purpose for this life will be the first step toward beginning and fulfilling your life path. Once you begin to work on your chosen life path, you will know a joy, contentment, abundance and fulfillment like you have never known before.

Your true self is your soul. Your soul knows only love because it was created in the likeness of God. Your soul is perfect in every way and remains totally connected to God whether you are consciously aware of it or not. It is only through your mind and ego that you feel less than perfect or separated from God. Your soul knows nothing of fear, judgment, hatred, resentment, betrayal or self ridicule. These are all acquired through the human mind and ego.

Even though your true self is perfect and God-like, your mind and ego are constantly challenging this truth within you. For that reason, Parts II, III and IV of this book will concentrate on breaking those destructive mind-ego patterns. Those patterns are what keep you from feeling connected to your true self and create a barrier, or amnesia that prevents you from following your life path. They are the biggest challenges you have to face here on earth. This is not

Chapter 1

because they are difficult to heal but because most people aren't even aware of them. As you break away from these self sabotaging patterns you will be able to go deep within yourself and discover your true self. Once you discover your true self you will be able to live your life through your soul once again.

Knowing the truth, that your soul is perfect and always connected to God is the first step to living an abundant, harmonious, peaceful and fulfilling life. It is not impossible to break the destructive ego/mind patterns you have developed. You can do it. Anyone and everyone can do it. All you need is the willingness to put some effort, intention and desire into achieving it. You will feel honored and thrilled to meet your true self and to see the perfection that is, and always has been, within you. As you get more and more acquainted with your true self and allow it to shine forth over your mind and ego, you will begin to remember the accomplishments and knowledge it already holds for you. This information and understanding is what enhances every aspect of your life.

It is important to find that place of truth and Light within yourself and allow it to be the pilot instead of the passenger of your flight through this life. It is through your true self that you will begin to unravel the secrets of your life purpose and unfold the map of your life path.

Chapter 2

Spiritual Contracts

*You have chosen to awaken others
to the love, Light, and gifts they have within.
The power is within all people;
the gift must be borne unto them.*

When your soul decided what your personal growth and development issues would be in this life, you also chose to have people in your life that would help you grow, learn and fulfill your lessons. The two of you made what's called a spiritual contract or sacred contract with each other.

A spiritual contract is simply an agreement between two souls to help each other with their life lessons here on earth. It would be difficult to learn our lessons on our own and without help. Without help from others we could not create the best circumstances needed to learn our lessons. You have made many contracts with many different people. They are your soul mates here on earth.

Even though you chose those people to help you, that does not mean they're all going to be wonderful, nurturing, loving teachers and friends. Most people have a vision of their soul mates as being adored friends or loved ones. Although we maintain a few kindred spirits like that to be in our life, many of our highly successful and important teachers are people we find to be most challenging and difficult to live with or be around. The truth is they are also your beloved soul mates. The two of you chose that type of relationship for this life in order to create the best circumstances for growth and learning. At a soul level your relationship is completely opposite.

This is why we are often drawn to people that don't seem to be our type. Our soul knows the truth and guides us to come together.

For instance, if you chose to learn self empowerment, your best teacher could be someone who challenges you to become powerful. That person could have an overbearing, dictator-type personality, and may even try to suppress your own power by making you feel unempowered. We all know this isn't a very enjoyable person to be around and if you do not choose to get busy on self empowerment, that person could actually make you lose your confidence, self esteem and self empowerment. What could be a better way to learn something than to be challenged with opposing strength? Therefore, a person like that would be doing a wonderful job at helping you learn self empowerment, despite the fact that you probably feel very angry and upset with how they treat you.

If you chose to learn love, who would be a better teacher than someone who challenges you with hate or lack of love? If you are here to learn about trust, who better to teach you than someone who is untrusting or not trustworthy? Thus, some of our best teachers are those that characterize the complete opposite of what we are here to learn. Think back on your life and see what types of learning lessons you may have been, or could still be, working on. Some examples are issues of independence, saying no, standing up for your self, setting boundaries, self empowerment, learning love, sharing, forgiving, being compassionate, or patience. We have all chosen more than one issue to work on in this life so don't be alarmed if you think of several lessons for yourself.

When you begin to look at your life in this way, it becomes easier to understand why things have happened to you and why certain people are in your life. It can actually be fun to look back at all the relationships you've had throughout your life and analyze what each person did for you and your growth. When I started to look back at my past it gave me an entirely new way of seeing the people themselves, as well as what they did for me. Now, I enjoy reflecting on events and people in my life and I feel a sense of gratitude to everyone that helped me grow and learn, even those I used to resent and feel anger towards.

Many times when looking back at your life you can see patterns that seem to recur over and over again. Perhaps you had several bad

Chapter 2

relationships with people who seemed to be terrible partners. You could have thought something like "I keep picking losers over and over again", or "I must be a poor judge of people". It is actually quite the contrary. You did an excellent job at choosing the perfect person for you at that time in your life. You were not just picking losers, you were guided or drawn to the same type of partner because they were the best at teaching you your life lessons. You may have been in several similar relationships because you never completely mastered the lesson with the first partner. You had to find another teacher to finish the job.

This happened to me in my first four relationships with men. Each one had their own unique way of teaching me, but each man deceived me. For years I couldn't understand why, or how, I could repeatedly fall for men who were cheaters and liars. No doubt everyone who knew me was wondering the same thing. Each relationship started out loving and trusting but in time the deceit surfaced once again. I ended the relationships before I had truly learned the lesson so I was drawn to the same type of person and situation in order to continue learning.

Just as you have made spiritual contracts with others to be your teachers, there are people who have contracted you to be a teacher for them. At a soul level, they asked you to come into their life at a certain point in time to help them learn and grow. You made a contract with them to be their teacher and guide here on earth. These people are depending on you to fulfill your contract with them. It is just as important for you to fulfill the contracts you made to help others as it is for others to help you. No doubt you have already fulfilled many contracts with many people. Every contract doesn't have to involve something huge and heroic and they don't all create life changing issues. It can be something as little as making someone stand up for them self and tell you 'no' without guilt.

Have you ever known someone who constantly demanded your time or attention when you didn't feel like you had the time for them? They could have been teaching you how to say no, or stand up for yourself. Often when we do say no, we immediately begin to feel guilty about it. Similar feelings occur when we stand up for ourselves. There's nothing wrong with taking care of yourself first and taking care of others needs second, yet we feel more compelled to help others than ourselves. We feel selfish or unloving when we say no. Learning to say no without guilt is a common lesson to learn. If someone is challenging these feelings in you, you may have a spiritual contract with them.

A contract could also be a matter of creating feelings of independence for someone else. A teacher like that could seem selfish or uncaring when in fact they are doing their job perfectly. The student could get mixed feelings of being pushed away or abandoned. The teacher may have to come across as cruel and selfish to allow the student to gain their own independence and power. My parents continually taught me independence. I can remember many instances when I felt as though they didn't love me anymore because they were pushing me to be more independent. The truth is they were doing their job very well.

It is important to respect and honor the needs of others and their need for you to help them identify and fulfill their own contracts. We often learn lessons ourselves by helping others with their issues. I have always believed that *the best way to learn something is to teach it*. Pay close attention to times when you feel you are assisting others with their issues. Turn the table around and look deep within yourself to see if you aren't learning something similar or completely opposite.

If you feel you are fulfilling a contract with someone and it is creating a difficult or uncomfortable situation between the two of you, try to be as loving and nurturing as you can without jeopardizing the lesson itself. In other words, instead of becoming impatient or irritated with the other person, be the teacher who is compassionate and understanding of their feelings while continuing to get their lesson learned and the contract fulfilled. Since you may not truly understand the lesson they are working on, try not to make assumptions or hold intentions for their lesson. Once you put your energy into the outcome of someone else's life lesson, you are stepping over your boundaries. Your job is simply to create an atmosphere for learning. They are the ones who determine what their lesson is and how they will learn from it. The only lessons you need to dissect and understand completely are your own.

Remember, we are all one, and we are no better or worse than anyone else. Each of us works best under conditions of love and compassion and we can help each other best when we incorporate these qualities. We all have our lessons to learn on this earth and we are all doing different things to accomplish them. Nobody's lesson is bigger or smaller than our own. No one's lesson is harder or easier than another. We all need to work together and work with love as our basic grid. Love will uncover the truth and the Light in all of us and will make our journey on this earthly plane much easier to follow.

Next time you find yourself in an uncomfortable situation with someone else, look at the whole picture. See if there could be a deeper meaning or life lesson involved. If you feel pushed to do something you really don't want to do, it could be a lesson in saying no. If you feel unjustly accused of something, it could be a call for you to stand up for yourself. Pay attention to all situations you encounter. Center yourself in your heart and do what you feel is right for you. As long as your reactions come from your heart you will be able to stand your ground without cruelty, guilt or over reaction. Remember that your soul holds as much importance over the contracts you made with others as with the contracts others have with you.

Chapter Two Exercise #1
Before going on to the next chapter, reflect back on your life and see what *recurring* relationship patterns you can see within your own life. Make a list of the recurring patterns or issues you've dealt with. Give your opinion of what the lesson may have been and identify which people were your best teachers. Decide if you might currently be working on certain issues. Try to figure out what you could do to resolve and master those issues so they don't have to keep recurring.

Chapter Two Exercise #2
Create another list of times you could have been fulfilling a spiritual contract for someone else. Be sure to go back as far as you can and include everyone you've ever known; siblings, parents, relatives, friends, teachers, bosses and co-workers. You may even discover a contract you are still working on. You will be surprised with what you come up with and how you will begin to view those people differently from this point forward.

Chapter 3

Your Future

Knowing the truth is the first step to living it.

Now you know you are more than just a body. In fact, before you came to this earth you were a soul with no body, mind, physical appearance, or human emotion. Once your soul was born unto this earth, you entered a body and acquired all of those things. When you can begin to see yourself as more than just a body and mind, your soul begins to take front and center stage in every aspect of life. I like to think of my body as simply the shell that houses my soul and allows me to stay connected to the earth. Each time my soul enters this earthly plane it takes on a new shell with a new personality, mind, emotions and appearances.

The object in each life is to look inside your shell and discover time and again who you really are, your true self. It is then that you can fulfill your true life purpose and enhance your ability to learn all you came back here to learn. Before we connect with our soul it is constantly banging against our body trying to communicate with us, causing us much unnecessary grief and misery. By reading this book it is evident to me that you are already on your way to fulfilling your life purpose and renewing a connection to your soul. You have already begun to set your soul free from the bondage of your body and mind.

Let's examine the life of our soul from this day forward. We all know that our body will die one day, but what happens to your soul when your body dies? Your soul is constantly learning and evolving and therefore it will continue, even after it leaves your physical body. In fact, your soul is eternal and it will never die. You may be wondering how your soul will continue to learn without a mind. A soul is not capable of thought. It is only capable of feeling; and its only emotion is love. Without the distraction of mental chatter and human emotion, our soul can feel and know a constant truth.

When your body dies your soul moves on to heaven or as I call it, the spirit world. I personally use spirit world because there is no hell or purgatory and the word heaven is usually a third party to them. Call it the spirit world or call it heaven, the bottom line is that we all go to the same place and it is a Divine place of love and Light with no suffering. The suffering we endure here on earth with some of the choices and circumstances we must make for our evolvement is surely hell enough for our souls. God would never forsake us and send us to an eternal hell or punish us by sentencing us to doing time in purgatory. God is not even able to consider such places.

It is God's wish that we continue to evolve, grow and learn. He is love and goodness. How would our soul be able to continue evolving if we became stuck in one place for eternity? If we make poor choices and do not fulfill our life purpose, we will simply choose to return to earth and try it again. Sometimes events that would cause some to say "you're going to hell for that" are actually brave and noble ways to learn the lesson we are here to learn.

When you die and reflect back on your life you will see that all things had purpose and meaning. Upon your return to the spirit world you will be looking back to see 'how well' you did on earth. What you accomplished and what you did not accomplish will be very important to you. For example, if you planned to learn seven lessons while on earth and you only achieved five of them, nothing different happens to you when you pass, other than the knowledge that you did not finish what you set out to do. You will just have to choose another life once again in which to learn those lessons. Your soul will be happiest with itself if you learn them when you had planned to.

Wouldn't it be wonderful to reflect back on your earthly life with pride in knowing you did everything you wanted to do? I rarely procrastinate and would rather get as much done as possible. As my Mother often said, "Why put off until tomorrow what you can get done today". The spirit world is a time of reflection and evaluation.

Chapter 3

Your soul will be extremely pleased to look back on your earthly life and see that it accomplished what it set out to do.

Our earthly visits are similar to going to college. We set goals and learning objectives for ourselves. If we don't pass a class we must take that class over again until we do pass. Why not pass the first time around? Our earthly visits are much more difficult learning experiences than in the spirit world. On earth your soul is learning and growing just as it does on the other side, but there are many more obstacles, pressures, and consequences to pay here. Finding the true self within us and connecting to the truth of our spirituality can take years in itself and some souls won't even achieve that much in their human life. Be gentle and compassionate with yourself while on earth.

The spirit world is a place in which all souls gather between their earthly lives to not only reflect and recharge but to continue learning and growing. This place is home to your soul. The spirit world is ten times greater than the most beautiful, peaceful, content place your ego mind can imagine. The pressures and physical restrictions you have while on this earth are gone. There is no fear, guilt, worry, doubt or anxiety. These things simply dissolve and truth, wisdom and understanding unravel. It is a place of utter peace, harmony and balance. Your soul recharges and begins to reflect back and evaluate the human life it just left. It easily makes note of what lessons were learned and what lessons are left to learn. Your soul charts and recognizes every event and relationship you had during your earthly stay and makes sense of, and gives meaning to, everything you experienced. This is a time when any questions you may have had are answered and you see your earthly life as a whole picture.

You will be your own judge when you pass to the spirit world. There isn't a big courtroom where a God or a string of judges determine what you did wrong or right. There is no sentencing of your soul to do time for your sins and crimes. You are your own judge and will be the hardest on yourself for any actions you feel were inappropriate. Remember, some of the things you view now as a sin may be an important part of your life lessons and growth. Even if you look back and see things that were not planned and were not in your best interest, you will feel compassion toward your soul for doing the best it could. You will understand everything you did on earth and why you did it.

After spending as much time as you need in the spirit world, your soul may decide to make an entry back to earth in order to continue its growth and development. The period of time between earth visits is entirely up to you. Some souls may come back in ten earth years, while others may wait as long as a hundred years. Longer stays in the spirit world are more common. The choice is all yours.

Time as we know it on earth does not exist in the spirit world. A year's time on earth is merely moments in the spirit world. Your soul is continually learning, growing, and preparing itself for the next life. To think that your soul merely lives the life you are having now and then goes off to simply float around in heaven for the rest of all time, would mean that your soul will not grow, learn, evolve or develop beyond what you do or learn in this lifetime.

Chapter Three Exercise #1
Think about the accomplishments you have already made in this life. Decide what your soul will be pleased with when you return home to the spirit world once again?

Chapter Three Exercise #2
Take time to imagine the peace, love and harmony of the spirit world. Picture an existence with no negativity, pain, anger, hatred, worry or fear. Try to connect to the blissful feeling of being freed of any restraints your physical body now has. Even if you can only catch a glimpse of heavens perfection, remember that it is home to your soul.

Chapter 4

A Closer Look at Death

*Heaven is home to your soul,
and there's no place like home.*

The idea of death frightens many people and I find that very sad indeed. Everyone wants to know exactly what happens when they die. Not knowing what to expect is what causes the fear of death for many. The truth is there is nothing to fear and it will feel like going home once again for your soul.

When your soul is contemplating entering the earthly world once again it begins to make spiritual contracts with others as Guides. These Guides assist us in fulfilling our learning objectives. Your soul also chooses what type of parents, siblings, environment, geographical location, social status, soulmate relationships and so on it will have. Every detail is carefully planned out by you including how and when you will die. You must realize that *you* alone have already chosen every detail of your passing.

How, when and why we will die is all part of our plan for this life. Oftentimes our passing is a lesson in itself. Sometimes it can be a lesson for us and other times it can be a lesson for the loved ones we leave behind. Every aspect of our life has purpose and meaning, including our passing. The soul that passes to the spirit world is rewarded with instantaneous peace and love.

Death is only unpleasant and sad to the people left behind. For that reason, we associate death and dying with the way we feel each time we lose a loved one. We feel great loss and abandonment without them in our life. If we can focus more on the joy and happiness our deceased loved one now experiences, we could heal much quicker. Knowing our loved one has moved back home where there is no more human suffering and their soul is free once again should make us feel happy for them.

What exactly happens when you die? As soon as your physical body expires, your soul *easily* exits your body and returns home. There's no struggle or effort to it. Remember that heaven is home to your soul and earth is a place you visit. The instant your soul leaves the body it feels a great sense of relief. No longer carrying the weight of the physical body, human emotions, mental distress or pain it will be free once again.

Upon your return you will be greeted by many kindred spirits and familiar souls. They will be waiting for you and anxious to see you return home once again. It will be a fantastic reunion and a time of great celebration. You have just successfully completed a stay on earth and you have arrived back home. It will feel wonderful to see everyone again, and they will give you all the support, love and comfort you need to make the transition.

Don't think that your only loved ones are here on earth. You are not only lovingly bound to those souls on earth that you call friends and family. There are many souls in the spirit world that are equally loved by you and that hold undying love, compassion and respect for you. You can't possibly share every life with every soul you hold dear. When you die you will be surrounded by loving souls and it will feel more like you are coming home than leaving home.

In cases of extremely difficult or traumatic lives there can be a short period of counseling and nurturing in order to soothe and comfort the soul. In extreme cases, it is possible to go into a safe and secure cocoon-type state, where you are allowed time to rest, heal, and be comforted. Within the security and safety of your cocoon you are filled with the constant healing Light and love of God.

Suicide is another way of passing. Sometimes life becomes too unbearable or difficult to endure and a person decides to cut it short with suicide. Although the soul will suffer regret upon passing because it did not finish what it planned for that lifetime, there is no punishment other than that. Normally, there is a period of counseling and reassurance for that soul. The length of which depends entirely on the healing of the soul. Again, you will be the only judge

Chapter 4

of yourself and the life you lived on earth. A soul that chooses suicide will realize that it not only dropped the ball on its own lessons but on the contracts it had with others. Those contracts will now remain unfulfilled by their passing. The souls they made contracts with will have to find someone else to fulfill their spiritual obligations. It is possible that, on rare occasions, suicide could be a planned destiny for a soul. There may be a lesson to learn by not only the deceased but by others who shared their life.

Abortion is believed to be a form of death. Even though a soul was probably already assigned to that body, and then the choice to abruptly end that life was made, the soul will continue on. We can not kill a soul. A soul lives on for eternity. You already know that the true self is found within the soul, so how could it be possible to end the true life of a person? It simply stopped the life of that soul, at that time, and in that specific body. The soul will continue on and choose another time to enter this world.

Oftentimes the soul will return to the same mother if she chooses to give birth later on. A soul normally enters a body shortly before the time of birth. It may be assigned to that body before then but it generally does not enter until late in the pregnancy or right before birth. Just as a soul continues to live after the death of a body, it will continue even after abortion.

It is important to understand that there is no punishment or penalty to pay for choosing to have an abortion upon return to the spirit world. We all have the freedom of choice, and that person did what they felt was right. Bringing a new life into the world when it can not be cared for adequately isn't always the best thing. If you had an abortion you may still be struggling with your decision. Stop it. Do not beat yourself up any longer for the decision you made. You did what you thought would be best. Let it go. There will be no other consequence to pay for your action other than the hell you have already put yourself through, and isn't that enough!

In summary, passing from this life and arriving back home in the spirit world is a birth to your soul. Upon your arrival to the spirit world, there will be a celebration of many souls that are delighted to see you return home. You will feel a love and joy ten times more powerful than anything you've experienced on earth. Your soul will be free again.

Chapter 5

A Closer Look at Birth

*Admire the courage of your soul
for choosing to be born into your body.*

When a soul enters the human body it is quite different than when it leaves. Upon leaving it simply floats out of the body and goes back home. As a soul enters a body it goes through some distress because it is leaving a place of peace, harmony, freedom, and constant connection with God. That tiny little newborn body feels constricting and helpless to the soul. Imagine yourself now, dropping into an infant body. You can't communicate with words, you have little control over your body movements and functions, and you can't even feed or care for yourself. You are totally dependent on others to care for you. It may feel as though you were just locked in a jail cell and all your freedom was taken away from you.

At the time of birth the soul of a baby remains very connected to the spirit world, but it slowly begins to loose that connection as time continues. A baby's physical life support depends entirely on earthly beings. To survive, it must begin to adapt to the environment and people who are raising it. Slowly it disconnects spiritually and reconnects to this new world.

As our soul connects to our new world, we begin to see ourselves the way others imagine us to be. In order to survive we accept and mirror their images, even if our soul feels otherwise. Our parents teach us how to act, what is wrong, what is right, how to think and feel, and so on. We have to learn everything about our environment and the world in which we live. The inner knowingness and knowledge of our soul gets pushed back more and more over time as we mirror ourselves through the eyes of others. Because of this, we slowly disconnect from the spirit world and begin to lose our true self.

It takes much courage and bravery to return to earth once again. Your soul knew what was going to happen when it made plans for a return visit. Imagine knowing the years of growth, learning, and detachment that would come with entering another human body, and still doing it! You have to pat yourself on the back for that alone. Now, imagine how happy your soul is when you've endured all those years and are beginning to awaken to the Truth within you once again. You made it. The power of your soul is re-ignited once again, despite all the obstacles and distractions along the way. Remembering the truth of your spirituality, your true self, is a major accomplishment for your soul. Way to go!

There are a few instances when a soul will enter a body that is not a newborn baby. This type of entry is called a "walk in". Walk-ins occur when the soul of a body decides it wants to go home early. To be brief, a soul may decide it has had enough of its human life and knows it will not get any more lessons learned. Perhaps it's just tired and has given up hope for finishing its learning objectives. Because that soul made spiritual contracts with others, it is important that those contracts be filled. At this time another soul can make the choice to enter that body and take over. That new soul will have to commit to living the life of the other person and fulfilling their contracts. The original soul floats off to the spirit world and the new soul takes over.

The switch often takes place at the time of an accident, illness or surgery. You will often notice a difference in the way that person acts, feels or thinks after the switch. Perhaps you know of someone that had a major shift in their personality. Often we will say that they seem like a whole new person. The person can seem full of life and spirituality after the switch. They can even display different characteristics about themselves. The old soul was feeling tired and therefore that weight was weighing heavy on their personality before the switch. The new soul is not tired and is eager to come to their aid. The new soul reflects a freshness and vitality that wasn't there before. Though this may seem very odd to you, it happens all the

Chapter 5

time. I had a difficult time with this concept at first but once I was aware that it could be possible, I began to notice evidence that it was true.

Miscarriage is way to stop the birth of a soul into human form. I have not had a miscarriage in this life but I understand how difficult it must be and how much pain it can cause a mother. Unlike an abortion where the mother makes the choice to stop the birth, miscarriage is a choice made by the soul of the unborn child. Knowing how difficult it must be to make the decision to come back to earth you must know that sometimes a soul will feel they need more time to prepare themselves for entry. This is called a 'pull out'. The soul had all the intentions of entering that body, but at the last minute made the choice to wait a little longer. The soul often comes back to the same mother, unless that mother decides not to have another child.

There can be many reasons for a soul to pull out including fear, birth order, lack of preparation, placement of the sun signs and more, but the important thing to remember is that it just wasn't ready yet. That soul wants to have the best circumstances and preparedness for its new life. It is unfortunate that the mother must endure such pain and heartache because of the pull out, but I'm sure the unborn soul would not choose to put its mother through this sorrow if it wasn't extremely important.

Chapter Five Exercise
Make a list the most difficult things you've already had to endure in this lifetime. Things like heartaches, depression, childhood traumas, illnesses, etc. Imagine the courage it took your soul to know what it was going to have to endure in this lifetime, yet it still made the decision to come back. Be proud of your soul's courage and be proud of what you've already achieved in this lifetime.

Chapter 6

Your Past

Listen to my soul rejoice,
for deep within I hear its voice.

When you realize that your soul continues to evolve even after this lifetime, it becomes easier to understand that this was probably not your first lifetime. Of course there are a handful of souls here for their first lifetime, but most of us have a past to our souls and many of us have thousands of past lives.

It may be hard to believe that your soul existed in another human form on this earth, but remember that it was merely your soul… not the physical body, mind and emotions that you currently have. You, in this human form, did not live a past life, your soul did. Your soul didn't have the personality you have now, and it lived in a completely different body doing different things in each life. In fact, you would be surprised to learn about the experiences your soul has been through. Some of those experiences may absolutely amaze you, while others may horrify you.

Since your soul has been continually growing, learning, and living different lives, it has a huge source of wisdom and understanding. Even though you may not consciously be aware of those past experiences, your soul remembers and therefore the knowledge is within you. Learning how to tap into these resources can aid you along in this life. The information of your soul is already a part of you, even if you aren't consciously aware of it.

Knowing you already possess a wealth of information from past experiences, you wouldn't want to re-learn and re-experience things you've already mastered. Without bringing that past knowledge into your consciousness this can happen time and again. That is why it is important to remember who you really are, your true self within.

Have you ever experienced a time when someone asked you a question and you came up with this unbelievably informative answer and you thought "now where did that come from?" You may have experienced picking up a new hobby, sport or interest and found that you were a natural at it. These are signals that you may have already learned these things. Even though the information may not be in your conscious mind, it can exist within your soul and can be most helpful to you during this lifetime.

When I first started learning about some of my past lives I was shocked to hear of those not-so-great lives. I was thinking that my past lives would have been similar to the way I see myself in my current life. I assumed that in most of my past lives I was happy, compassionate, loving, intelligent, and successful and that I was basically a good person. I figured that if I had thousands of past lives, I was probably always an evolved, enlightened, wonderful person, full of love and Light. If we continuously chose only wonderfully happy lives to live we would not be setting ourselves up for the best learning circumstances.

Sometimes the best way to learn a lesson is in living with, or being, the opposite. Therefore, as you begin recalling your past lives do not be surprised if you see many of them as far from pleasant. For instance, if you recall a past life in which you murdered someone, try to understand the lesson it held for your soul or even someone else's soul. Do not dwell on the fact that you would never, ever, consider doing something like that in this life, or that you feel very strongly against that sort of thing. There was an underlying lesson that your soul chose to learn from the experience and your soul was very brave to have chosen such a life in which to learn it.

Even if you can't think of the lesson it held, pat yourself on the back and thank your soul for enduring such a life in order to learn, grow and evolve to where you are today. Imagine the courage and bravery it would take to make the commitment in the spirit world to learn such major lessons by enduring a tragic or dramatic lifetime.

We all have our lessons to learn and we have chosen lives in which we will best learn them. Do not judge others and the life they live, even if they seem to be bad people, for it took much courage,

Chapter 6

determination and bravery to choose that life and follow through with it. It would be much more difficult to choose a life in which you committed a crime and had to endure the circumstances of that deed, than to live a carefree life of contentment and abundance. Which life holds more importance as far as learning lessons? Neither. Each and every life is as important as another. The lessons are just different. The importance is equal.

When I first started looking back at my past lives I was amazed at some of the things I'd already been through, disease, murder, war, and famine to name a few. I became so thankful I had already experienced those things and didn't have to experience anything like that again. I honored the courage of my soul for enduring those lives. It also helped me realize that this life was a piece of cake compared to most of my past lives. How could I complain and whine about the trivial things brought before me in this life?

The world has never been a better place to live despite its problems now, especially in America. Women have never had as much equality. Prejudices are beginning to heal and mend. We have health care, financial aid, low income housing, and social security. Education is getting better and becoming available to more people. We have the right to free speech and we are able to make our own choices. Everything is continually getting better for us.

As you look back into your past you will see the expanse of improvement. Seeing the way it was then, allows you to be more thankful for all that we have now.

Chapter 7

Cell Memory

*Release the baggage of negative memories.
Admire and respect the wisdom of all
memories.*

All the experiences your soul has ever encountered remain within your soul. When you enter into a new body those experiences come with your soul. Your body is made up of billions of cells and upon entry of your soul all the past experiences, knowledge and memories of your soul are downloaded into those cells. This information is then stored within your cellular structure and remains within your body in what is called cell memory.

Cell memory is quite interesting because generally we aren't at all conscious of the memory since it originated in a past life, yet our subconscious will continue to hold it eternally. Despite not being aware of it, our soul and spirit carry all the positive and negative energy of many events and many lives, creating cell memory that affects our current life.

The memories of past lives can influence us mentally, emotionally, physically or spiritually in this lifetime. Sometimes it's just a matter of having a mental thought that pops up over and over and either helps us enormously, confuses us, or seems to get in the way of how we would normally think. It can also be as simple as a smell or sound that floods our emotions for reasons we can't understand. Other times we have the memory of deeply buried physical pains, phobias, illnesses or traumas that are like scars carried over into this life. Emotional issues that carry no weight in the events of this life have probably been carried over and can include fears such as dying, disease, heights, small places or distrust to name a few. Everything that our soul has ever experienced becomes a memory and thus is stored within the cells of every human body we enter.

We all have good cell memories or experiences and bad ones. Of course the positive cell memories are much easier to admire and deal with, but what about the negative cell memories? What do we do with the information and memory of those negative, not-so-wonderful events? All of that wisdom, information and memory is also instantaneously infused into the cells of our physical body the moment we are born.

Much of our cell memory can be good for us to hold on to, continue using, and reflect back on, but a lot of it is simply baggage because it holds no value to this lifetime. Although every experience your soul has had was important and useful at the time, holding on to negative fragments that do us no good in the here and now is like carrying around a disease. In time it can grow and manifest into something worse than it originally was. The event itself was a lesson but often there is no need to hold on to the feelings or pain associated with that event.

It is important to release this type of negative cell memory so that it can't cloud or interfere with your current life. Releasing negative cell memories can greatly enhance your present life and the way you view your life and yourself. Currently, you may be holding on to memories from another time and place that create an illusion to your current reality. These illusions distort our truth and can become crippling to us in the here and now.

If you think about history and how difficult and traumatic people's lives were during all the different eras and periods of time, you will be able to see the magnitude of negative energies that can be lodged in your soul. As I've already pointed out, we have it made now compared to years ago. It wasn't that long ago when women had no rights and it was acceptable to suppress or physically and emotionally abuse them. People fought tragic wars where enemies stood face to face with their rivals, slaughtering hundreds of people without lifting an eyebrow. Some were burned at the stake, beheaded and hung for their actions. Diseases took many lives and there was no understanding of them or of inventing a cure for them.

Chapter 7

Famine and starvation were common. Poverty, homelessness and losing your entire family were also the case many times.

When you look back at the history of civilization, the world today is a wonderful place compared to then. Think about the cruelties and the lack of information hundreds and thousands of years ago.

You had many past lives in which you experienced and/or witnessed many of these terrible things. Imagine having those experiences locked in your cell memory. Try to understand the impact they can have on your current life and how wonderful it would be to release the negativity of those memories from your cells so that you could start fresh with this life and carry no old baggage from times that are irrelevant to the now.

I will be teaching you ways to cleanse your own body of these memories later in this book, but for now let's take a closer look at some examples of the impact cell memories can have on you.

Chapter 8

Past Lives

The lessons forever last when you let go of the past, but the pain cannot go on and inner peace will soon dawn.

The following past lives were all revealed to me within a six month period. At that time I was working through issues of speaking my truth and remembering my true self. Generally, the past lives that are revealed to you are ones that hold some importance and relevance to your current life situations and issues. The following past lives all relate to the issues I was working on at that time.

The Oracle at Del Phi
A gifted psychic told me that I was an Oracle at Del Phi. I was so excited to hear this information because I imagined a wonderful life, dedicating myself to helping others by channeling and staying spiritually connected. At first I thought it would have been the best life I've ever had. Interestingly, it was the opposite. It was one of my most difficult lives, mostly due to the opposition of some people and the rejection I felt from those that did not believe in channeling. There were many people that hated and feared my powers and felt threatened by me. Although I was loved by the people I helped with my spiritual gifts, there were many that feared me and thought of me as evil and different.

The same thing has happened many times over the years with gifted psychics who were labeled witches or evil and killed for that reason. This is sad and seems to make no sense to me now, and no doubt then. What better way to stay on track spiritually than to hear the direction and support of spirit working through us.

From this lifetime long, long ago I continued to carry a cell memory which caused me to be fearful that I would not be accepted by others if I channeled and spoke the truth given to me. That fear was suppressing my natural gift and ability in this life even though I wasn't conscious of it and the circumstances were much different now.

Joan of Arc

A second experience I had with a past life involving speaking my truth and channeling was a life in which I fought side by side with Joan of Arc. Brave Joan, spoke her truth and channeled information without fear or hesitation. This scared many of the people at that time and the fact that she was a woman who was taking charge was also not taken well. Joan channeled for me often and prayed with me.

In case you aren't familiar with Joan of Arc, her young life was ended when she was burned at the stake. Even though her life was dedicated to helping others and following her Divine guidance, her life ended tragically. She paid a high price for speaking her truth. This, no doubt, was also locked into my cell memory and was an important memory for me to release. Coincidentally, my current mother named me Joanne after Joan of Arc. In the Catholic religion it is common to be named after a patron saint. I'm honored to have Joan of Arc as my patron saint.

The Holocaust

In my most recent past life, I was a twelve year old Polish girl during the Holocaust. Despite my young age, I was taken from my family and placed in a political concentration camp. I was quite mouthy, standing up for myself and my people. I created quite a fuss by constantly trying to get the other prisoners to stand up for themselves and not believe the condescending words of the soldiers. This caused fear of rebellion amongst the soldiers and they threatened to kill me if I didn't stop. I didn't stop and continued on until the moment they hung me in front of everyone.

Chapter 8

The soldiers actually did a wonderful thing for those people by killing me. The remaining prisoners had renewed strength and hope for themselves. Several of them even mustered the courage to successfully escape from camp after my death. The words I spoke caused me suffering but gave Light to others. This past life was probably the most important one to release since it was my most recent. There again, I was releasing issues with speaking my truth.

Still to this day, I am very proud of the bravery, courage and fine work I did during that life. It makes my current life path seem like no big deal. By releasing the cell memories of those lifetimes I began to channel and speak my truth once again.

Hit and Run
Through a dream, I experienced being the driver of some sort of vehicle. My vehicle hit someone. When I looked back I could tell they were badly injured. Instead of stopping I drove off, scared to admit what I'd done. I saw the whole accident happen and actually relived the feelings that flooded over me after I drove off.

When I woke up I couldn't believe that I would do anything like that. For a while I was ashamed of myself and couldn't figure out why I didn't confess to what I'd done since it was an accident. From this, I was to understand that I did not hit and run because I was a bad person. I had so much fear about the accident, I was unable to speak the truth and confess to my guilt. I spent the rest of that life miserable and non-forgiving of myself.

Releasing that cell memory helped me to release fear associated with speaking the truth... no matter what the consequence may be. This memory brought a balance to the other two past lives in which there were serious consequences to speaking the truth, for now I realized that *not* speaking your truth has it's consequences as well.

Indian Warrior
A past life regressionist told me of a life I had as an Indian warrior. I can still feel and see exactly what it was like with all of nature's beauty and peace in my life. Although I suffered a serious injury from an attack which kept me from ever being the brave warrior I once was, that life still remains the most wonderful I can remember.

In an attack to our tribal camp, I was hit with a spear in my left shoulder. The wound was very serious and I was never able to ride a horse again, much less be the warrior I once was because of the pain. I ended up spending my days at the camp with the women instead of riding with the other braves. That was very sad and difficult for the brave warrior in me.

During my time in camp I became known as the wise one, channeling guidance and healing words for the rest of the tribe. Despite the shame I felt from being the wounded warrior, I found a new joy and fulfillment through speaking my truth and helping others in a different way.

Interestingly, I had been having a lot of problems with pain in my back in my current life up until that session, yet I never thought to mention this to the regressionist that day. I asked her where the spear entered my body. She described it as the exact area of my current pain. Once I was able to realize that this pain was just a cell memory and it played no part in my current life, I was able to release that cell memory and the pain disappeared.

The Pub
In another dream I was a drunk in a pub. The pub felt like my second home. I was very fond of the bartender however I'm quite sure he didn't feel the same way about me. I believe he was probably my only friend in that life as I was quite a repulsive person.

As the bartender was walking a bag of money to a back office I followed him, rambling on, slurring unimportant chatter all the way. I was rude and obnoxious as I called out silly, crude, stupid things to other people passing by. While I was dreaming this I was thinking what a disgusting man he was.

As the bartender entered the office with his bag of money a man came out of nowhere with a knife. He started moving toward the bartender. I had the sense that I couldn't react quick enough and I wasn't mentally alert enough because of my intoxicated state. I felt my drunkenness kept me from doing as much as I could have, but managed to lurch forward toward the thief. At that moment he stabbed me in the stomach. I felt the pain as though it was real and I can still remember that moment. Time seemed to stand still as I stood there with a blade in my belly. My last thoughts were that if I hadn't been a blubbering drunk I may not have been killed.

Chapter 8

The fact is I saved my friend's life by sacrificing my own. The attacker ran off after he killed me and the bartender lived. In analyzing this dream, I realized that despite my disgust over this blubbering alcoholic of a man, he still had the love and bravery inside of him to save his friends life. This dream helped me to see drug and alcohol addicts in a different way and to realize that we truly are all one, and we are all love. The outer shell and the story line may be different for all of us, but inside we are all the same. Once I realized this, I looked back at this man with respect for what he did out of love.

Chapter 9

Remembering Your Past Lives

The past had much to teach you,
Hurt and anger can still reach you,
But let it go you must,
This method you need to trust.

There are many ways in which you can learn of your past lives. The past lives that are revealed to you hold some significance in where you are in your current life. For instance, when I was beginning to channel, I was reminded of past lives that involved channeling and speaking my truth. When I was suffering with severe back pain I was reminded of a past life with back pain and suffering. Some information was given to me by other people and some came to me during meditation and dreams.

Dreams
When there is something you need to recall, it will come to you. If you are recalling it in your dreams, it is important to pay attention to them. One way to know if a dream is about a past life is the way in which you remember the dream the next day. Past life dreams are vivid, detailed, crystal clear, and you usually remember every detail about them. The dreams will seem very real and you usually have feelings about the events that happened. When you wake up, they are extremely hard to shake off and forget about, sometimes lingering on in your mind for days.

Depending on the type of life you are recalling, past life dreams can feel like nightmares. Some of them seem so far fetched that it can be difficult for you to believe you had a life like that. Most of the time, I know or feel, deep inside of me, that it was a part of my past.

Past Life Regressionists
If you have some doubt as to whether or not a dream was a past life, you can visit a past life regressionist. A regressionist will help you to recall it again. There are several types of regressionists. Some put you into a hypnotic state and allow *you* to pull up and answer your own questions. Generally, they will make an audio tape of the session for you so that you can hear your own words after you are out of the hypnotic state.

Other regressionists are able to hold a piece of your jewelry, or a personal item of yours, and simply tell you about the life. With this method you aren't as connected emotionally and it seems more like hearing a story than re-living the event. Either way, you will feel a sense of truth or connection to the life as the scenario is played out.

One time I was getting a massage from someone I'd never been to before. As she was working on my back she told me that she found pieces of a spearhead in my shoulder. I had already been to the regressionist and knew that the spear was from my warrior days. I thought I'd released the memory but apparently there were still fragments left there. I told her about the past life and she helped me remove those left over bits and pieces.

Moving on, the massage therapist began working on my leg. There again, she picked up on another injury. As she rubbed my leg to release the memory, I received a vision of a gray wolf but didn't share this with her. I asked her if she knew how I was injured. Because of my vision, I expected to hear that I was attacked and possibly bitten by a wolf. She paused for a moment and said she saw a Native American Indian who's name was Gray Wolf. The injury was a bullet hole from a battle with him.

You can imagine how amazed and surprised I was. Not only had the massage therapist told me of a past life, but I received a vision which confirmed her words.

Chapter 9

Psychics and Channels

Another way to receive information about past lives is through a psychic or channel. I was personally guided to Kim O'Neill. She was my first experience with channeling. I must admit there was some skepticism and doubt in me when I first decided to see her. The only psychics I'd ever known about were the ones you see along the roadside. Kim's talents for channeling fascinated me and I fell in love with her immediately. Aside from telling me about some of my past lives, she clearly and accurately passed on large amounts of information from my Guides. This was extremely helpful to me when I didn't know how to channel for myself, and then again when I needed confirmation and reassurance that I was getting the correct information. Though the words she spoke were not her own, but words from my Guides, Kim made a huge impact on my life by passing this information on and directing me onto my life path.

I think of Kim as one of my Earth Angels and will always be grateful to her for the help, support and motivation she's given me. I was guided to her by Spirit and I believe you will be guided to the person best suited for you. Kim is located in Houston, Texas and offers many wonderful classes in the area. She can give you a reading in person or over the telephone. If you feel guided toward her, or are curious about psychics and channeling, you can visit her website at www.kimoneillpsychic.com.

I highly recommend being very careful when choosing a psychic. Do not be driven by low prices or roadside convenience. If the information you receive doesn't seem to ring true for you, it may not have come through correctly. Remember, psychics are here to connect us to our Guides but they are only human and we can all misinterpret or make mistakes. Your Guides want to help, assist and teach you in order to make your life productive and fulfilling. Never let a psychic tell you that you someone put a spell or curse on you, or that you need to come back for follow up sessions in order to finish any type of business regarding those things. That is a big lie. For one thing, it is not possible for anyone to put a spell or curse on you and secondly there is no need to have follow-up visits 'to finish anything' unless you simply desire more information.

Chapter Nine Exercise

Think about any dreams or recurring thought patterns you've had that could be past life experiences. Write them down, in detail, and allow yourself some quiet time or meditation time to reflect on each of them. See if you can 'feel' any inner connection to those events. Decide which ones could be important to your life now. Take note of any that could be causing you unnecessary suffering in any way.

Chapter 10

Communicating With Your Soul

Release anything that is inauthentic.
Let go of all that does not mirror your
highest intentions.

Fear not the illogical, irrational
and unexplained for the
answers lie within and an
awakening emerges from.

Be a courier of all that is True and Divine.

    It is a magnificent experience to tap in to your soul and after some practice you can remain consciously connected all of the time. I've already explained why and how your soul holds so much information, now it's time to learn how to tap into that wealth of knowledge. The truth is you are already constantly accessing that information even though you are not fully conscious of it. Some of the information you receive is from your Spirit Guides, Angels and others in the spirit world, but your soul, or higher self guides and directs you as well.
    In our human form, we are made up of a soul and an ego mind. The biggest enemy you will encounter when first beginning to tap in to your soul is your ego mind. This is because your mind is con-

stantly thinking of the past or the future and seldom focuses on the present moment.

Your soul is the only place of true power within you because it is your true essence and always stays in the present moment. When you allow your mind to constantly chatter it keeps you from hearing the voice of your soul. Learning to quiet the mind and tune into the soul it is called enlightenment. When you become fully enlightened, you are able to be in the present moment and feel total contentment with all things. Worry, doubt and fear diminish when you stay in the present moment because those things are only created by dwelling on the past and future. The voice within will guide you without fear, anger or judgment.

Becoming fully conscious of communicating with your soul is actually quite simple, but it will take time and practice to feel completely confident. When I first started listening to my soul I found it extremely difficult to turn off my mind. In order to hear your soul you must turn off your mind and stay in the present moment. Your mind is not able to be in the present because it is constantly thinking about the past and the future. This causes your mind to fight with your inner voice constantly. Your mind creates thought and thought creates distraction from the voice of your soul.

The soul is not capable of creating thought. The soul communicates through feelings. If the soul were to take on thought it would not be in the present moment. Think about what most of your thoughts are about. You will notice that much of your energy is being used in repetitive, obsessive thought. This is robbing you of communication with your soul and the place of true power and inner peace. Your mind will strip you of your true power and inner peace with its negative comments and constant chatter.

Here is an example. Imagine having a wonderful lunch with an old friend you haven't seen for a long time. Your mind may keep you from fully enjoying the moment because it is still bouncing off thoughts such as "I wonder if I remembered to turn off the coffee pot", or "I can't forget to go by the cleaners on the way home". With all this background chatter going on in your mind and constantly creating illusions for you, how can you totally enjoy lunch and be in the present with your beloved friend?

Chapter 10

You must learn to *identify with your soul instead of your mind*. Throughout life you have identified yourself through your mind, your physical body and your environment. From the moment of our birth on this earthly plane, we are programmed to think, feel and react to our new world in certain ways. Through this programming we eventually disconnect more and more with our higher self.

As children we identify with the role we play in our family or with the way the other family members see us. Later we identify with our surroundings, our physical appearance, the face we show to the world and our emotional state. As adults we often identify with our careers, family, financial abundance, neighborhoods and material possessions. All of these things are temporary and inauthentic. The real you, your true self, is your soul.

The exciting truth is that you have always had and will continue to have that true self within you. The exterior has just muddied the water and made it more difficult to see what is at the bottom. By clearing the waters, you will be able to vividly see and connect to your true self once again. Quieting the mind helps settle the mud and clear the water. I am not saying your mind is not a powerful and useful tool at times, but it can become quite destructive to you if it is running your life. Allowing your thoughts to consume and identify you exhausts your energy level as well.

Learning to stay in the present, the place where thoughts can not exist is the first step. Since the mind is only capable of thinking, and all thought is either of past or future, you need to learn how to stay in the present. If you are fully in the now, there can be no thought of future or past.

To practice staying in the present, become aware of everything you do, as you do it. If for example, you are pulling weeds, bring yourself to that moment and put all your attention on the weeds coming out of the ground, one at a time. Do not think ahead or behind that very moment. Feel your body and what it's experiencing in that moment. Feel the dirt on your fingers, the sun on your back or the breeze in your hair. If you catch yourself thinking, become a watcher of the thought rather than give any energy to the thought. Do not allow it to continue by giving energy to it and focusing on it.

If you do not give any energy to a thought it can not continue and will dissipate. When you are practicing staying in the present moment, and you catch yourself with thought over and over again, simply put yourself back in the present moment and start again. Keep working at it every day and as often as possible. You will get more successful at being in the moment and it will become easier to remain there. Whatever you are doing, be there fully and completely.

I elaborate more on staying in the present moment in Chapter 20.

Chapter 11

The Many Voices of Your Soul

Center yourself in your heart,
the place of love.
It is there that you will hear
the voice of your soul.

Your soul was created in the likeness of God. God is pure love and therefore your soul is pure love. Centering yourself in your heart, the place of true love, opens you up to communicating with your soul.

Have you ever verbally lashed out at someone who made you really upset or angry, and then heard a tiny voice within say, "Gee, I feel kind of sorry for what I said", or "Maybe my words were a bit too harsh". Your mind and your soul were at battle. In your soul there is no hate and anger. The conflicts you had when you were trying to remain upset and angry are the inner voice of your soul arguing with the words of your mind.

Remembering that your soul is your true self, you must learn to stop connecting with the thoughts of your mind. Instead, center or listen to the love of your soul. Love is what life is about and the Light and love within you are found in your soul. Practice opening your heart and then begin listening to your heart. Staying centered in your heart keeps you connected to the Light and love of your soul. There are many ways in which the soul can communicate.

Gut Feelings

One way the soul communicates is through feelings or intuition. When people talk about their intuition or gut feelings, they are communicating with their soul. Many times our gut feelings tell us to do something and then the ego mind steps in and talks us right out of doing it. It can sound something like this.

You are reading a college brochure and the Yoga class jumps out at you and catches your attention. Immediately, without thought, your gut feeling is that you want to do it. You get excited and actually start to see yourself doing Yoga. Then the dreaded ego mind steps in and starts telling you things like, "You shouldn't spend the money", "You haven't exercised in so long you probably won't be able to do it", or "Yoga is too difficult, you'll never be able to do it". What do you think you would end up doing? Probably blowing it off and then regretting you didn't do it.

Since your soul originally told you it would be good, you will be irritated and bothered over and over again with the fact that you didn't take it. It isn't easy to trust in your gut feeling and for some people it can be difficult to even be aware of their gut feeling.

Your Inner Voice

Another way your soul communicates with you is similar to an inner voice. This can be confusing at first because you will wonder if it's your soul or a mental thought. There have probably been several times in your life when you wanted to do something, say something, buy something or go somewhere and a little voice inside of you said "no". Perhaps there was a time when you ignored this voice only to find that something negative happened or there was a serious consequence as a result of it.

When my body was going through a natural detoxification, it no longer wanted me to eat certain foods. Even though I knew this, I had strong desires to consume them anyway. Every time I reached out for the wrong foods I could hear my inner voice say, "You shouldn't do that, it will make you sick". When my cravings got the best of me and I chose not to listen, I suffered with stomach aches, sometimes lasting for two or three days. My inner self knew it would be bad for me, yet I did not listen, and therefore I suffered unnecessary discomfort and pain.

Chapter 11

Your soul knows best and it is in your best interest to tune in to it. You may not like what you hear but believe me there is a good reason for it. Advice like this on a larger scale can keep you safe from injuries, accidents or heartaches. Center yourself in your heart and listen. If you find yourself confused about whether the voice or feeling is that of your soul or ego mind, try the following exercises for confirmation.

Pendulums

Pendulums are a way to communicate with your soul and receive visible feedback. Pendulums are inexpensive and quite easy to use. You can use a pendant and a chain if you don't want to buy a pendulum, but I have found that the store bought pendulums move much faster, have more definition, and are much easier to use. They can be made with crystals, rocks or metal. Rocks and crystals carry a lot of energy themselves and can easily be charged with your own energy, making them very personalized.

When picking out a pendulum the best advice I can give you is to pick the one that you feel attracted to. I prefer rocks or crystals but the metal ones I have used work very well too. You will be attracted to the one that will work best for you.

<u>Cleaning your pendulum</u>

If you purchase a rock or crystal pendulum it is important to first wash it to remove any old energies it may be carrying.

There are many beliefs on how to cleanse your rocks and crystals. Personally, I prefer to soak mine in salt water overnight or for at least three hours to cleanse them. Then I place them in direct sunlight for several hours to recharge them. Occasionally, on a full moon, I put them out in the moonlight overnight.

Once you have cleansed your pendulum of outside energies and charged it, keep it in your pocket or near your body for the next two or three days so it can pick up your energy. It will work best for you if it resonates to your energy, and keeping it close to your body will do that.

Cleansing and charging your rocks and crystals may seem time consuming and tedious, but it is extremely important and should always be done before using a new one. I will discuss rocks and crystals with more detail in Chapter 34 of this book.

Using the Pendulum

Begin using your pendulum by holding the top of the chain with your fingers and allowing it to swing freely. Some people may find it more effective if they keep no more than two or three inches of chain below your fingers. We all have our own technique, and there is no right or wrong way to do it. You must find what works best for you. In time, you will be guided to use your pendulum in your own style for maximum effectiveness.

At first, I started draping mine over my index finger and found that method worked best for me. Now, I feel more comfortable using the full extension of the chain.

Once the pendulum is hanging freely ask it to give you a 'yes'. Be patient and don't expect any type of movement. When it begins to move notice what direction it is going. Next, ask it for a 'no' and again, note the direction it moves. Never think you can't do this. Everyone can do it. Be careful not to hold any expectations while you are working with the pendulum. This will involve your ego mind and push back the voice of your true self or soul.

If you aren't having any success with getting your pendulum to move, start by swinging it before you ask a question. Be patient and allow it time to begin its own movement. My sister-in-law receives a yes on one pendulum differently than she receives a yes on her other pendulum. There is no correct or incorrect way to get your answer. Every time you use your pendulum, start by asking for a yes and a no to verify it's response.

Once you clearly get a no and yes response you are ready to begin asking questions. Again, be sure not to hold expectations of the answer you may wish to see, or expect to see. If you allow your ego mind to get in the way you will not get an accurate reading. The pendulum will tell you what is best for your soul and what your soul's truest desire is.

At first it also helps to follow up any answer you get with the question, "Is this answer from my higher self?" If the pendulum says no, you have engaged your mind into the outcome. Simply re-

Chapter 11

phrase your question with the words, 'What does my higher self say about ....?".

It is a lot of fun using a pendulum and you will begin to find many uses for it, including helping others. When you use your pendulum to help others, be sure to hold the intent of that person. Mentally say their name and be sure the questions include their name. For instance, "Are these vitamins good for John Doe?", instead of, "Are these vitamins good?". They may be good vitamins, but John Doe may not need them.

You can use the pendulum for advice on buying certain herbs, vitamins, essential oils, flower essences or medicine. You can also ask the pendulum for dosage amounts. To do this, simply ask, "Should I take one tablet?" If it says no, ask it if you should take two. Continue asking until you receive a yes.

Your pendulum can tell you what foods are good and bad for you, as well as answer any other questions you may have regarding your life. I like to use my pendulum to diagnose illnesses and pain as well. When you're feeling sick and aren't sure what it is, simply write down some possible causes such as virus, staph, strep, yeast, bacteria, and allergy on a piece of paper. Ask the pendulum to tell you what is wrong with you. Point your finger to each word, one at a time, allowing the pendulum to answer yes or no. If you find that you have a virus you will know to take Echinacea and Vitamin C to help combat it. If your pendulum swings to allergy you can write down a variety of possible allergens on paper and again, point your finger to one at a time for a diagnosis.

If you are having difficulty diagnosing an illness, include such causes as mental, emotional, energetic or chemical to your list.

There are many health food stores that carry herbal and homeopathic remedies for just about everything. If you've tried and tried but still can't get an answer from your pendulum, go to the health food store and use the pendulum as you touch different remedies. Remember to trust your gut instinct to help direct you to the correct shelf.

Once you locate the proper healing remedy, ask the pendulum for the correct dosage to take. There is a lot of comfort in diagnosing yourself and your loved ones and avoiding trips to the doctor for every little thing. It works wonderfully on animals and children too.

Don't feel disappointed if you can't get a diagnosis. Sometimes it is necessary to go to a doctor but I have found that most of the time I can treat myself quite effectively. It takes a lot less time and money than I'd spend seeing a doctor. Western medicine is not my chosen favorite because I believe they treat the symptoms and don't cure the problem.

I will always try the natural approach before I resort to the western style of medicine. The natural approach is much friendlier to your body than chemicals. With natural healing, your body is given what it needs to return to its state of good health while healing the problem at the same time. Many times we have a deficiency of some sort that may be the cause of our illness or a product of the illness. If we do not heal the body of its deficiencies, it will remain in a weakened state and we could be prone to another outbreak or recurrence soon after our believed recovery. I will talk more about that in Part IV of this book.

If you want to learn more about using the pendulum there are many wonderful books available. One of my personal favorites is a workbook called *Energy Therapy*, by Sheila Hollingshead, but you may find one that suits you better. Ms. Hollingshead's book has nearly 300 pages of useful charts, techniques and information regarding releasing, healing and charting energy, along with specific instructions and answers to using a pendulum.

Meditation

Meditation is another excellent way to connect to the voice of your soul and quiet the mind. This is something you should make time for every day. Think of meditation as your quiet time all to yourself. Life can get pretty stressful and the times we feel like we haven't got a minute to ourselves are the most important times to find and make quiet time. It is important to your mental, physical and spiritual health that you make time for yourself every day. Meditating is wonderfully refreshing.

My favorite way to meditate is to get comfortable in our big recliner or lie down flat on the floor or a bed, but many people believe in sitting upright in a lotus position or Indian-style. The important thing is to be comfortable so that your body and mind can relax. It

Chapter 11

is also recommended that you don't try meditating when you're extremely tired as you could end up falling asleep.

The amount of time you devote to meditating isn't that important. I can get just as much out of ten minutes as thirty minutes. It all depends on your schedule and what you are trying to achieve through meditating. Most importantly, make *some* time, and remember any amount of time is better than nothing at all. The following is my method. You may change it to fit your desires and needs in any way.

After getting comfortable, close your eyes and make sure every muscle in your body is relaxed. If you are sitting upright, be sure your back is fairly straight and your shoulders are relaxed. I like to start at the top of my head and scan down slowly, relaxing any part of my body that seems to be holding tension along the way. Relax your facial muscles, neck, spine, arms, hands, stomach, legs and feet. You will be surprised at how many times you think you are relaxed and find certain parts still holding tension when you take the time to scan your body.

Next I tell my mind to turn off. This can take some practice. No sooner do you tell your mind to stop and it's already trying to create thought again, *sometimes just the thought of how to not have thought*! Stay persistent with turning your thoughts off. Repeating a word or phrase can help distract your mind. You do not need to say the word aloud, simply repeat it mentally over and over again. The word 'hue' is great to use if you can't think of another word.

As thought pops into your mind become an observer of the thought. Do not hold on to it. Allow it to drift in and out of your mind. Begin to breathe deeply, using your belly as you inhale. It helps to place your hand on your stomach to be sure it moves out with each inhale and in with each exhale. Allowing your belly to move with each breath instead of your chest alone will fill and expel your lungs completely. If you look at a baby breathe you will notice they use their belly. We are all born to this type of breathing method. It is through the years that we've lost it. When we only use our chest we are limiting our intake to shallow breathing. Take deep breaths and long exhales, putting all your focus on your breathing. This will help calm the mind.

If I'm having a lot of difficulty turning off my mind, I visualize the air coming into my lungs and then passing back out of my body. You can add a color to the visualized air moving in and out. When you feel completely relaxed in body and mind, simply look out into the darkness before you and *be*. This means you should hold no expectations or anticipations, just relax, breathe and be in the moment.

As you do this you may begin to see colors, much like a kaleidoscope, waving in and out, back and forth, or you may begin to see faint images or pictures. Do not put thought to these things, simply enjoy the moment and be like an outsider watching it happen and unfold. This is a good place to stay and maintain until it becomes easy for you to get there, hold it and stay relaxed. Your soul can communicate at this time even though you may not consciously know what it's saying.

Once you have master this part, you can begin to ask questions. Again, do not anticipate or expect anything specific. Sometimes you will receive information and sometimes you won't. The more you keep your mind from engaging in thought, the sooner you will receive information.

When I first started practicing meditation I saw the colors purple and green waving and moving. I felt these colors represented Archangel Michael and Archangel Raphael. My gut feeling told me they were with me and they were busy cleansing and healing me.

After that period of time I began to see images. The first images I saw all the time were an eye and a small dot of light. The eye represented connecting to my third eye and the light was the Light of God and the universe. Any pictures, feelings or experiences you have are wonderful. It does not matter what, if any, you experience. Stay relaxed, breathe, turn your mind off, and the rest will happen for you as it should.

Never judge your meditation techniques and experiences with someone else. We are all different and unique. What is important for me may not be important for you. You will receive what you need to receive. Sometimes meditation can simply be a time to recharge and energize your self. Often I feel surges of energy wave through my body when I meditate. I start to feel as though I'm lighter and full of God's Light and loving energy. Happiness and peace flood through my body and that is all that happens.

Chapter 11

The method I just explained is a wonderful way to begin experiencing meditating for the simple joy and contentment of it, as well as allowing time and space for communicating with your soul.

I will teach you more meditation styles and techniques in Chapter 19.

Chapter Eleven Exercise #1

Try meditating as often as you can over the next several days. Make an appointment with your soul to schedule daily meditation time. Remember, you can give yourself five minutes if that's all you have time for. Anything is better than nothing. You will begin to feel much better in a variety of ways once you make time for meditating.

Chapter Eleven Exercise #2

Practice using a pendulum. Be patient and consistent. Start asking it questions that you already know the answers to. Then play around with different types of questions. Use it as often as you can, even if you still don't completely trust in the answers. The more you use it the more confident you will become and the handier it will be for you.

Chapter 12

Oneness With God

God is love.
He is the light within you and around you.
He is the essence of all that is.
Your soul was made in the likeness of Him.
There is no separation between you and God.
You are filled with the Light and love of God.
You are one with Him.

These are facts that cannot be changed no matter how you feel or what you believe. You are here because God created you. His voice speaks to you and within you constantly. You have conversations with Him everyday and all day long. He has been guiding you and encouraging you since your soul was first created. He hears every prayer and request you make to Him. He is everywhere and can hear everyone at the same time. His love for you is unconditional and undying. God will never forsake you or abandon you. It is only you that can create the feeling of separation from God.

When we are young we communicate openly and easily with God. As we get older we create blockages and fears that cause us to feel disconnected from Him, when in fact, there is never any separation between you and God. You always have the voice of God within you and it is possible to turn up the volume and hear His words once again. God will not punish you, reprimand you or cause pain or suffering to come your way.

Religions often impress upon us to be fearful of God or that there will be severe punishments for the bad things we've done in life. This type of 'hell and damnation' information is wrong and is exactly why we build up a wall between our Divine Father and ourselves. It is sad and unfair for us to place this wall between our Father and us. God wants us to be happy, healthy and loving to ourselves and all creatures. He wants us to have abundance in our life. God holds unconditional love for all. God is love and His Light shines within each and every one of us.

When I was a child I felt strongly connected to God, Jesus and Mary and always prayed to them and asked them for help. As a child I attended a Catholic school and my family devotedly went to church each Sunday. It didn't make sense to me that God was to be feared or that He would punish us for our sins by sending us to purgatory or hell. The whole thing seemed quite contradictory, yet I was very afraid of going to purgatory or hell if I did one thing wrong. The thought of these places often troubled me so much that I would pray and pray to God to forgive me. Sometimes I would obsess over wondering where I was going when I died. It scared me so much to think I may not make it through the gates of heaven.

As with most children, my big sin then was lying and I didn't even do that much of it for fear of going to hell. I was also taught that God forgave us and loved us and this just didn't seem to fit into the fearful, punishing image I was also constantly taught.

As I grew older I began to feel separated from God. Throughout my teens and early twenties I began to feel worse and worse about myself. I did some unacceptable things throughout these years. I knew that all of those things were looked down upon by my church and felt they would most likely keep me from getting into heaven.

It wasn't completely conscious, but I slowly began to feel that God could never forgive me for *everything* I'd done wrong. I soon started to think of myself as nothing more than a sinner and began pulling away from the church and from my spirituality. Thinking that this would be the best thing for me to do since there was no way to go back and make things right again, I remained spiritually dead for many years.

When I had children, I made sure they were baptized and sent them to religion classes, knowing they must learn about God. We went to church occasionally.

Nearly every time we went to church, I was brought to tears before the mass was over. Most often, it happened during a song. I

Chapter 12

never really understood what the tears were about. I would get this uncontrollably strong feeling of love and peace inside of me as I sat in my pew. That warm feeling made me very emotional and brought on the tears. Looking back, I see that it was my feeling of separation that caused the emotions. I desperately needed and wanted to feel completely spiritual once again, however I stayed detached from God for twenty more years as I remained confused and spiritually lost.

Later in my life, a dear soul mate I'd never met walked into my life. Out of the blue, she asked me if I'd like to have an Angel card reading. She told me she would be able to receive messages for me from deceased loved ones after the reading. I didn't even know what she was talking about but I quickly said yes and became very excited at the possibility of hearing from my deceased father, who had died several years before then.

I had never heard of Angel cards before that day and was a little skeptical about the whole thing. The accuracy of the card reading left me totally amazed and astonished. When she later channeled words from my father to me I could no longer control my emotions This woman didn't know me and certainly never knew my father or the relationship I had with him, yet she was telling me about times and events my father and I shared. There was no doubt in my mind that the words she channeled were his words, meant just for me.

That event sparked a rebirth of my own spirituality. From that day on, I studied, read and learned everything I could get my hands on. To my amazement, everything I read and learned seemed vaguely familiar and I knew it was the truth and of the Light, even though it was quite different from the Catholic religion I grew up with. I found myself reading book after book and soon my entire life was changing. With each day, abundance, peace and happiness were getting stronger and stronger. There seemed to be miracles happening everyday for me, little signs of encouragement and support from above. I knew then that I had found the way to my life path and my life purpose. There was never any doubt in my mind. My spirituality was re-ignited that day and will remain a strong, pure, white flame forever now.

That is my story, but there are many other reasons why we can feel detached from God. Perhaps you have lost a loved one and feel that God has taken that person from you. You may also feel like God is more loving and giving to others who have more than you. There may also be a feeling that God has neglected you in unanswered prayers. You may feel ashamed and unworthy of God's love because of things you have done in the past. There are many ways in which we can separate ourselves from feeling the God within us.

God needs to hear you. He loves to chat with you. By talking to Him and telling Him exactly how you feel and why you feel that way, the barriers will begin to fall apart. God already knows how you feel, you just need to realize it yourself and express it to Him. God sees the true you, the Light and love inside of you, and He knows the real reason for your behaviors and actions. He knows that deep down you are pure love, and your human body and mind can get in the way at times.

Trust in Him to be with you and to love you all the time. Be honest with Him and true to yourself. He will never leave you. God knows what you think, how you feel, your biggest fears and worries, your angers and judgments of self and others. Do not try to hide anything from Him when you talk to Him. He knows the true you, loves you unconditionally, and sees the Light within you.

Never think that you have to make a special time slot for talking or praying to God. Going to church once a week and praying is wonderful, but you should talk to Him all day, every day.

You don't need a flowery prayer to talk to God either, just communicate as you would with anyone else and speak your truth. If you think He has neglected you or forsaken you in any way, tell Him. Be honest and your prayers will be answered. Speak your truth and He will comfort you and heal your pain.

You can hear the voice of God if you listen. At first it may seem like a faint whisper and you may even wonder if you are just imagining it or creating it yourself. Ask God to 'turn up the volume' and tell Him you need a much clearer line of communication. He will be more than happy to help you hear him more clearly. Remember He is right there inside of you, and His words have always been with you, you just stopped listening.

Since God has been guiding you all your life, His voice will not be that unfamiliar to you. Realizing it is His voice is the only thing you have to familiarize yourself with. Don't strain to hear His

Chapter 12

words and don't be surprised with what you hear. His words are often spoken in ways that you can best understand and will be spoken through your soul.

I was always expecting to hear dramatic, powerful words like those in the bible. It surprised me that God's words sounded no different than if I were talking to my best friend; plain, simple words. Speaking to God is not going to be a big, earth shaking event. It is soft and subtle and often sounds like your own voice. Remember, He is within you and the essence of your soul. There is no separation between your soul and His Light. Because you have the right to make your own decisions, God will not interfere with your life unless you ask Him for help. God is love and His answers are of love, forgiveness, support and comfort.

Many people feel that God is off in heaven somewhere, far, far away. Creating this distance between you and God causes feelings of separation. These feelings can make it difficult to believe that He hears you, can talk to you, and is with you at all times. You may feel that your problems and questions aren't important enough for Him, or that He is just too busy with everyone else to make time for you. The truth is He is with you and in you at all times. He can be with everyone at the same time. Separation from Him is created only in your mind.

Realizing this, opens you up to the fact that we are all one because we all have God within us. No one person is better or worse than another. We are all filled with His Light and therefore we should all be considered equal. Every person you meet has the Light of God within them and you need to honor that fact.

It is important to see the Light and love in all people, even in those that make your stomach turn or your skin crawl. Deep down, they are no different than you.

We are all called back to this earth to continue evolving and learning. Each of us has different lessons to learn and different ways to learn them. Do not judge others, their life style or their appearances. Try to see the Light within all people. We should not point fingers or judge others, for their life's mission is as important as ours.

When you can honestly look at every person you meet and feel the love and Light within them, you will be able to understand that

God is everywhere. Remember, you have had many past lives and some were far from wonderful or spiritual, yet you were here to learn and grow from the person you were.

When someone gets under your skin and you find it hard to see the Light of God in them, stop for a minute and try to understand what they may be here to learn. Put yourself in their shoes as if you had no choice about it. Their life could have been the life you chose for yourself this time around.

Be forgiving and understanding of all people. We all have our 'cross to bear' in this life and we all handle things differently. Let your Light shine into their life and give nothing but love to them. Know that we are all in God's hands and He will take care of them just as He takes care of you.

Chapter Twelve Exercise #1
Take some time to evaluate your life and any events that occurred in which you may have felt a separation from God or felt abandoned by Him. Don't feel bad that you had these feelings, simply tell God about them and ask Him to help heal you now. Forgive yourself and forgive others for creating these feelings. Let it go and know that you can connect right here and now with God once again. It's that easy.

Chapter Twelve Exercise #2
Over the next few days, practice hearing the voice of God within yourself. Talk to Him as much as you can. Be honest and open. Listen and be patient. Keep talking even if you don't hear an answer. Remember that God answers all questions, we just need to ask. Know that sometimes His answer may not come through words but rather signs and events. Stay connected and tuned in. Know that everything will be perfect and you are always safe
.

Chapter 13

Channeling With Your Guides

*For He will command His
Angels concerning you
to guard you in all your ways.
Psalm 91:11*

    In addition to God, there are many beautiful spirit forms out there that want to, and do, help us constantly. They are gifts from God and are purely and completely of God's love and Light and include the Holy Spirit, Ascended Masters, Archangels, Angels, Guides and deceased loved ones. I will refer to all of them as Guides, since that is what they do for us. Never think that your Guides are less important than God or that you are ignoring God when you talk to them and ask for their help instead of asking God directly. Your Guides are one with God just as you are. They are Lightworkers for God. Serving you, in the name of God, is their purpose.

    Before we came into this life, each of us assigned ourselves Guides to help us along the way. The Guides you chose are some of your dearest loved ones. While some of your loved ones share your life in human form, there are many others that remain in the spirit world. You chose them to guide you, protect you, and share your human life from the spirit world. Imagine the magnitude of love and trust you hold for these beautiful souls to assign them the job of guiding and protecting you here on earth. They are to be thanked for accepting the job and for all their help and love toward you.

Your Guides understand what you are going through and can help you see what you must do along the way. They know what you intended for your life purpose and life path before you entered your body. They want to help you find and follow your path. Your Guides will be with you the entire time you are here on earth. You chose your Guides for the life you were coming into, and you chose the best Guides to help you with the issues you came here to deal with.

I currently have fifty seven Guides helping me. You will have as many Guides as you need to fulfill your life path and purpose. Having more doesn't mean you're more important or more protected; it's just what you chose to have according to what you felt you needed.

You can talk to your Guides as often as you like. In fact, they love it when you communicate with them. They are never too busy or too far away to hear you. They are completely devoted to you, have endless patience with you, and will forever hold unconditional love for you. They want you to express your desires, fears and worries. No request is too small or insignificant for them. Please talk to them as much as you can. If there is something that you desire, ask your Guides.

Your Guides cannot interfere with your life unless you ask them for help. Once you hold the intent or wish, you open the door for them to step in and lend you a helping hand. It doesn't matter how insignificant or small your request may seem. You can ask for something as small as a good parking space or a short line in the checkout area. When I have to go to the post office I ask my Guides, as I'm leaving my house, to clear the lines at the post office for me. I've been doing this for years now and it has worked every time. If you are running late to an appointment, sit back, relax and ask your Guides for help with green lights or whatever else they can do to get you there on time.

Remember, you must ask for help or they can not intervene. It is so much fun asking and receiving because you begin to realize that they truly are with you and helping you all the time. It's very comforting when you maintain that connection consistently. The most important thing you can do for them, aside from asking for their help, is to always be thankful and appreciative of their help. Just

Chapter 13

like you, they love to be acknowledged and thanked. Start asking for help and guidance now. Don't hold back, ask for anything and see what happens. You will be surprised at how often your requests will be answered.

Occasionally you may request something and it doesn't happen. Do not think that your Guides did not hear you or are punishing you by not granting your request. There is always good reason for your unanswered requests. You may not always see the whole picture or the end result. You may assume that your request is the best thing for you when it is not. Your Guides know the truth, what you really need, and what is best. Asking to be the winner of a million dollar lotto is okay, but do not expect that you will win just because you asked. Some things can be changed easily and some things can change your entire destiny and are not in your best interest or even a considerable option. Trust that your Guides already know what is best for you. You just have to ask, sit back, wait, and then be thankful.

Channeling information means that you talk to your Guides and they respond back to you. This is something we all do, every day, all the time. In fact, channeling is just another way to pray, however in this form of prayer you not only ask questions and talk, but you receive an answer as well. Wouldn't you rather hear the answers to your prayers? If you are praying and asking without channeling you will feel more separated from God and your Guides. You will wonder if they heard you and if they are truly with you.

The truth is, your Guides are always communicating with you even when you don't consciously hear them. You have been receiving their information since the moment you were born. Sometimes the information they give you can be confused by your ego mind. That is why it is wonderful to become aware of channeled information. Once you open that line of communication and listen more consciously it greatly improves your life and the lives of others.

Soon after I began channeling, I noticed that other Guides began asking for my assistance in communicating verbally for them. It is a wonderful thing to pass on helpful, supportive and protective information to others. If you are getting a clear message for someone else you should pass it on. If it doesn't seem to make sense to you it usually does to the recipient. Try to remain an open channel not just for yourself but for everyone. I am always very thankful when other people channel information for me. It amazes me when someone else gets important information for me and I welcome it anytime.

An intuitive friend once told me that she had a feeling my husband and I were going to get a big refund from the IRS. Since we'd been paying big bucks to them each year, for many years, I didn't 'think' her information sounded right. She said there was an error in computing the numbers in an interest calculation. She advised me to have someone else look over our past returns and check their accuracy. We always paid a CPA to do our tax returns and I had faith in his work so I didn't give it much more thought. Besides, I was much too busy to go through all the work of pulling out the old tax records on our business for nothing.

Within the next month, two different people approached me and told me how they had their old tax returns reviewed and ended up getting an extremely large refund. When the first person told me their story I asked for the name of the tax person who looked it over. I decided it might be worth a try, but I procrastinated again and never got around to it. When a second person told of their big refund I again asked for the name of the person who did it. To my surprise and amazement it was the same bookkeeping company. It was then that I decided to follow through with it and to my astonishment we did, in fact, have a large refund coming to us because of a miscalculation in our returns over the last three years.

Many times when you pass information on the recipient will say something like, "I was thinking of that", or "I had a feeling about that". The reason they respond like that is because they already channeled this information from their Guides. They most likely didn't realize it was channeled and therefore they lacked the confidence to proceed with it themselves.

To channel you must turn off your mind. Our mental thoughts create a lot of distraction from the truth. Truth is mixed in with our mental chatter. Our mental chatter is so constant and can quickly respond negatively to our channeled information. For this reason we are constantly leery of where the information actually comes from.

When first starting to channel it helps to understand that mental chatter carries more of a negative vibration than channeled information. The information you channel sounds so beautiful, uplifting and

Chapter 13

positive that it seems almost unreal to your mind at first. When you become fluent at channeling you easily recognize the difference between your mind and channeled information just by the 'sound' of the words.

Everyone can consciously channel information from their Guides. Practice is the only way to become confident and successful. If you are thinking there is no way you'll ever be able to do it, you are wrong. I remember the first time someone told me I could channel. I was fascinated because I really, really wanted to do it, but I had so much doubt about it and the thought of failing or getting wrong information kept me from even trying. When someone finally told me that I'd have to just *do it*, I finally mustered up the courage to give it a try and to my amazement it went very well. I was able to 'feel' the energy, much like you feel when you get very excited. I also saw a beautiful Angel off to the side of me throughout the session. These two things gave me confirmation that I was channeling.

That was my personal experience and certainly not something you should expect to happen when you first try. You will definitely have your own style and experiences, and many times people feel or see nothing different. I personally asked for verification that I was really doing it and I my Guides chose those two ways to reassure me.

Channeling also happens while you're sleeping. Dreams often carry messages from your Guides, information that you are not picking up while you are awake. One night I dreamt that I saw my horse standing in front of me on the other side of a fence. I remember 'feeling' as though she was on the outside rather than the inside of the pasture. The dream was short and not too alarming but I did remember it the next morning. I didn't pay much attention to the dream because it didn't make sense to my ego mind. Later that day my horses got out of the pasture. I hadn't secured the lock on the gate the previous day and they managed to get it open. If I had given that dream more consideration when I woke up, I would have checked the gate and fences to be sure something like that couldn't happen.

In another dream I saw myself with a new hairstyle. I had been wrestling around with new ideas for my hair for weeks. I couldn't find any pictures that seemed like the right cut for me. In my dream

I saw myself with this new haircut and loved it. There is certainly nothing earth shattering about a new hairstyle, but it was something I was having trouble with and at the time it was very helpful. Ask for anything. Nothing is too small or too big.

Chapter Thirteen Exercise

Before you go on to the next chapter, make a list of things friends, family or even strangers may have said to you lately that have stayed on your mind. If you find any duplicate messages it's a big heads up to start listening. See if you can remember a time when someone told you important information that helped you tremendously. From this day forward begin to pay attention to any repetitious messages, feelings or signs you receive from others.

Chapter 14

Methods of Channeling

Listen with all your senses, not just your ears.

There are many ways to channel information from those in the spirit world. As I outline the various methods in this chapter, you may find that you feel familiarity with a certain style. You may even feel like you've had a past experience with one or more of the methods I describe. That isn't your imagination. You have been channeling all your life. Your conscious mind just hasn't been involved.

Before learning that anyone and everyone can channel, it is common to describe channeling events as 'something weird' or 'just coincidence'. The truth is, you have the ability to use all of the channeling methods in this book. There will be some that come easier to you than others, but with practice you can develop your skills in each of the areas. Everyone can consciously channel and everyone can channel in every way possible. To begin, I will explain the different methods of channeling.

Clairvoyance

You can receive Divine Guidance through *clairvoyance*, which means visions, pictures or images. These can come to you at anytime, including through dreams. Clairvoyants see images, shapes or pictures. Some even see events as though they are a motion picture. Like watching a movie, all the details are displayed visually for them. These visions can be quick flashes or simply float into your consciousness. When I channel I usually receive still pictures and images, followed by a knowingness or feeling. To me it seems as though the visual image helps clarify my feelings and knowingness by giving me confirmation.

Naturally clairvoyant people generally notice every detail of the world around them. They walk into a room and visually scan every part of that room, taking in everything there is to see. A visual person will notice everything about you, including what you are wearing, the color of your nail polish, your shoes, earrings, etc. If you find yourself to be a very visual person, you may channel best through clairvoyance.

Clairsentience

Another method of receiving guidance is by *clairsentience*, which means through your feelings. Feeling guidance can involve a physical feeling as well as a gut feeling or a hunch. Feelings are felt in the body rather than the mind. Your gift is clairsentience if you generally feel everything you experience. These people will have a feeling when they meet someone. The feeling can be in the pit of their stomach or all over their body. You often hear them say something like, 'I had a funny feeling about that', or 'That guy made me feel uncomfortable'.

Clairsentients can take on the actual feeling of another person they are with or thinking about. If they are with someone feeling ill they may be able to feel their pain and then feel what can be done for them. Clairsentients are extremely sensitive to the energy of different people and places. It is important for feelers to remain in their own space and to feel without attaching themselves to the feeling.

Clairaudience

Another way to receive guidance is through *clairaudience*, meaning hearing sound or voices. The words you hear can be loud or soft and they can seem to be coming from outside or inside of your head, often sounding like your own voice. No doubt you have had this happen to you at least once in your life, especially in a moment of crisis or danger.

My stepson was in a bad car accident. His car went off the road into a bayou and landed upside down under water. He claims to have heard a voice in his head that told him what to do and saved his life. You may have been in a dangerous situation and heard the word 'stop' or 'run'. Since these words can sound like your own voice it's easy to doubt that they are Divine Guidance.

When I first started channeling, my clairaudience was always backed up with a visual word. Receiving messages with two or more methods was very helpful for me in gaining confidence in my new way of hearing. My suggestion is, if you hear any words of caution, direction, guidance or anything else, listen to them. Whether they are coming from God, your Guides, or your higher self, they are meant to protect you and are of the utmost importance.

Claircognizance
The last form of channeling information is called *claircognizance* or 'knowingness', in which you simply have the thought or idea and know, with complete certainty, that it is so. This was my strongest method at first and it was extremely difficult to feel confident with. Even though I 'knew' it, there was the constant question of 'How would I know that', or 'What if I'm just hoping it's true'?

Claircognizant people can seem like little Miss know it all's. No matter what you are talking to them about, they always have an answer *and* most of the time they are right. One thing I noticed about myself was that when a question was given to me, initially I thought "I don't know this", but it was only a matter of a few seconds before the whole answer came out of my mouth with much detail, clarity and certainty. I wouldn't know where the answer came from but I knew in my heart and soul that it was the truth.

You must learn to trust your own knowledge, especially if the words ring true to your ears and your heart.

When you first begin to channel one of these methods will be your specialty, meaning one will be the most common way in which you receive guidance. The more you practice, the more you will notice other methods beginning to develop as well. It can get frustrating at first because you tend to try too hard. Straining to hear and trying too hard can put up a block. You must relax and just listen. If you don't hear, see, feel or know an answer do not give up and think you can't do it. Be patient, ask for help, and keep trying.

Many times you *are* hearing, it's just that your mind won't believe it to be true. The answers you receive will sound vaguely familiar and many times you will think, "I knew that". For this reason it can be quite confusing to trust and have confidence in your new listening skill, but with practice you will soon be quite confident.

I found it quite helpful to get outside help with channeling when I first started practicing. I would verify and confirm that the answers I got were the same as what a professional Channel told me. You have been listening to God and your Guides all your life so their voices will not be that unfamiliar to you. Realizing it's them and not your mind is the only thing you have to familiarize yourself with. Don't strain to hear their words and don't be surprised with what you hear. Their voices are generally soft and subtle, and can sound like your own voice.

Practicing Channeling

There are many ways to practice channeling for your self and for others. When I first started to practice, I lacked confidence when channeling for myself because I continually doubted whether it was coming from my Guides or from my own mind. So much of the information sounded like something I would think. For me, it was easier to get the lines of communication flowing by channeling for others. In that way, you don't have as much emotional and mental attachment to the outcome. Everything you receive is relayed to another person and it is up to them to make sense of it. Their response is good confirmation that the information is correct and personalized for them. We are all unique and you will have your own method and style of channeling. I suggest trying all of the techniques to see which one feels best.

Keeping your body relaxed and not straining to get an answer is very important. The only other extremely important key is keeping your mind turned off. If your mind is chattering away you will be distracted and interrupted by your own thought. Once you quiet the thoughts and stay in touch with only what is happening in the moment, you will be able to receive guidance. Focusing on your body, breath and everything that is in the now, keeps your mind from bouncing around thoughts of the future and the past. Just relax, breathe and bring your self to the here and now.

Once you have mastered these things it's time to ask a question. After you ask the question go back to relaxing, breathing, and keeping your mind free of thought. Do not anticipate or worry about an answer. If you don't get one right away, be patient and wait. If you still get nothing after a minute or so, ask another question. Expect nothing. Just be open to receive.

It may help to close your eyes, especially if you are a visual person. When your eyes are closed you won't have the distraction of the world around you. At this point it's important to notice any feelings, pictures or sounds that pop up. Be an observer of all that you experience. Do not give it any thought. Let it keep flowing and just watch and listen. Ask your Guides to help you or to turn up the volume when needed. They will be happy to help you develop your skills so that they can communicate better with you. Practice as often as you can. You will get better and more confident each time you practice.

The following list suggests different physical environments to experiment with. The object is to choose an environment that allows your mind to relax and stay out of it.

<u>Meditative State</u>

You can practice channeling when in a meditative state. Sometimes this is easier because you have put more effort into being calm and quieting your mind. Once you are relaxed, ask a question and expect no response. Resume your meditative state and just 'be'. If there is an answer for you it will come when you are relaxed and without thought.

<u>Soaking in the Bathtub</u>

Another wonderful time to try channeling is when you're soaking in a bath. The water will help calm you and open your energetic field. Follow the same steps for relaxing, breathing and clearing your mind first. Lighting a candle and looking at the flame often helps calm the mind.

<u>Amidst Nature</u>

Sitting outside in nature is also a wonderful place to practice channeling. The energies of the trees and plants will help you connect. You don't have to drive to the park, your own backyard is just as good. Let your eyes relax and take in everything around you. Bring your thoughts to how wonderful it feels to breathe fresh air, smell the sweet fragrances of nature, and see the beauty of all living things.

At the Keyboard

Another place to channel is in front of the computer. Without going into a meditative state, allow your mind to calm and place your hands on the keyboard. Breathe deeply and ask a question. Type whatever comes to your mind. Even if it makes no sense, type it. Don't try to understand or put thought into what you are typing. You can read it when you're finished. The important thing is to type *everything*. I found this method to be the easiest for me at first. I found that as soon as I started typing, the information began to flow more freely. The more I typed the faster and clearer the information came. This method is called automatic writing.

Pen and Paper

If you don't type well, try automatic writing with a pen and paper. You can sit anywhere you'd like, indoors or outdoors. This is the same as sitting in front of the computer except that you will write everything instead of type it. If you can type, it's easier to keep up with the thoughts by typing. When I write I feel like I'm not doing it fast enough to keep up with the information coming to me. If this happens simply ask your Guides to repeat what they said or to talk a little slower.

Channeling for Someone Else

If you want to channel for someone else you can use any of the above methods by stating the name of the person, their age and where they live. The information will come through in the same way.

You can also sit with them and channel. I was very nervous and doubtful the first time I channeled for someone else. My dearest friend Jill was my first experience. We went into a room by ourselves and sat on the bed. I was so worried that it wouldn't work but Jill was patient, supportive and encouraging. She asked a question and I closed my eyes. We sat there a few moments and then it started coming to me. Slowly the words came out of my mouth and honestly I couldn't believe it. In a matter of seconds the words were rolling off my tongue faster and faster. My eyes were shut to avoid distraction. I started to feel a flutter inside of me and then I saw an image of the most beautiful angel in front of me. That beautiful image gave me confirmation and encouragement and I went on channeling for the next twenty minutes. Once I broke the ice with that experience my channeling abilities remained open and flowing from that day on.

There are many ways to receive guidance. Try them all to see which method feels most comfortable to you. Don't worry if you have trouble learning to channel. It will happen. Be patient and never stop trying. Your Guides can, and do, communicate with you already. They have always been, and will continue to, guide you for the rest of your life. While channeling allows you to consciously communicate, you will still receive their information at a subconscious level. The following experiences should help you understand the diversity of communication and Divine intervention.

Personal Experiences

The very first time I experienced channeling I wasn't even trying to. It all happened one Easter morning when I was typing an email to my new friend. She was the person that gave me an Angel card reading and at that time she was already channeling. We hadn't known each other more than a couple of weeks and we'd never talked about channeling. In fact, I had no knowledge of channeling whatsoever. I didn't know how it worked or that I could even do it.

As I typed an email to her I began to feel odd. I felt a strange energetic sensation deep inside me that I couldn't explain. All of a sudden I knew her deceased husband was with me. I had never met him yet I knew it was him. Without any effort on my part my fingers began typing words from him. I sat there in a semi-shocked state and continued typing. My mind was reeling with thoughts of me possibly going crazy and I was getting scared because I didn't understand what was going on. It was as if I had no control over my hands until he finished what he wanted to channel. The entire time, I had no idea of what I was typing. In fact, I assumed that it would make no sense at all. When it ended I went back and read the words. I realized that this was information intended for my friend so I forwarded the e-mail to her with an explanation of what happened.

It is sad, but that experience scared me so much because I didn't understand what was going on. If I had known about channeling I would have been so excited to be a 'channel'. I was scared to get back on the computer again after that. I felt confused and upset about the whole thing and I certainly didn't want it to happen again. Once my friend reassured me and explained what happened I began to feel honored that I was able to pick up and pass on information.

Shortly after that experience her deceased husband channeled to me during one of my meditations. I had only been practicing meditating for a few weeks and wasn't even sure I was doing it correctly. All of a sudden my body felt icy cold and I could feel his presence once again. This time I experienced hearing, seeing and feeling his message. To be honest with you, I was 'freaked out', but I let it continue until he was finished and left. After that I was shook up and scared all over again. Once again, my friend reassured me and explained that it was okay. From then on I began reading every book I could find on channeling.

Another time, I had an absolutely amazing and awesome experience with butterflies for several weeks. It all started just after I was first introduced to this new spiritual way of life. Someone had told me that butterflies are a sign of new beginnings. I thought that sounded sweet but I never thought much more about it. We all see butterflies and how was I to know it was a 'sign' and not just a butterfly flying around. Shortly thereafter, literally hundreds of butterflies crossed my path during a six week period of time. I'd never seen anything like it before. It was so amazing that I would ask other people if they were seeing an unusual amount of butterflies, thinking that it may just be a record year for them. It was not happening for others and that is when I realized it was a special way my Guides chose to communicate with me.

Butterflies would fly directly in front of me, sometimes circling around me several times. Others brushed across my skin or landed on me. One time my husband and I were fishing in the middle of a big lake. It was almost dark and we were far from the shore. A huge butterfly flew all the way out there, circled our boat and flew

Chapter 14

off. I even had one fly right in front of me in the dark one night. You may have never noticed, but butterflies seldom fly around at night. The last butterfly I saw before this amazing phenomenon ended was an enormous four inches wide. It drifted past me and left me standing there with my mouth hanging open. It flew into my garage and I followed it to take a second look. I never found it. I searched the entire garage and never saw it again. That was the last of my butterfly experience.

Another time I received a visual sign from above was when I was moving car loads of odds and ends to our new house. I pulled up to the new house and began emptying the car. When I had finished unloading I stood in my new home and said a prayer of thanks to God and my Guides for sending me to this wonderful new home. I was overflowing with joy and gratitude. I returned to my car and opened the door. There, on the driver's seat were two coins. They seemed to be strategically placed side by side and face up. One was a solid silver dollar and the other was a Susan B. Anthony dollar. I hadn't unloaded anything across my seat and I didn't move anything that could have held such coins in the first place. There was no explanation for how the coins got there. I took this experience as a 'you're welcome' from my Guides.

After telling my story to others, several people told me that our Angels and Guides often drop coins in our path to let us know they are near. As I am writing this I am reminded, from above, of my father's love for coin collecting and his mother's name. My grandmother's name is Susan Antony. Both of them have passed.

Clairaudience means to hear guidance. The following experience demonstrates how our Guides can communicate in that way. We had just bought our new home but we had not sold our old home yet. Financial stability was a concern for us as we became worried about the possibility of paying the mortgage on two homes for a while. I already knew that God wanted us to have abundance in our life, and I knew that I was divinely guided to buy our new home, however I was still consumed with doubt and worry over getting ourselves over-extended financially.

One week after we moved into our new home we were watching television. My husband was flipping around the channels and stopped on a channel that was a Lakewood Church sermon. We never watched this before but that sermon caught our attention. The whole thing was about letting go of the negative feelings that keep us from receiving the financial abundance we deserve. It reinforced the fact that God wants us to be financially free and that it's okay to have success and money.

We felt better after watching that but it was three days later when I was unpacking some books that I received another confirmation. I came across a book I hadn't seen in a long time. The book had spiritual passages for each day of the year. I opened it up to the current date and the message I read was exactly the same as the message in the Lakewood Church sermon. Confirmation for sure!

I have experienced some Divine interventions while shopping too. One day, my husband and I were shopping for televisions, trying to figure out how to choose one brand over the other brand when they all seemed to be very similar. We had been in the store for quite some time and were becoming tired of shopping and confused about how to make our decision. I finally gave up and told him to choose whichever one he wanted.

As I stood there waiting for him to decide, the remote control of one of the televisions jumped out from *behind* the TV and landed about three feet in front of it. I immediately said, 'Did you see that?' My husband quickly answered, 'I guess we found our TV'. That was it. We marched right over to check out and bought that one.

Another time I was shopping with my daughter-in-law, Erica. I've never been the type to enjoy shopping, especially in a mall. My wardrobe suffers greatly because of this, so about twice a year I take Erica shopping with me. She has an eye for fashion and she loves shopping. We were near the end of our shopping spree *and* my patience level. I wanted to get some new earrings before we finished. As Erica happily browsed, I stood there thinking, 'Who cares, just pick something so we can get out of here'. Just then she came around the corner holding a pair of earrings. Her eyes were big as she said they literally jumped right off the rack and landed in front of her. I loved them and we were out of there.

For some time I'd been seeing the same vision during my meditation. I drew a picture of it in my journal. The object was a tree stump. It made no sense to me. We live in the woods so I walked

Chapter 14

the property looking for something similar but never saw it. I eventually put it out of my mind, announcing in my journal that 'I was stumped' with this information. Shortly after that we had a massive tree fall over next to our house. It didn't hit the house but the stump that remained looked exactly like my vision. Since it did us no harm or damage, my vision was simply a confirmation that we are always in constant communication with our Guides. They can help us see the past, present and the future.

Sometimes our Guides intervene in our lives through human form, and assist us as a Guardian Angel would. One day my husband and I were out in our new boat enjoying the day. We started to notice a lot of boats flying past us and going to shore. We were irritated with them and thought they were rude for coming so close and going so fast. A few minutes later we noticed a massive, dark cloud in the Western sky. It looked like it was a long way off so we weren't too concerned, however, in no time at all the cloud was nearly over our head. Finally it clicked! Everyone was getting off the lake because of the storm cloud rolling in. We quickly began pulling up anchor and heading toward shore. The sky got darker and the waves got stronger. Soon it was pouring sheets of rain and the waves were pushing our little boat around like a rubber duck.

By the time we reached land the storm was pounding us with rain and the waves were slamming over the deck of the boat. Knowing we had to get the boat out of the water or the waves would wash it too far up on shore, my husband jumped out and headed for the boat trailer. He shouted to me to keep the boat from getting stuck on the beach. The waves were stronger than I was. They were literally washing over the back of the boat and pushing the boat into me. With each wave the boat slammed into me harder, working its way farther up on shore.

Out of nowhere, a tiny, elderly lady walked up to me. Despite the raging storm she looked calm and undisturbed by the weather. I glanced at her but I had my hands full fighting the boat and waves. She said, 'It looks like you need an Angel'. Without taking my eyes off my job I replied, 'I sure do!' I thought it was sweet of her to be concerned but I was thinking it would be better if she were a big, strong man so I could get some help.

Then she said, 'Is there anything I can do?' I looked around and saw an old tire on the beach. The day before I had commented to my husband about how awful it was that someone littered the beach with a tire. My husband explained that the tire was there to put under the front of your boat while it was on shore so that it wouldn't get pushed up on the beach by the waves. Realizing the tire could help, I looked back at the frail little lady. I was sure she couldn't even lift the tire much less bring it to me under these serious weather conditions.

I was getting tired struggling with the boat but mumbled my thoughts of using the tire. Like a miracle she walked up to me and held the boat. She told me to hurry and get the tire. Reluctantly I turned the boat over to her and ran as fast as I could for the tire. When I rushed back to the boat I noticed she looked as if it were no strain for her to hold it.

Amazed, but still in a panic, I threw the tire down and the next wave pushed the boat right on it. It was easy to stabilize the boat after that but the pounding waves were quickly filling the boat with water. I saw my husband coming toward the boat ramp with the trailer and breathed a sigh of relief. I looked up to thank the sweet lady for her help but she was gone.

It was still quite a few more minutes before we got the boat out of the water. The waves were pushing the trailer around and a part of the boat support broke off when we finally got the boat on it. For the rest of the weekend I kept looking around for the lady but never saw her again. I asked several people if they had seen her but no one had.

When my husband was about four years old he had a similar experience. He was with his brother and they were walking home. It was getting dark and as they walked they noticed someone following them on the other side of the street. They looked back but it was too dark to make out anything other than the silhouette of a man.

They started to feel afraid and began walking faster. The faster they walked the faster the man walked. The man crossed the street and started getting closer to them. In the pit of their stomach they knew that something was wrong. They began to get very scared.

Just then a lady appeared in front of them. She was older and had a shawl on. He remembers her face looked sweet and friendly and

Chapter 14

she was smiling at them. As they walked up to her, she opened her shawl and wrapped it around the boys as if shielding them. She started walking with them. My husband looked back over her shawl at the man but he had turned around and was walking the other direction. The lady got them safely home that night. They never saw her again.

My husband also vividly remembers another experience he had when he was about four years old. There was a tree house across the street from his home. He was too little to climb up it but he wanted to go over there anyway. He was not allowed to cross the busy street but he snuck over there and played beneath the tree house for a while.

It started to get dark and he heard his Mom calling him. Quickly he started back home. He remembers a big ditch just before the street. As soon as he reached the ditch he noticed a lot of cars coming down the road. Just then a bright light came out of the sky. He looked at it and it got brighter and bigger. Soon it was like an enormous beacon or beam of light shooting down. The light seemed to get right in front of his face and he stood there staring at it. As he looked he began to see the image of a face. Soon the face turned into a man's body. The image became clearer and he realized it was Jesus. After a brief moment of shock he got real scared and took off, jumping over the ditch and running across the street. It wasn't until after he crossed the street that he realized there were no more cars on the road.

Telepathy

Telepathy is much like channeling but it is an exchange of energies between two earthly beings. I think it is absolutely fascinating but many people, including myself for years, are very confused about telepathy and channeling which creates fear and skepticism. There is nothing to fear about either one. In fact you have had telepathic experiences many times in your life.

Have you ever been talking to someone and thought "I knew they were going to say that' or while someone is describing something you actually 'caught a glimpse' of it clearly in your mind? Telepathy is a projection of energy from one person to another. Channeling is picking up the energy and wisdom of deceased or spirit world friends. No one can really get in your mind; they can only pick up on your energy.

Emotions and thoughts are carried in your energy and that is why it is possible to pick up on them in other people. Telepathy is nothing supernatural or frightening. We all do it to some degree quite often. Practicing and working with your telepathic abilities can enhance your channeling and psychic abilities.

When we begin to channel we seldom have immediate confirmation that we actually picked up the right information. With telepathic exercises, you can work together with another person and receive immediate feedback and confirmation. There are many fun exercises you can do to test and develop your telepathic abilities. I highly recommend trying them as a way to increase your ability to connect energetically with others on earth or in the spirit world. The most challenging part will be finding a partner who's open to the idea. Here are a couple of telepathic experiences I had.

I took a class on telepathy and the third eye one day. Though it was fascinating to me, I wasn't very familiar with either one at that time. In one exercise we were supposed to close our eyes and try to telepathically pick up on what our instructor was thinking. Apparently not paying full attention, I thought we were supposed to send our thought to him. As we began, I held my thought and vision and pictured sending it out to the instructor. I was slightly agitated because another picture kept popping up in my mind. Time and again, I would push it aside and return my focus to the picture I was sending to my instructor.

Thank goodness I wasn't called on first to explain what I saw. To my surprise everyone ahead of me was describing what they *received* from the instructor. I panicked because I had the whole lesson confused. Just as he called on me to give my answer I remembered the vision that kept interrupting me and explained it in detail. When everyone was done describing their visions the instructor explained the picture he was sending to us. I was shocked to find out that I had picked it up the best, and with the most detail, and I didn't even know I was supposed to. To this day, I still chuckle when I think about it.

The most surprising experience I had with telepathy happened before I even knew what it was. I was curling my hair in the bath-

Chapter 14

room and my husband was in the other room watching television. He said, 'Honey, you've got to come in here and see this'. Not wanting to stop what I was doing and feeling a little irritated at being summoned when I was obviously busy, I made a comment under my breath. I mumbled, 'The only way I'm going to see that is if you send it to me because I'm not leaving this bathroom right now'.

Well, I never dreamed it would actually happen but it did. Immediately, I had a crystal clear flash of a picture in my mind. I saw the people, and their mouths moved to the same words I heard from the television in the other room. It was so vivid and so real that I quickly put my curling iron down and, still carefully holding the picture in my mind, ran into the other room. I was amazed that the same exact picture was on the television screen. Everything was identical. The background, the color of each person's hair, the body shapes and size, and the objects in the room were all the same. I saw what he was seeing!

The following exercises are fun ways to test and develop your telepathic abilities. Practice them with a partner so you can get instant confirmation on how you're doing. Once you feel good about your telepathic abilities you will be able to trust and feel confident with your channeling as well.

Telepathy Exercise #1

Begin sitting across from someone else with your knees touching. If you feel comfortable with this, you can even hold each other's hands. One person closes their eyes and tries to pick up on any information or feelings the other person has.

When you first start doing this it is important to say *everything* that comes to you. Sometimes the information you receive will make no sense to you but it will to them. If all you see a flower, tell them. If you feel an ache in your belly, tell them. Whatever you feel, know, see or hear should be put into words. Who cares if neither one of you can make sense of it right then and there. Sometimes you will find that you have picked up on information that pertains to a future event. Other times your partner may not understand the meaning until much later.

Telepathy Exercise #2

Begin sitting with your partner in the same way as the last exercise. This time, one person thinks of an object. That person visualizes it in their mind and continues to hold that vision while the other person tries to pick up on what it is.

When you're first starting this, it's better to pick one simple object instead of visualizing something complex like a forest of trees, plants and bushes. The simpler your visualization is, the easier it will be for the other person to pick up. As you get better at it, you can make your visualizations more complex and detailed.

Telepathy Exercise #3

Make a set of color cards. On each card make a big circle and color it in with one solid color. You can have as many cards as you'd like but be sure there's just one colored circle on each card. Have your partner hold a card and look at the colored circle. As they look at the card they need to put all their attention and thought into the color of the circle. You will try to telepathically pick up on what they are seeing.

You can do this exercise without a partner by laying a card face down on the table. Look at the card and hold your hand over the card. Try to sense what color it is. When you get good at doing one card at a time, try laying out two, three, or four cards and picking each one's color.

To change this exercise up a little, you can make a deck of cards with different shapes. Each card should have only one shape. Draw a square, circle, triangle or rectangle on each card. Make the shape with a dark pen or marker and do not fill it in with color.

Telepathy Exercise #4

Another way to practice telepathy is by holding a piece of your partner's jewelry or their watch. It can be anything they keep close to their body all the time. If you have a group, each person can place their personal item in a basket. Pass the basket around and have everyone pick an item. If you only have one partner, you can practice picking up on their energy like you did in exercise #1. By holding the energy of the jewelry, it may be easier for you to connect.

You can also ask your partner to bring in a piece of jewelry from someone else if it's possible. Don't let them tell you who it belongs to. Pick up whatever you can and see if it fits the owner.

Telepathy Exercise #5
In this exercise you give your partner a photo of someone they don't know. While looking at the photo and holding it, see what information comes to you. Remember to say everything you pick up on. It may help to get their name, but try it both ways and see what happens.

If you don't have a photo, give your partner the name of someone they don't know. When you do this, it's best to write the persons name, city and state and approximate age on paper first. Look at the words and see what you pick up.

We all have the ability to tune in to other energies. Be creative and practice channeling and telepathy. Once you start feeling comfortable with listening and connecting to other energies, you will notice how often you channel and have telepathic experiences. You will also begin to trust in the guidance and channeled information you receive from the spirit world more.

Nothing is impossible and if there is a message you need to hear from your Guides they will get it to you one way or another. Take nothing for granted and remember there are no coincidences. Everything happens for a reason. We need to pay attention to everything around us and within us. Once you begin to realize that there is a constant flow of communication you will have so much fun recognizing and receiving it.

Chapter Fourteen Exercise
Think back on events that could have been Divine intervention in your life. You have had some, you just need to remember them. The more you think about it the more you will remember.

A Soul's Guide to Abundance, Health And Happiness

Watch closely for new communications as well. Once you start paying attention you receive more. Your Guides love communicating with you and they'll be happy to start giving you more confirmations now that you're paying attention.

# Chapter 15

Surrendering to God

Release your fears, worries and troubles to God, for only then can Divine Light enter and a miracle happen. Let go completely to God and He will guide you in all that you do.
If you let go a little, you will have a little peace. If you let go a lot, you will have a lot of peace. If you let go completely, you will know complete peace and freedom.
Your struggles with the world will have come to an end.

How often do you find yourself worrying about all the things you need to get done and the little time you have to do them? How often are you afraid that something is going to, or not going to happen? How often do you dwell on problems you face or difficult situations you find yourself in?

These feelings enter into all our lives nearly every day. Sometimes just the thought of one extra item on our 'to do' list can put us over the edge. Our fears, worries and troubles can consume a lot of our energy and thought. Worrying about something can create hours of mental struggling, juggling and turmoil. Fear can cause us to feel unsafe, helpless, defenseless and powerless. Aside from creating a great amount of negativity within us, it is also a waste of our time and energy to allow ourselves to react this way.

God takes care of you all the time. Everything you need is given to you. You have nothing to fear. I read a sign the other day that said, "If God is your co-pilot, switch seats". We have to surrender everything to Him in order to have peace in our life. Here's an example. You are stressing out and worrying about a big lecture you have to give. You hate speaking to groups and the thought of standing up there and blacking out or stumbling through it keeps running through your mind. The lecture isn't until next week but you can't stop worrying about it. Does your worry have any impact on the lecture? Will the lecture be better because you are spending so much time worrying? No, in fact you can make it worse by allowing those negative thoughts to keep banging around in your head. Worry comes from fear. Fear comes from not trusting that God will take care of us and everything we do. Fear and worry won't make the lecture go away and it won't help you to feel better about giving it. It's a waste of time and energy.

We must learn to surrender to God. Whenever I find myself obsessing over something that is doing me no good I ask God to take it from me. I remind myself that God already has everything perfectly planned, in perfect order, and in perfect timing. Allow yourself to release your own fears, anxieties, worries and troubles to Him. Once you pass it on to God, you feel a great sense of relief and peace within yourself. Let it go and truly trust in God to take care of you. He does all the time anyway.

This is not to say you only need to surrender difficult situations or crisis to Him. Let go of the feeling that you alone control your life. The truth is that you do not. God is in the driver's seat and He alone is in control.

Your mind cannot stop hashing through every detail and thus it makes you feel as though you are alone and in total control. When this happens you are being controlled by your mind. Your mind is not real and it is not of the present moment. That busy little brain of yours is constantly tossing around thoughts of the past or future. These thoughts are what create your fears. Stop letting your mind control your life and give the control to God. He is an expert at protecting you, guiding you, supporting you, and knowing what is best for you. When you can surrender everything to God it changes your entire life.

Have you ever heard the phrase, "Go with the flow"? There is a natural rhythm to the universe and to your life. Surrendering to God allows you to live in the natural rhythm of things. Is it easier to swim upstream or downstream? Of course, downstream is much easier because you barely have to swim to move with the natural flow of the water.

Chapter 15

It is the same with your life. Struggling and fighting with schedules, commitments and demands is much more difficult than trusting the natural flow and rhythm and gliding smoothly along. Why is it then, that most people are fighting that rhythm? It is because they believe they are in complete control of their lives and it becomes overwhelming, overbearing, and at times impossible.

Stop fighting the natural rhythm. Everything will get done in the same time frame anyway. If there is only enough time for you to do four of the jobs on your list, there is only time for four. Worrying and fretting over not getting those last jobs done won't change a thing anyway. The only thing it will do is rob you of your energy, create more negative energy within you, and leave you feeling upset and stressed out.

This is not to say that when you surrender your tasks to God you won't get as much done. It is quite the contrary, you seem to get twice as much done and it gets done with *ease*. Start practicing surrendering your life to God. Try for just an hour or two at first, working up to several hours and then an entire day. The shorter you make your first attempts the easier it will be to get the hang of it.

I can still remember the very first time I did it. I had two hours worth of errands to run in one hour's time. I had to get these things done and get to work in a specific time frame. Normally, I would find myself fighting with the clock, worrying constantly about whether or not I'll get it all done, and getting irritated and frustrated with traffic.

This day was entirely different. I started out thinking there was no way it would all get done but I was willing to surrender to God and let go of some of my errands just for the experience. Well, everything got done and there was time to spare. In fact, I allowed myself to chat with people along the way and enjoy each stop instead of rushing through like a crazed maniac. It was absolutely amazing. That was when I realized how much easier it was to surrender *everything* to God.

My example may sound pretty simple but that is why I chose to tell you about it. Rather than waking up one day and announcing that you are going to surrender your entire life to God from this moment on, take it slower. It isn't that easy to make the change. You have probably been flying solo for many years, taking on all the responsibility, worry and pressures of life and calling on God only in times of crisis. When you surrender completely to Him, you not only call on Him during difficult times, but all day, every day.

Practice with an hour or two and then work up to a full day. Once you feel the peace, harmony and ease it brings to your life it will feel natural to surrender at all times. No longer will you feel that constant struggle and frustration. You will feel lighter, safer and freer. Your mind can stop the constant negative chatter of worry and fear. Each event of your day will unfold with ease and you will no longer feel the stress and pressure of time.

Next time you're late for an important appointment and traffic is slowing you down just say out loud, "I surrender this to you, God". The burden you remove from yourself will instantly make you feel lighter and will bring you peace. You may find that you encounter a string of green lights and end up getting there on time after all. This has happened to me numerous times. If the green lights do not happen, know that there is a reason for everything and you are going to arrive at your perfect time. You will have eliminated stress and worry and you will be there no later or earlier than if you had arrived carrying all that negative garbage with you. Imagine feeling refreshed, calm and happy instead of stressed, agitated and angry when you get to your appointment. I know that if I end up running late even after I've surrendered to God, there was good reason.

One day I was in a hurry to get somewhere. Just as I was leaving, someone stopped me and started talking to me about their troubles. My first thought was, "I have to get going now or I'll be late". As soon as I realized what I was doing I stopped myself and surrendered the whole thing to God. We ended up having a wonderful conversation. Ten minutes later I was on my way. A few miles down the road there was a serious accident involving an RV and a motorcycle. It had happened about ten minutes before I got there and I later found out that someone had been killed in the accident. I thanked God for protecting me.

Surrendering to God opens up the opportunity for miracles to happen. Sometimes it is hard to understand why things happen as they do, but you must trust that everything is perfect and happens for a reason. When you know that God is in the drivers seat of your life you no longer have to worry about anything. Who knows better than God what is good and perfect for you. Your mind *thinks* it knows but it is only basing that knowledge on past events. God knows the now and the future of your life. Give Him the steering wheel so you can sit back and enjoy the scenery.

Life is to be enjoyed and it's impossible to fully enjoy life if you're constantly fighting the natural flow of things. When you find you're working way too hard to make something happen and it just isn't happening, it's time to get out of the drivers seat. Perhaps there is something even better awaiting you, or you will be spared some unnecessary hardship.

Chapter Fifteen Exercise

Try surrendering just an hour or two of your life to God. Give yourself small time frames to practice the way it feels. Be sure to completely surrender. Trust with *certainty* that God will take care of your every need and desire. Do not worry or hold any doubt that it won't work. Trust, believe and then surrender completely.

Chapter 15

Surrender to God

*When we're always on the go,
But we'd rather take things slow,*

*Take time to really see things,
And notice the joy it brings.*

*Surrender to God your tasks,
Remove that worrisome mask,*

*Just relax, be calm and breathe,
And handle each day with ease.*

*So next time it's go, go, go,
Trust in the natural flow,*

*New peace will come to your life
No longer will you know strife.*

Part II

Your Mind

Grant yourself a wish today,
Let nothing get in the way.
Hopes and dreams can all come true,
The job is all up to you.

For anything you may wish
A house, a job, or big fish,
Is simply a thought away,
A thought to hold every day.

Affirm your wish all day long,
And soon you'll sing a new song,
For your mind holds much power,
And gifts soon start to shower.

Pick one wish and start today,
Soon all things will go your way.
Don't delay!

Chapter 16

Positive Thoughts

What do you think about your thoughts?

Have you ever taken the time to think about your thoughts? We think thousand of different thoughts a day, yet we seldom put much thought into our thoughts themselves.

In the previous chapters I explained that the mind is not a reflection of our true self and it can get in the way of communicating with our higher self, God and our Guides. This is true but it would be unrealistic to think of turning our minds off all the time. For this reason I want to teach you how to use your mind in a way that will enhance and fulfill your life even more.

We all have a mind that holds thought constantly. What we need to do is make sure our thoughts are working *for* us and not *against* us. This means we may have to change the way in which we think. First, know that *you choose* every thought your mind has. You are in complete control of what thoughts you decide to hold. Secondly, every thought you have creates a mental reality for you.

You believe your thoughts to be true, therefore they become the truth or reality. When you piece together all of your mental realities they create your life and your future. If you're not happy with your life all you need to do is change your thoughts. Remember, you make the choice because you create your own thoughts. You control your mind. Your mind does not control you. You must be the creator of only good, positive thoughts.

To begin, think about the mind. What a powerful tool mankind has been given. Reflect on all the good things the power of the mind has done for us and for our world. There have been fabulous inventions, remarkable solutions, and amazing ideas created in the mind. The abilities of the mind are truly awesome. Think back to a time when your mind played a powerful role in your life. Perhaps you remember a class that you aced in school, or an idea you came up with at work that everyone loved, or you figured out a solution to a major problem. You might even remember a time when your mind helped someone else who was having trouble thinking for themselves. Thank yourself for your active, healthy, strong mind.

Your thoughts hold tremendous power over your life emotionally, spiritually and physically. For this reason it is important to pay attention to *all* of them. Just as your mind has the ability to create wonderful thoughts, it also creates destructive, negative thoughts. Negative thoughts are self sabotaging. They affect your life in many ways. Your thoughts can create illness or heal illness. They can create wealth and abundance or keep you from ever having it. Thoughts can create fear or the feeling of power. If we create positive thoughts we will have positive reactions. When we engage our mind in negative chatter we create negative reactions.

The following prayer by St. Francis of Assisi speaks of giving the positive to eliminate the negative.

> Lord, make me an instrument of Your peace.
> Where there is hatred, let me sow love;
> Where there is injury, pardon,
> Where there is doubt, faith;
> Where there is despair, hope;
> Where there is darkness, light; and
> Where there is sadness, joy.
> Oh Divine Master, grant that I may not so much
> seek to be consoled, as to console;
> To be understood, as to understand;
> To be loved, as to love.
> For it is in giving that we receive
> It is in pardoning that we are pardoned;
> And it is in dying that we are born to eternal life.

Notice that St. Francis has touched on many self sabotaging mental realities such as hatred, injury, doubt, despair, darkness of the

Chapter 16

soul, and sadness. I've always loved that prayer but I assumed he was speaking only about giving to others. Now I see that it applies to healing our own mental realities as well. It works the same way. By replacing the negative with the positive, you trigger a positive mental change. The bottom line is that we need to pay attention to all negative reactions and feelings in ourselves and others, then quickly replace them with positive thoughts.

Take a moment to look into your own mind and see if you are holding any negative thoughts about your body, your financial status, or your life in any way. Try this quick exercise:

Get a piece of paper and a pen. Write the numbers one through five as I have below. Now answer these five questions as quickly as you can. Write down your first response to the question. Try to use only one or two sentences per answer.

1. When you look in the mirror, how do you feel about your body?
2. What do you think of your job?
3. What is your financial situation like right now?
4. Explain your relationship with your spouse or partner?
5. How do you feel about your parents?

Take a look at your answers to these questions and draw a line through any answer that carries a negative response or thought. Scratch out anything that sounds negative. How many answers are left unscratched? Do the majority of your answers hold negativity?

You can not continue to allow negative thoughts to control your life. It is important to keep cleansing your mind by immediately replacing negative thoughts with positive thoughts.

You also need to pay attention to what you project outward. Your thoughts have tremendous power over others because you transfer them constantly. When we transfer negative thoughts we create more of the same in others. When we transfer positive thoughts we benefit ourselves and everyone else by creating more of the same.

Thoughts are also created from past experiences. Some thoughts will continue to pop up over and over again for years even though they hold no relevance to us in the here and now. Carrying around the baggage of old, worn out, negative thoughts, suppresses your ability to be the perfect person you truly are and to have the perfect life you deserve. Some of the negative comments we heard as a child still linger in our minds because we are a product of our environment. We can continue to carry around things that were said to us many, many years ago like 'She's not that smart', 'He's always been chubby', 'She's so uncoordinated', 'He's absentminded', or 'She never applies herself'. Even if you don't consciously remember hearing those words, their energy can remain locked in your mind for years. Those words may have become your mental reality to some extent. Your life will be a reflection of those thoughts.

Think for a moment on some of the repetitive negative thoughts your mind holds about yourself. Thoughts such as 'I can't do anything right', 'I hate my hair', 'I'm fat', or 'I always forget things'. I also hear people make comments such as, "I hate my boss', "I have a rotten job', 'I never have any money', 'My house is too small' and so on. The list is endless. Anything you can talk about can be spoken in negative words or positive words. What do you hear yourself say time after time?

It's possible to analyze how and when those thoughts became a part of you. I'm not going there in this book, mainly because my intention is to briefly introduce you to each topic, however there are many good books and workbooks available that can help you evaluate the source of your thoughts. Louise Hay has several wonderful books and workbooks that can help you diagnose these issues further. I have listed some of her books in the Suggested Reading section at the end of this book.

The important thing is to get rid of them once and for all. It doesn't matter to me where they came from. They simply are no longer welcome in my mind. I refuse to allow them to exist. I will not give them any more of my time and energy. It's as simple as that and you can do the same thing right now.

Every time you allow yourself to listen to these words they cause more self destruction. When you replace them with positive words you open the door for joy, abundance, peace, self-love, self confidence and fulfillment in your life. The first step is to consciously pay attention to the thoughts racing around in your head all day. Pick out the negative thoughts as soon as you notice them.

Chapter 16

Don't be surprised if there are many and if you find yourself picking out most of your thoughts for a while. This is very normal. Those thoughts have been bouncing around in your mind for many years. They have become your way of thinking now.

The reality is that you do not need to hold on to them any longer. There is no ball and chain attached to you and those thoughts. You must refuse to listen to that garbage. It's time to say *stop* to the negative words and replace them with positive words. Anytime you hear your self thinking or speaking negatively, simply make note of it, stop yourself immediately, and rephrase or rethink the sentence in a positive way.

As easy as it sounds it can take some time and practice, but the reward is well worth your effort. I don't mind working at it for the rest of my life if it enhances and fulfills every part of my life. When you begin to think more positively you will experience a major shift in yourself, your life, your relationship with others and your attitude toward life.

Thought creates reality. If you are constantly thinking you'll never have enough money, you won't. If you think you'll never be thin again, you won't. Anything you think becomes your reality. You create everything about your life through your thoughts. Because of that, you can change anything and everything to a more positive reality by holding only positive thoughts. In the same way, you can also deny yourself of anything through negative thoughts. How can you knowingly deny yourself of the happiness, abundance and fulfillment you desire and deserve?

Here's a personal example to explain the power of your thoughts. We had our house up for sale and had already found our new home. We were worried that closing would come and go on the new home and we'd still be stuck with the old house. We kept thinking "What if we get stuck with two homes?" and "How will we pay two mortgages?", and "What if we don't get a buyer for our house?"

A friend of mine told me that we may not be letting go of the old house completely. She explained that we may be emotionally attached to our home and not willing to let go. It sounded crazy because we desperately wanted it to sell it and move to a better house. When we thought about it, we realized that there were a lot of old memories with our kids and our own relationship that occurred in that house. Every now and then we'd catch ourselves feeling guilty and sad about leaving this home that was so much a part of all our lives.

My friend suggested we write down the word 'sold' on a piece of paper and keep it somewhere where we would see it from time to time. When we wrote the word sold we visualized the house selling and visualized ourselves detaching from the house. We also began to visualize ourselves in the new home and projected our energy toward that house instead. Letting go of the emotional and energetic attachment to our old house, and affirming the sale and move into the new house, cleared the way for a buyer to come along just two weeks later.

Becoming aware of your negative thoughts is the first step to change. The moment you catch yourself thinking negatively, you've already started a major shift toward being more positive. Knowing is the first step to changing.

Chapter Sixteen Exercise

From this day on, pay attention to all your thoughts. Whenever you catch yourself thinking negatively just say 'stop', and replace the negative with positive. Be extra careful that you do not fall into the trap of other people's negative words. If negative words are spoken to you by someone else, do not give them any of your energy. Do not allow them to become part of your thoughts. As long as you do not allow yourself to *hold* the thought, it can not become your truth.

Chapter 17

Positive Affirmations

*I have all the abundance I need to feel safe.
I have all the Angels and Guides I need
to steer me down the right path.
I have all the love and kindness I need
to share with others who need it.
I clearly see, hear, feel, and know my
Divine guidance.
I have all the wisdom and power I need to achieve my life purpose.
I only have positive thoughts and feelings.
I quickly and completely give any negative thoughts or fears to God.*

The above is an example of a positive affirmation. An affirmation is a statement. It can be negative or positive. When we allow our mind to think negatively we are holding and creating negative affirmations. Holding positive affirmations will help you remove negative thought patterns by replacing them with positive thoughts.

Begin to acknowledge and change your negative thought patterns by writing your own positive affirmations. As soon as you write down positive thoughts you hold the *intent* of that thought. When you go back and read them you place the thoughts into your mind and your entire being. If you practice reciting them daily they will become your reality and truth. Holding intent, followed by reciting positive affirmations, will manifest all your desires.

Affirmations should be recited as often as possible. I believe it is important to recite your affirmations aloud at least once a day. Hearing your own voice say the words helps make them more concrete and real. It's similar to forcing yourself to smile when you're really upset or angry. If you make yourself smile, and make the smile genuine, it immediately becomes difficult to hang on to your anger. If you can maintain that genuine smile, you find yourself relaxing and healing from the anger quickly and completely. Try that next time you get upset or angry. A positive thought is like that smile. If you hold on to it, it will trigger a change in the way you think and feel. It's inevitable. It works all the time.

At first our positive affirmations are the complete opposite of how we actually perceive our reality to be. This is because we are trying to change our thought pattern from negative to positive. For this reason, it will seem odd and untrue when you first start saying them. Remember, what you think becomes your reality. If you have been holding thoughts of how awful your job is, saying that you love it would be the opposite. You wouldn't be creating that positive affirmation if it weren't something you needed to change or improve. When there is a need for positive affirmations it means you have negative thoughts to change. Therefore, the positive affirmation will sound the opposite of how you actually think.

You're affirmations need to be worded in the *present tense*. For instance, if you never have enough money you would say, 'I have all the money I need to be happy'. If you despise your job you would say, "I have the most rewarding and fulfilling job". You don't want to make your affirmation in the future tense by saying 'Someday I'll have a rewarding and fulfilling job', or "I will soon have all the money I need", because that desire will always remain in the future. Make your affirmations in the now.

You may be thinking that's ridiculous because you'll never love the job you have, no matter how many times you say it. Positive affirmations can also *create* whatever it takes to make the statement true. Keep saying it and believing it. If there is no way of finding that ultimate happiness in your current job, a new job offer may come your way that fits the bill. The affirmation will become the truth if you say it and believe it.

Saying it and meaning what you say is the biggest secret to making it work. If you are working on self love affirmations they can be extremely difficult to get out of your mouth. If your old thought pattern was 'I'm ugly" or "I'm fat", saying that you are beautiful and perfect in every way can make you cringe. This is because you

Chapter 17

don't believe it yet. You've never allowed your mind to hold positive, loving thoughts like those toward yourself and it feels untrue. Your thoughts create the truth for you and you created that fat, ugly person to begin with. Now it's time to create that perfect and beautiful person you truly are.

Whenever you have an affirmation that seems exceptionally difficult to verbalize, it is a very important one. It's a signal that you've struck a sore spot that needs some attention. To me, the harder it is to say, the more I know I need to say it in order to begin believing it.

It also helps to put your affirmations on paper and post them in places you'll see them often. You can post them on the refrigerator, the bathroom mirror, next to your computer or next to the television screen. This will remind you to read them as often as you can.

Blow drying your hair is a wonderful time to recite your affirmation. Waiting for the microwave to heat your food or during a TV commercial are perfect opportunities. You can even tape record yourself saying them and listen to it while you're in the car or falling asleep at night. Listening to them or saying them right before you go to bed and then again as soon as you wake up is ideal. Saying them aloud while looking at your self in the mirror is also a powerful method.

Write your own personalized affirmation. It can be just one sentence or an entire sheet of paper. Stick with the affirmation for at least four weeks before changing it. A good rule of thumb is thirty days. It takes thirty days to break a habit. Changing your thought patterns are just like breaking habits. Remember to mean it when you say it and to say it as often as you can.

The following is an affirmation I created for my students. It's quite long but it was intended to cover many things, providing a variety of examples. Take what you feel would be good for you, or use it to create your own affirmations. Be sure to stay in the present tense when making your personalized affirmations.

Daily Affirmation

"In my life where I am, all is perfect, whole and complete. I am always protected, guided and safe. I never fear life or its changes because I know and trust the natural flow of life and realize that it is always perfect.

It is safe for me to be financially free and I deserve to have the money that I need in order to be happy and feel safe. I now release all fears I have about money and I trust that I will always have as much as I need.

I openly love all people. I quickly forgive others of their imperfections and know that in forgiving others I also forgive myself. I release all self blame, self hatred and self guilt. I love myself for all that I am. I am perfect, beautiful, and full of love and life. I share my love. I give my love to everyone I come in contact with. I know that everyone needs my love. I openly allow myself to receive love from others. I quickly accept their compliments and thanks, knowing that I deserve them and I am as they say.

I do not fear my own empowerment. I am strong. I am very powerful. I do not let others control me, my thoughts or my emotions. I take total control of my own life. I am always in control of my emotions and I choose to always think positively.

I now release negative thoughts from my mind and my life. I quickly replace all negative thoughts with positive thoughts. I rise above my problems. I realize that I am the cause of all my problems and problems only arise because I allow them to in my own mind. I have the power to see all things as problem free, for everything is perfect.

I love my life. I love everyone and everything in my life. I love all people and see that even those people who have caused me hurt, anger or rejection in the past, only helped me become a better person today. I forgive them and thank them now. I love myself. I love others. I allow others to love me. I am powerful. I am strong. I forgive myself. I am perfect in every way. Everything in my life is perfect. I am in total control of my life. I love me."

Chapter Seventeen Exercise #1

Before going on to the next chapter, spend some time creating your own affirmations. Feel free to use my examples, but in time I know that you will be able to, and will want to, create your own personalized affirmation. Post your affirmations on your bathroom mirror, at your desk, on the refrigerator, anywhere and everywhere.

Chapter 17

Chapter Seventeen Exercise #2
Try adding visualization to your affirmations. See it the way you are saying it. Make the picture clear and see it as if it were already true.

Chapter Seventeen Exercise #3
Try the smile technique. Next time you find yourself upset, angry, worried, or afraid make yourself smile. Be genuine and give a heart felt smile to the world. Keep smiling even if you don't feel like it. It's amazingly powerful.

Chapter Seventeen Exercise #4
Pay attention to the thoughts you hold just before going to sleep at night. Notice the thoughts you create the moment you wake up. Be sure you are not holding negative thoughts at these times. Consciously think positively and notice how it affects your quality of sleep and your attitude throughout the day.

Chapter 18

Dreams and Sleep

*In the stillness of the night,
Your soul soon takes to flight.*

*In dreams and visions so real,
It sends messages to heal.*

*Listen to your voice within,
Your life anew will begin.*

*Sleep in peace beloved one,
Your soul is having so much fun!*

*And when tomorrows light shine,
Give thanks for all that is thine..*

*And throughout the light of day,
Remember, to always play.*

*Your soul does it every night,
As you hold your pillow tight.*

How often have you fallen asleep perplexed with a conflicting thought or question, only to awaken the next day with the answer? Or perhaps you've gone to bed with illness or pain and awakened the next morning feeling healthy, refreshed and pain free. There's a lot more going on when you're asleep than you can imagine. True, your body is getting the rest it needs physically, but your soul and subconscious are up all night. This is one reason it's important to hold positive thoughts just before going to sleep. Your subconscious will hold on to the last thoughts of the day.

When we sleep our conscious mind goes on vacation. Relieved of the mental chatter of our mind, our soul embarks on a journey of its own. Free from the bondage of our human body and mind, the soul connects to that place of oneness with God and the universe. Those hours of slumber allow our soul to communicate with God and connect to His Divine Light, energy, and healing powers.

While on earth, sleep is the closest our soul gets to spending time in the spirit world. Meditation can connect you, but seldom do we devote six to eight hours to it. Imagine eight hours of your waking day. That's an entire day at work! You can get a lot done in a day on the job. In the spirit world time is much different. A year to us on earth can be just moments in the spirit world. Regardless, one nights sleep is the longest period of time we allow our soul to go out and play.

Many things occur in your sleep and often these events can be revealed to you as dreams. Your conscious mind can get answers, guidance and direction through your soul. Your physical body can restore its healthy state. Your emotions can be diagnosed, explained, and repaired during the night. Your body benefits physically, mentally, emotionally and spiritually from your sleeping hours. I believe my dreams are reflections of my soul, my thoughts, my emotions, my body and my life in general. Whether your dreams are mending, guiding or teaching you, they help you dramatically.

During sleep, your soul can reunite with others in the spirit world and even visit other people and places. Did you ever wake up feeling exhausted and tired? Perhaps that was a busy night for your soul. It could also mean you slept lightly or restlessly, and because of your shallow sleep your souls was denied its usual freedom, freedom that would have energized you rather than exhausted you.

Sometimes your soul leaves your body to visit another place or time while you sleep. When it returns to your body some people experience the feeling of falling. Sometimes we dream of falling and landing on the ground. This can even cause your body to jump

Chapter 18

slightly and wake you up. That is what I call a rough landing. I used to be concerned because I frequently had dreams of falling, many of which would wake me when I hit ground. For many years I feared it meant I was going to actually fall, or die like that later in life. I was very relieved to hear that this was just a re-entry period and that the fall was not significant to my life now.

Dream significance isn't new information by any means. In fact, it is basic knowledge in its most condensed form. Throughout the Old Testament there are stories like *Jacob's Ladder* and *Daniel in the Lions Den*, that tell of receiving Divine guidance through dreams. The prophet Mohammed learned about most of the Koran in his dreams. Buddhism has many stories and legends involving dreams. The Greeks and Egyptians believed that dreams could heal people. Zeus, Plato and Aristotle all studied the importance of dreams. Even the founder of modern medicine, Hippocrates, used dreams for diagnosing and treating his patients.

People have been studying dreams and trying to interpret them since the beginning of time. There are a number of books on dream interpretation available. I have fanned through many myself but have found that *you* are the best interpreter of your own dreams. You understand yourself and your current life situations best. Years ago, I had fun looking up my dreams in books and trying to find answers to them, yet it seldom gave me much insight. We are all so unique and different and so are our dreams. I don't believe that dreaming of a waterfall means the same thing for me as it would for someone else. For that reason, I am not going to give you a long list of possible interpretations.

The best way to analyze your dreams is to write them down as soon as you wake up. Include every detail you can remember. Generally, this can be done in a short amount of time, like waiting for the coffee to brew or your body to fully awaken. If you don't have time to ponder its meaning at that time, you will have it in writing for some other time. Sometimes just putting it down on paper will reveal the interpretation. Other times giving yourself some space between the dream and the interpretation allows enough time for the answer to come naturally and in great detail to you. I have received interpretations immediately following a dream, while other times it was several hours or even days later before I understood its meaning.

If the answer does not come to you, go back and read your dream. Keep your conscious mind from getting too involved. That wonderful imagination you have can conjure up all sorts of misinformation. Relax and pass the interpreting over to your soul to explain. You can do this through meditation if you find it difficult to communicate directly with your higher self just yet. Generally, within a few minutes of just relaxing, quieting the mind and listening, an answer will come. It was your soul that was awake and creating the dream, so it would be best to get the diagnosis from the creator rather than from your ego mind. If you still aren't having any luck, ask your Guides to assist you. If there's a message you need to know or understand they will be glad to pass it on. If you don't get the message from your dream, they will reiterate the message to you in another way.

There may be times when it isn't important to analyze a dream. Some of our dreams in the earlier hours of sleep incorporate our mind. As you sleep you fall deeper and deeper into the sleep. There are phases to the depth of your sleep. It's a transition from your conscious mind to disengaged from your unconscious mind. By the REM state, you are disengaged with your mind as much as possible.

Some dreams seem to directly relate to the events of the prior day, such as a TV show, something you saw on the news, or things you heard or read about the day before. Although the idea came from a thought your conscious mind held, ask yourself why you chose to hold that thought. Perhaps you connected to it on another level, either emotionally or spiritually. Since we store things like fear, resentment, anger and worry in our conscious mind, your dream may be revealing an issue with one of those things.

I rarely diagnose my dreams. I am not recommending that, it's just that I seldom remember my dreams. It used to bother me. I thought something was wrong with me. I wanted to remember my dreams every night so I could analyze them. I believe, for me, it isn't that important. This could be because I stay very connected to my soul and my Guides throughout the day and I automatically pick up any needed information by channeling while I'm awake. Information is still downloaded to my higher self through the night,

Chapter 18

but I either just 'know it' to be true the following day, or pull it into my conscious mind through communicating with my higher self the next day. When I remember a dream well enough to write it down, I do. Remembering the dream gives me a big heads up that it is important to analyze it.

Some nights I do a lot of self healing during my sleep. This is evident the moment I wake up. Sometimes my healing slumbers are miraculous, to say the least. When I go to sleep I ask for my health and healing. I rarely have any pain or illness longer than a day. It's normally gone by morning. If it isn't, I take a good look at my life, emotionally and mentally and see why I didn't *allow* myself to heal. Yes, I said allow myself to heal. We all create illness and pain for ourselves in order to achieve something we are lacking emotionally or spiritually. Examples would be, needing sympathy, down time, or pampering. All illnesses are created by us. I will get into more specifics about that in Part IV.

The intent of this book is to introduce you briefly to everything I know. To keep this brief, I will close this chapter with some personal dreams and their interpretations.

Personal Dreams

One night my husband and I had similar dreams. We both dreamt that we were in a prison. While sharing the details of each of our dreams the next morning, we realized that we were dreaming of the same place, and the same events.

In our dreams we were transported by a large truck. We felt like prisoners, yet we loved and felt quite attached to the other prisoners. We thought it would be odd to feel such love for fellow prisoners. Our prison cells were dark, dirty, nasty and empty. We saw the corridors and our surroundings with much detail. It was a miserable place and we remembered wanting to get out of there, but we both felt the love between the inmates.

Soon after this dream I was told of my time in the political concentration camp. This dream was definitely about that past life. It made sense to me then that I would feel love toward the other prisoners because they weren't criminals and felons, they were my people locked up just like me.

Another night my husband had a dream in which there were police in our home. They were searching for someone and looking around our house. My husband went out to the garage and saw even more police out there. He was wondering why the dogs didn't bark at them, then he noticed two long lines of people in the back yard. He called me to come see this amazing sight.

In one line were his deceased loved ones and in the other line were mine. They had all come to tell us they loved us and were happy for us. As we stood at the head of our lines greeting them one by one, my husband thought to himself, "How will I ever have enough time to speak with each one personally?." He was overcome with loving memories and emotions for everyone who came to see him. He didn't want to run out of time and miss visiting each person individually.

Through this dream, time was explained to him as just a flash of a second in the spirit world. I believe we were visited by our deceased loved ones that night. I think the police represented our ego mind, looking around for answers to how and why we could have visitors on this level. The police never found their suspect because it wasn't of this earthly realm. The dogs not barking also represented the fact that this event took place on the spiritual level, not the visual level we are used to. The dogs did not see them because their presence was only in spirit form. Although I believe that animals are able to pick up on other levels, this was just representing the difference between the two.

In another dream I was in icy cold water on a rubber raft. I was looking for a missing person. Others were looking too. It was very cold but we kept searching and searching. I woke up freezing cold, shivering and sweating. I wasn't sick with fever or anything like that. For some reason my husband woke up at the same time. I told him about my dream and he told me his.

In his dream our house was freezing cold. He said I asked him to come closer to me and warm me up but he couldn't touch me. He said just before he touched me he felt paralyzed and couldn't move. At the same time he felt a powerful surge of energy that felt evil. Feeling rather disturbed over my dream and still feeling very cold, I got out of bed and went outside where it was warm. I asked my

Chapter 18

Guides to help explain our odd dreams and this is what they channeled to me.

They told me I was going through a natural detoxification in my sleep. My body was releasing negative energies as a way to purify itself. The person I was searching for was my higher self. On a subconscious level, my husband was aware that this was happening. He was paralyzed when he reached out to me because the process needed to be completed without interference. The evil he felt was the negative energy being released from my body during the detoxification process.

After I channeled this, while still sitting outside, I looked up and saw a huge bird on the antenna attached to our house. It stayed there a long time, looking down at me. I'd never seen a bird that looked like that around our house before. A few days earlier I had bought a book called *Animal Speak*. This book was about animal totems. It explains that there is a relationship between us and the animals that come into our life. It teaches that each animal carries a different message for us. Even though I owned the book I never got to read it. Just after I bought it, I passed it on to my friend Jill to read. I already had a pile of books to read and I knew she was very interested in animals.

Knowing that I would want to read about this bird when I got the book back, I decided to draw a picture of it so I wouldn't forget how it looked. I went inside to get a pen and paper. Amazingly, when I came back outside the bird was still there. The bird never flew off as I drew every detail about him on paper. As soon as I finished my drawing, it flew away. When it flew off I realized how huge it was. The wing span was about two and a half feet wide. I was feeling exhausted by this time and it was only 6:00 a.m. on a Saturday morning. I decided to try going back to sleep on the couch.

While dreaming, I saw myself wake up. I saw many people in my house. I didn't know who they were. They were eating, laughing and talking to my husband. Pardon my description but they looked like 'back woods' folks and I asked my husband, "Who are these people and why are they in our house"? He said I was rude to say such a thing in front of them so I began conversing with them myself. I ended up having a wonderful time.

I *thought* I woke up but soon realized it was a dream. Worried that I'd slept a long time, and knowing my husband had an early appointment that day, I ran into the bedroom to wake him up. I shook him and told him over and over to get up. I asked him what time it was because my eyes were still blurry from sleep and I couldn't see the clock. He said it was okay but I felt like he was late. I dreamt that I was standing directly in front of the clock but I still couldn't see the time. Every clock I looked at in the house was blurry. It was then that I realized I never really woke up.

I began trying to wake myself up then and thought I really had this time. I got off the couch and looked outside. I saw my horses rubbing themselves on the fence and biting each other as if scratching. They started biting each other harder and harder. Just then, I saw what appeared to be smoke down the road. As I watched, the smoke moved closer and closer. I soon realized it wasn't smoke but rain. It was a downpour and as it crossed over the horses they received instant relief of their itching. They started frolicking and rolling in the mud.

The rain was coming down in sheets now so I went to the door and opened it for a better look. When I looked outside there were ducks everywhere; in the trees, perched on our cars and all over the ground. I saw an owl fly in and start fighting with a duck. I called for my husband to come and see this amazing sight but he just smiled like he already knew it and went back to sleep. It was then that I realized I still hadn't really woken up.

I started to get a little scared then. I wondered why I wasn't able to wake myself up. I called out to my husband. I tried to project my voice and move my lips but all that was coming out was a soft, mumbling murmur. I knew there was no way he could hear me in the bedroom so I fought and fought to wake myself up. Finally I did it. I was really awake. I looked at the clock and only 15 minutes had gone by.

As you can imagine, I was pretty shook up after that. I was confused by how real my supposed wake ups seemed in the dream. I was shocked at how many times I thought I was awake when I was not. I quickly channeled to find some answers. I wrote down my channel session to be sure I would remember everything and these are the exact words given to me.

Chapter 18

'Look closer at your dreams and notice their meaning. The animals have strong messages for you. The bird you saw earlier was a loon. Look up the horse, duck and owl in your book as well. The strangers in your home represent the need to be kind and welcoming to others, even if they seem strange or different from you. You must love all people. We are all one. The horses itching terribly and then soothed by rain represents the power of Mother Nature to cleanse the world of its pain and misery, just as you have been cleansed through your natural detoxification last night. Not seeing the clock clearly represents that time is not of importance. It is more important to stay in the perfect and natural rhythm of life. Do not become a slave to time. Trying to wake up your husband with no luck and trying to get him to look outside represents not feeling so responsible for others. Others must, and can, take care of themselves. Take the responsibility of others off your shoulders."

You can imagine how excited I was to get my hands on the *Animal Speak* book at this point. The problem was my friend was on vacation. After several hours I did manage to contact her daughter and get the book back. To be brief, this is what each animal totem message was for me.

<u>Loon.</u> Pay attention to your dreams. They are very important. Hopes, wishes and dreams will come true. The loon teaches you a new state of consciousness and various states to open you to new dimensions and other life forms such as the Fairy Realm. Imagination and dreaming ability while awake or asleep are powerful. Images and visions are life like and it may be hard to tell real from unreal. Loons remind us to shift into our altered states of consciousness. The loon can lead you back to your greatest dreams and imaginings.
Note: Remember, I saw the loon while I was awake. It was also before I had my series of dreams that involved the following animals.

<u>Horse.</u> The horse was given Divination. They are clairvoyant and they recognize those in magic. They express our magical side.

The horse represents movement and can help you move along in life. They bring new journeys and teach you to ride into new directions to awaken and discover your own freedom and power.

<u>Owl.</u> The owl is a symbol of higher wisdom. Owl totems are associated with clairvoyance, astral projection and magic. It hears as well as it sees. You will hear what's being said and see what's in the shadows. Visions and hearing capacities have metaphysical links to gifts of clairvoyance.

<u>Ducks.</u> Ducks represent emotional comfort and protection. They remind us to drink of the water of life as well as nurture our emotions. They reflect an inability to be comfortable with most people in your life. They reflect a need to find comfort in your own element and with those of like mind and spirit. They remind us to return to those parts of ourselves, or activities, that we feel safe and comfortable in. They help you handle your emotions with grace and comfort. They teach you how to maneuver through various waters of life. They help you through tangled emotions.

While visiting my 84 year old Mom, I had another vivid dream. It was so vivid that in the morning I wasn't sure if I dreamt it or if I was awake as it played out. Prior to this dream, I had taken a Reiki II class where I learned how to do long distance energy work and healing on others. I had been successfully using Reiki one-on-one but hadn't practiced much long distance healing. The few times I had done long distance healing I wasn't able to get any feedback from the patient so I still had my doubts and reservations about its effectiveness. As I slept in my Mother's house, I dreamt that I gave her a full Reiki healing session. In the dream she was right in front of me, not long distance. When I awoke the next morning I immediately wondered if I really had given her a session. Soon after she woke up I received confirmation. She walked out of her bedroom, rubbing her tummy. Her first words were, "I feel so warm and happy inside today".

At the end of a rocky twelve year marriage I had a dream that changed my life. Although there were good times in our

Chapter 18

relationship, there had been an ongoing issue with cheating on my husband's part. For years I tried to hold on to the relationship, thinking I was to blame and not wanting to face a divorce. My desire to make it work blinded me from reality. The reality was that I began to loose my own self confidence, self esteem, self worth, self love and self power. I had a growing lack of trust, hope, faith and love in others and myself.

As a result of holding on, anger, resentment, fear and unhappiness were festering like a disease inside of me. I began to get feedback from friends and loved ones that I should stand up for myself and what I believed in. I knew they were right but lacked the strength and courage to do anything about it. I prayed for help in getting myself through it all.

My children and I joined a martial arts class and had been going for months. Through the martial arts I slowly began to feel my old self return. With the new bonds of friendship I was making, and the personal accomplishments I was achieving in class, I began to feel the return of my self esteem and confidence.

One night I dreamt that my sons and I were out of town at a Tae Kwon Do tournament. We were staying in a hotel with all the other Tae Kwon Do students. All of a sudden the hotel became infested with rats. They were everywhere. My new friends and children were screaming in fear. Soon, mass hysteria broke out amongst everyone. I couldn't bear to see all my loved ones like that. Despite the fact that I feared and despised rats, I began to tell everyone that I would save them. I started to grab rats with both hands and toss them out the windows. My stomach turned and my skin crawled each time I grabbed a rat but I knew it was up to me to save everyone and get rid of their fear. On and on I went through the entire hotel until the rats no longer bothered me and were completely gone.

Everyone was relieved, including me. We all began to laugh and smile once again. I felt a tremendous amount of courage, pride and self worth in myself. By conquering my own fears and taking matters 'into my own hands', I was able to not only help others feel safe and happy, but remind myself of the power, determination and bravery I still had within me.

I'll never forget the moment I woke up from that dream. I sat straight up in bed, turned to my sleeping husband, shook him and said, "That's it, I've had enough. I'm leaving you." Initially I was surprised at the words that flew out of my mouth. I couldn't believe I said them. I was totally shocked yet I knew it was what I had to do. From that moment on I never looked back or doubted myself as I filed for divorce.

I now have a wonderfully loving husband named Johnny. At the beginning of our relationship eleven years ago, we lived in a tiny two bedroom apartment with my teenage sons. Financially, times were tough. We longed to give ourselves and my sons a house of our own and a piece of land but with our low income it seemed impossible.

For months I had a recurring dream of a small, white farmhouse. In my dream I loved the house even though it was old and run down. In each dream I would walk around the house and discover new corridors and rooms that I'd never seen before. I would repeatedly think, "Wow, this house is nicer and bigger than it looks". The dreams went on for months and I figured they were just that, a dream of having our own home someday. Sometimes when I woke up I would feel more depressed and hopeless knowing it wasn't real. I never mentioned the dream to anyone because I didn't think it meant anything. After experiencing this dream for several months, my husband woke up one day and told me he had the following dream.

He dreamt he took my oldest son, Josh, to a little white, run down house. The two of them walked around the house. When their tour was finished my husband asked Josh, "Well, do you think your Mom will like it?" Josh replied, "It needs a lot of work but I think she will". That was the whole dream.

A month or two later I received a check from my Teacher Retirement Fund. I had worked for the school district for eight years and money was automatically taken out of each check. Since I no longer worked there, and because we were having so much financial difficulty, I requested a refund. I had no idea how much money was in there and it took months to get my check. I was shocked to find a check for $10,000 in my mailbox one day. Prior to this, we had

Chapter 18

been looking at houses as a weekend hobby. It was more of a Sunday drive activity. We imagined our dream house and prayed we could afford to buy one day. The day before my refund check came we had driven by a house that was unbelievably inexpensive. As soon as we saw it I said, "Keep driving, it's a dump!"

Holding my big refund check a day later, I suggested we go look at the dumpy house. I figured we'd been looking at homes way above our price range and it was time to see exactly what the other end of the spectrum looked like. We met a real estate agent at the house the next day. Within seconds of getting out of the car I said, "I want this house. I can feel it. It's got to be ours". My husband's mouth dropped open in shock but he agreed that if I believed in it, he would support me.

Miraculously we ended up getting the house and I think our entire family thought we were crazy. There was no central heat or air, there were holes in the floor, it was filthy, and some areas were rotting. It had three acres and a pond out back but the grass was nearly four feet high and you could barely see it all through the thick overgrowth of weeds, vines, trees and bushes. It truly was a dump, but it was now our dump and it only cost us $40,000.

The house started off as a tiny home moved onto the land. Over the years, each owner had built on new additions. Because of that, it was like a long, winding series of corridors and rooms instead of the traditional square or rectangular shaped home. When we would show the house to people they would feel lost in it, not knowing where they were and feeling surprised that there were more rooms and space than appeared from the outside. That is when my recurring dream and my husband's dream started to make sense. I also realized that since we'd moved in, I no longer had the dream.

We labored for years on that house and despite the fact that we felt pride in every completed renovation, there was a constant feeling of overwhelming amounts of work still to be done. After eight years we sold the house for $150,000. We were so pleased, and surprised, to get that much for it. All our dreams and hard work had literally paid off. Looking back we see how much more that house gave us than just a roof over our heads, and we'll never forget the dreams we had before we found it.

Dreams can help you deal with current situations, heal from the past, or give you a glimpse of the future. You will have your own dreams and your own interpretations of them. Be open-minded and try to get help from your Guides when you can't understand them. Keep in mind that although your conscious mind is snoozing while you sleep, your soul and subconscious mind are still active and busy. If you remember a dream, there is good reason. Meditating on it or analyzing it, opens the line of communication between your higher self and Guides. While you sleep, information is downloaded into your consciousness to heal, help, guide, teach, or comfort you. Extract that information and use it to your advantage. Remember to always be thankful for receiving it.

Chapter Eighteen Exercise #1
Try interpreting your dreams. In the morning, be sure to write down every detail of it first. Keep in mind things like:
- What was the outcome of the dream? Did you win, lose, end up happy, or feel sad?
- How did you feel when as the events played out; scared, lost, happy, or peaceful?
- The people and places in a dream often come from the association of them through your conscious mind. Look at the dream closer than who and where it took place. Often it doesn't have anything to do with the person you actually dreamt about.
- Analyze your emotional state when you went to sleep. Try to never go to sleep upset, angry or agitated.
- Associate your emotional reactions to the event. If you dreamt about a big, new home it may have nothing to do with a real home. It could signify general feelings about your life.

Chapter Eighteen Exercise #2
Just before you drift off to sleep try doing some of the following:
1. Ask your Guides for an answer to a specific question you have.
2. Ask for healing of an illness or pain, or ask for the cause of it.

Chapter 18

3. Pray for knowledge that will be useful to you the next day.
4. <u>Always</u> hold happy, peaceful, loving thoughts right before you fall asleep.

Chapter 19

Meditation

*Disconnect from mind, body and matter.
Connect to the universe and all its wisdom.*

Meditation is an excellent way to quiet the mental chatter of your mind and connect to the infinite wisdom of the universe and your true self. If I had to describe meditation in just one word it would be bliss.

Physically speaking, it's like going on vacation without leaving home. Spiritually speaking, it's like visiting the spirit world without leaving the earthly plane. Meditation disconnects you from all that is your human form... body, mind and matter. It connects you to all that is your spiritual form, God, your Guides, universal energy, and the wisdom and inner voice of your soul.

When you meditate your body feels light and weightless as if you are floating on air. Free of the burdens your mind creates, you feel total joy, contentment, security and harmony.

Through meditation you actually shut down or turn off all that is human about your self. With that shut down, you open yourself up to all that is spiritual and of your spiritually true self. It is the most divine state you can put yourself into as a human being. For me, each time I meditate it is a spiritual experience. Time and again I am overwhelmed and awestruck at the feelings of complete peace, understanding and harmony it creates within me. Personally, it feels less like I'm turning off my mind and more like I'm taking a break from mental stimulation. As I allow my mind to relax and calm, I visualize myself going to the spirit world. Remember, you communicate with 'feeling' rather than 'thought' at the soul level. Once I feel connected to this other dimension my mind automatically slows down because I am enjoying the blissful new *feelings* occurring.

Depending on your individual needs at the time, meditation can be useful for many different things.

- It creates a time and place for you to shut off the mental chatter of your mind and practice just 'being' without thought.
- It reduces stress, anxiety and completely calms and relaxes you.
- It helps you center and balance yourself.
- It opens you up to hearing guidance from the spirit world.
- It opens you up to hearing the voice of your soul.
- It allows you to hear the answers to your prayers and questions.
- It energizes you and recharges you with universal energy.
- It allows your soul time to go out and play.
- It puts you in the present moment.
- It makes you look younger physically because it removes the stress lines from your face.
- Twenty minutes of meditation is equivalent to eight hours of sleep.

There is no limit to what you can achieve and experience through meditation. There are no boundaries or guidelines to follow. It is the mind that creates those things. When we turn off our mind those things no longer exist. Removed of all that is limiting us physically, mentally and emotionally we enter the place that is of our soul and spirituality. That place is the essence of our true self and where we came from.

Don't let this scare you. It's not like you actually leave your body and float off to some other realm. You still stay completely connected to your physical body. At any time you can quickly return to your mentally conscious state. You are never so far gone that you can not return. You hear everything that is going on around you as you meditate. You have total control of yourself and your conscious state at every given moment. In fact, it is much easier to disengage yourself from meditation than it is to remain in the meditative state. It will take some practice to silence that brain of yours.

As you begin to practice quieting your mental chatter you will be annoyed with how many outside distractions challenge you to pull back into to your conscious mind. Turning *off* your mind takes practice and your conscious effort, while turning it back *on* is quite natural and is as quick and easy as snapping your fingers. Remember, you've been letting your mind control your life for years and it won't like giving up that control. As you work to suppress it, it will constantly keep trying to take back its control. You will spend much more time and effort on meditating then on calling your mind back into the driver's seat. There will be no delay in reconnecting with your mind state.

Everyone has their own style, and individual beliefs about meditating vary greatly. There are no rules to meditating. Meditation is a very personal thing. We are all unique and different and what you like may not be something anyone else is going to like. The important thing is that you are comfortable and relaxed. Certain meditative postures I've read about feel unnatural and uncomfortable to me. You won't be able to meditate if you are distracted with feeling uncomfortable.

It helps to find a quiet area free from as much auditory distraction as possible. You may enjoy being outdoors more than indoors. Darkness may be easier for you than a brightly lit room. You can meditate in the bathtub or while floating in a pool. I've even meditated in my car at the park over lunch hour. You can sit on the floor or in your favorite chair. You can lie on the floor or in your bed. My favorite position is sitting on our big recliner while it's fully reclined.

You can also meditate with soft music playing or in complete silence. There are a number of guided meditation CD's and tapes available too. These guided meditations talk to you every step of the way. They can be very helpful if you find it difficult to meditate. The length of time you give your meditation is entirely up to you and your schedule. I've had ten minute meditations that were just as good as thirty minute sessions. If it's hard to find ten minutes, go for five. Anything is better than nothing. Once you feel the wonderful effects of meditation, you will want to increase your time whenever possible.

If you begin your meditation with the background worry of time, it will distract you. Time flies when you're in a meditative state but you can still control how long you want to be there. As a back up, I will tell my Guides how much time I want to spend meditating. They are always eager to make meditation time as worry free and productive as possible. I ask them to be sure I am finished in time. I never go past the time period I planned, and I don't feel distracted worrying about the clock.

No matter how or where you meditate, try to keep your torso straight. If you are bent or hunched over, you squish and put pressure on your internal organs. This restricts the blood flow and energy flow throughout your body.

The following is a method that I have used. It's not the only way. I have included it as an example for you to try. Do what feels right and true for you.

Meditation Method
First, I begin to breathe deeply and rhythmically. Starting at the top of my head, I relax every muscle in my body. I mentally talk myself through it like this. Relax your scalp, your forehead and your facial muscles. Relax your neck and shoulders. Relax your arms and hands. Relax your chest and stomach. Relax your hips, thighs, calves, ankles and feet. I move slowly down my body, paying attention to areas that have more tension than others. After going down the body from head to toe I do one last scan from the feet to the head in order to double check that everything is truly limp and relaxed. If I find tension in any area, I stop along the way to work a bit longer on that area. Don't short change yourself on this very important step. As tedious as it may seem, it sets the tone for your entire meditation.

Once your physical body is relaxed, put all your attention on your breathing. This gives your mind a little something to hold on to as well. Make each inhale deep and pull the air all the way down to your belly. I call this belly breathing. If you put your hand on your belly while you breathe you should be able to feel the belly push out as you inhale and pull in when you exhale. This is your body's

Chapter 19

natural breathing technique. A baby breathes this way and it's how we all took our first breath in life. It is our instinctive and natural way to breathe. Through the years we became conscious of holding our tummy in and began changing to chest breaths. When you breathe with the chest alone you take shallow breaths and do not allow the lungs to completely fill and exhale. As you inhale, allow the air to fill your lungs from the bottom up. As you exhale, expel the air from the bottom to the top. It's like filling a glass of water. Even though the water enters the glass from the top, it begins to fill from the bottom up. When you pour the water out it comes out of the top, but empties from the bottom first.

Once you have your belly breaths, put all your focus on the air going in and out. Actually visualize the air going in and out of your body. This helps keep you in touch with the here and now and you will begin to relax more with each breath. If you have difficulty putting all your focus on your breathing, picture the air going in and out as a color. See the flowing color sweep up into your nose and move down into your lungs. Visualize color coming out of the lung, moving up through the airway and out of the mouth. Again, concentrating on your breathing helps you quiet your mind by giving it something to hold on to. Even though your mind is holding on to your breathing it doesn't require detailed thought.

When you feel completely comfortable with breathing and relaxing, start to pull your mind off visualizing the air of your breaths. At that time, give your mind *nothing* to focus on. It is a time to simply *be*. Connect to your body and the way it feels. Be in the moment totally. Give no thought to the moment, just be aware of how you feel as you breathe naturally and relax. Notice *every* detail of how your body feels. Stay connected to feeling rather than thinking. Remember that your soul holds no thought. It is only capable of feeling. When you can be a feeler instead of a thinker you connect to your soul rather than your mind.

At this point your mind may start to fight you. You may begin to notice pesky thoughts popping into your mind. Don't worry about it. This is very normal, but as soon as you realize your mind is trying to engage in thought stop it. Give no energy to the thought. If you give no energy to a thought it can not exist. See the thought float through your mind and right out the other side. Don't feel as though you are a failure if the thoughts won't stop. You can still meditate effectively even if you have thoughts popping up. Simply keep pushing them aside by giving no attention to them and start again. Do this over and over again and soon you will have longer and longer periods without thought. Don't worry if it takes days, weeks or months to feel like you are successful at controlling your thoughts the majority of the time. You have been a thinking being for many years so it will take some work. You should be very proud and happy with yourself for even a few seconds of thoughtlessness. If you are able to hold a minute without thought, you're doing fantastic!

When I first started meditation it was extremely difficult to turn off my thoughts. It would be several seconds before I even caught myself thinking. It felt so natural to hold constant thought that I didn't even notice I was doing it. The more I thought about not having thoughts the worse it got. It helped me to just look out at the darkness in front of me and enjoy it as I would enjoy the feeling of closing my eyes and going to bed after a long, tiring day. After a rough day the last thing you feel like doing is thinking. You want to just lie there and do nothing but relax and enjoy the comfort of your body in that wonderful bed.

When I first practiced looking out into the darkness I began to see colors, shapes, objects or waves. I looked at them without giving them thought. Sometimes all I saw were beautiful colors. It usually started with the color purple. Then the purple would start waving back and forth, in and out. Shortly after that, another color would start to appear. It was a very relaxing time for me to just *be* and *watch* the colors. It reminded me of looking into a kaleidoscope when I was a little girl. There's really nothing to think about. You just enjoy watching the colors change. Concentrate on being a watcher to help you stay disconnected from thought. That way, even though you continue to have thoughts, they will not connect with you.

Make sure to hold no expectations of what you will see or experience. Every meditation is quite different. You can hear, see, feel or sense anything. Just watch and experience whatever comes your way. Do not let anyone tell you there are specific things you should experience or see. Nothing is abnormal because you are your own

Chapter 19

unique self. For a while, all my meditations held the picture of an eye. Then there were weeks when all I saw were faces that looked holographic or ghost like. Other times I saw nothing but felt energy, love or comfort. Sometimes you will understand your experience and other times you may not have a clue. It doesn't matter. Just meditate. You will receive anything you are supposed to receive. It could be that your needs are that of just relaxing and connecting to your soul's inner peace. Hold no expectations.

As you become more comfortable with meditating, you will begin to receive guidance and messages. When you begin to receive, it's easy to get excited and disengage from your thoughtless state. Stay relaxed. Be thankful for the information and then quickly let it go so that you remain thoughtless and open. Do not start analyzing or thinking further about the experience. Putting a large amount of thought to each idea or message that springs up will be allowing your ego mind to enter into the meditation and you don't need that. Once you are feeling pretty good about your meditation time, you can begin to ask simple questions. It is important not to hold any thoughts or expectations regarding the answer. Just relax, watch and feel for the response or answer. Sometimes you may not get an answer and that is okay. Simply ask another question and wait. Keep reminding yourself to stay thought free and totally relaxed.

Chapter Nineteen Exercise

I'm sure you can guess what this one is going to be. Practice meditating. Try to make time to meditate at least once a day, twice a day if you can. Don't be upset if you can't find time some days. It's not mandatory that you meditate. It's just a wonderful gift to give to you self. You can give five minutes to meditating or sixty minutes. Just do it!

If you can't get to a thoughtless state it doesn't matter. You can always stay focused on your breathing the entire time. Some people find it helpful to repeat a word or phrase in their mind. This is called chanting and it will give your mind something to hold on to that does not cause thought. Try different things. Allow yourself to be guided to what suits you best. Nothing is abnormal and nothing is normal. It's all up to you.

Chapter 20

Live in the Moment

Time is borne of the human mind,
For in the spirit world there are no clocks.
Stop holding on to what WAS
and what WILL BE..
Realize that your life is only what IS.

    The quality of your entire existence is affected and determined by your ability to be in the present moment at all times. The past is over. The future is not here yet. The now is where you always are. The present moment is your life. Your reality exists only in the now.

    As I explained earlier in this book, the mind spends most of it's time in the past or future, yet the present moment is where you always are. Very seldom do you allow yourself to enjoy the here and now. The present moment is your true connection to life and to your higher self. It is the place to stay in order to enjoy each glorious moment of your life.

    When your mind is filled with thoughts of past events it identifies you and your current life with that time period. This robs you of living in the true time period of the now. Past events create an illusion based on prior experiences and their consequences. Your mind will repeatedly relive those memories and in turn, create the same reality for the now. It is human nature to identify ourselves with past experiences. Although those experiences *were* your reality back then, they are *not* your reality now. The only place it remains a reality is in your mind. The now is a whole different set of events and circumstances. The now is what is important because each second is creating the real truth of your identity and your life. Stop holding on to what was, and realize that your life is only what is.

When your mind is thinking of the future it identifies your life with what will be, not what is now. You begin to think that you must get to a certain point, or achieve a certain goal, before you can be completely happy and fulfilled. Yet even if that goal is achieved your mind will not rest because it continues to set new goals and dreams. Therefore your happiness remains just out of reach.

How often do you spend Sunday afternoon and evening thinking about, or dreading, Monday morning? I used to feel a sense of doom every Sunday because I was already focusing my thoughts on going back to work Monday. This ruins your enjoyment of Sunday... your glorious day off! Your mind does the same thing with every thought of the future. It robs you of enjoying the now and begins to affect the quality of your consciousness.

If you can keep your mind in the present, everything you do becomes exciting, new and important. Everything you do should be that way because each moment is creating a part of your life. Life is to be enjoyed to the fullest. Being in the present moment is the only way to fully enjoy every moment of your life.

When you first start practicing being in the present moment it can scare you a little. You may have the feeling that you won't be able to remember all the things you have to do in the future. You can also feel as though you won't be as productive or efficient because your mind isn't focused on all the things you need to get done. Your mind can hold a thought to the point of obsession.

For example, if you know you need to get bread and milk before you go home from work, your mind can bring that thought up over and over again all day long so you won't forget it. If you could count how many times that one thought will repeat itself to you in just a few hours you'd be amazed. Now imagine all the future thoughts you have that do the same thing over and over again. I have to do this, I can't forget about that. You can see how much time and energy you spend thinking about the future.

The truth is, those obsessive thoughts aren't necessary. If you had less of them running through your mind you wouldn't have any trouble recalling the things you really need for each moment. Obsessing over the future wastes your time and energy.

When your mind is filled with thoughts of the future it makes your life seem like a reward system. If you get this done, you will achieve that. How often have you begun your day with a list of things to do? You need to get the kids to school, run to the bank and get gas before work. Then you begin the list of duties you must get done before you can have lunch. After lunch, there's the afternoon duty list that needs to be finished before you can go home. On the way home you have to stop by the cleaners, pick up some groceries and get your hair cut. Once you're home you have to cook dinner, do homework with the kids, run a load of laundry, get the kids to bed, fold clothes and pay bills before you can relax.

By the time you can relax you're so exhausted you fall asleep before you actually enjoy your relaxing time. What happens then? You start a new day and the same scenario plays out. It will never end because there will always be something else to do. That is life. I doubt you'll ever wake up one day and have absolutely nothing to do and no plans for the future.

Staying in the moment removes the burdens of your daily chores and responsibilities. With these burdens lifted off your shoulders you have a sense of lightness, peace and ease in everything you do. It removes the feelings of struggling, juggling and fighting to get everything done. Your mind creates those feelings when it lives through the past and the future. When you live in the now you can enjoy every moment no matter what you are doing. You do not base every moment on the outcome or end result. The end result will still happen even if you stop dwelling on it, but you will *enjoy* each step of the way.

Many times we feel overcome with problems. When this happens you have to ask yourself, "Is the problem actually affecting this very moment?" When you put your self into the now and ask, "What are my problems right now", or 'What is bothering me this very moment?' you usually realize that the problem is not of the now but of the future. You can always easily cope with the now. It is the future that you can not cope with, because it isn't here yet. Your mind creates projected thoughts about the future that are not real. Those projections will never be real because they are not happening in the present moment. The only problems you have are those that affect you now, in this very moment.

Children easily and naturally live in the now. How often have you thought, 'Life was great when I was a child. I didn't have a care or worry.' That's not true, because even children have responsibility, demands, and worry. They just don't dwell on it as much as adults do. They take things as they come and enjoy the now much more. They adopt an 'I'll worry about that when the time comes' attitude.

I feel like children today are loosing that natural ability at a much younger age than ever before. Parents are passing on their stress and worry to their children. I saw a difference between my childhood in the 60's and my children's in the 80's. Now I see it even more pronounced with kids of the 2000's. I have worked with children for the last fifteen years of my life and there are more and more stressed out kids today than ever before. They are under much more pressure, have become obsessive worriers, and have reached serious levels of anxiety. This is all a reflection of their environment because we know children are not born that way. It's time to be role models for our kids. We need to stop passing on our own pressures and demands to them by removing ourselves of the same.

Our own thought obsessiveness is spreading like a disease and it's affecting the entire planet. Look at the increase in suicide, crime and depression today. People as a whole are reaching their limits and it's causing them to feel overwhelmed and hopeless. This is all being created within the human mind. We can change this by changing our thoughts and living in the now. By staying in the present moment we remove fear, anxiety and worry because these things are only created when the mind thinks of the past and future.

In the now, you find an *ease* to everything and you discover a feeling of freedom. This ease and freedom creates joy, self empowerment, self confidence, fulfillment and inner peace, to name just a few. You'll find that your anxieties, worries and problems dissolve because they don't exist in the now. They come from projected thoughts of other times irrelevant to the now. Without presumptions and projections of the future, each new moment is easy to handle. Events unfold slowly and are easy to deal with. You give your full attention to every moment of your life. You enter each moment re-

Chapter 20

freshed because you haven't spent hours agonizing over the outcome before in even happens.

Staying in the now will seem so foreign to you that it may cause you frustration and impatience. You may get upset at your lack of ability to stay there. Don't do that to yourself! Just keep practicing pulling yourself back to the now. Who cares if it takes one, two or ten years to get the hang of it. Once you begin to realize you are not in the moment, you are already beginning to change. Acknowledgment alone, instantly puts you in the now. The only way to effectively change your life long pattern of living outside the now is to take one step at a time toward being in the now.

Meditation is an excellent way to put your self in the moment, but ultimately, you will want to hold that same feeling as you go about your entire day. Start practicing by paying attention and re-directing your thoughts to the now as often as you can. Don't get frustrated every time you catch yourself outside of the now. Be thankful for all the times you are in it. It will get easier with practice. Your intent and awareness will make it happen more often.

If you find this practice extremely challenging at first, begin by consciously committing to a few moments at a time. Whenever you want to practice, mentally announce your intention to yourself. All you have to do is say something like, "I want to be in the now". Take a few deep breaths and start to notice the world around you. Observe and put all your attention to the *details* of all you see in that very moment. All the visual images in front of you will become clearer and more pronounced when you do this. You will have a sense that the world is more vivid and beautiful and you will see so much more than you did when you were out of the moment.

Next, quiet your mind as much as you can by beginning to *feel* your world. Be an observer yet feel what you're observing rather than put thought to it. Now, center your feelings on your own body. Notice exactly and precisely what every inch of your physical body feels. You may start to notice your heart beating or feel every inch of your body functioning at this point. Breathe deeply and continue to let go of all that is not in the present moment. Keep feeling.

When you truly connect with the now, you will feel a surge of energy rushing through your body. It feels as though you're full of energy, yet completely peaceful, calm and relaxed. You begin to feel lighter, almost as if you're floating. You'll experience feelings of bliss, joy and contentment. Time will feel as though it is slowing down. When I first started to experience being in the now it was almost more than I could handle. The overwhelmingly euphoric feeling was odd to me. I'd worry that it would stop because I didn't want it to. I wanted to remain in that state so much, yet it took a considerable amount of conscious effort to hold on to it.

Do not try to hold on. Avoid putting any thought or worry into it. You are doing it, and that's what you wanted. If you get pulled away it's no big deal. You have the ability to return whenever you wish. The now is always there for you. Each time you practice putting yourself back in the present moment it will become easier and you will be able to stay there longer. Since it will feel so wonderful, you will want to make it happen more often. In time, it will happen naturally. Short moments will occur when you weren't even expecting it. Practice is the only way to start the connection. If you practice, it will happen and soon it will become very natural for you to remain there.

Chapter Twenty Exercise

Start paying attention to your thoughts. Bring yourself back to the now as often as you can. Begin with short time periods and work up to longer stretches. Be gentle and nurturing to your self as you practicing this. Baby steps will get you there. You have your whole life to work on it. There's no rush to mastering this, just keep moving forward, taking one step at a time. You'll get there as long as you keep moving forward.

Chapter 20

Living in the Moment

*It often creates a fuss,
When the past keeps haunting us,*

*And our dreams of things to come,
Make us want to get more done..*

*Living in the here and now,
Often leaves you saying "How"?*

*But when you stop and see,
The gifts God brings to thee,*

*Each precious moment given,
Is all a part of living.*

*So stop yourself and take note,
And I'm sure that you will vote,*

*That living in the moment,
Improves your life's enjoyment.*

Chapter 21

Be Creative

You are the Creator of a healthy, balanced mind.

Creativity calms the mind and nourishes the soul. It brings balance to your life. Through it, you allow your soul to express itself. It occupies your mind with the total involvement of a pleasurable activity. Creativity is magically refreshing and nurturing.

As adults, we can forget the pleasure and importance of creativity. Our lives get so hectic and busy with all the necessities that we keep pushing back time for creativity. We push it back so far that it ends up in a corner filled with cob webs. By denying your mind of creativity, you build a corner of cob webs in it. When this happens, a piece of your mind will be rotting away in the back somewhere. Your mind can not work at its peek performance level if it's missing a piece of itself.

If we even find it, our free time is often spent sitting in front of the television or relaxing on the couch doing nothing. Spending these precious times engaged in a creative project would be much more beneficial to us. Making time to express ourselves creatively is refreshing and energizing to our mind, body and soul. Many people think that doing nothing is how we relax and recharge, when all it creates is the same...stagnation. Stagnation of the mind is self destructive.

You may be thinking you're not a creative person. That is not true. As a child you were always creative. The imagination runs wild in our youth. We create with our mind the majority of our childhood. Whether it's making mud pies, coloring, or having imaginary tea parties, kids create all the time. When we become adults we slowly move away from that and make less and less time for creativity.

Think about all the creative things you've done in your life. The farther you look back in years the more you will remember. Now, remember and feel the joy it gave you. You were totally involved mentally with that creation. It was fun and you didn't want to stop doing it. Time flew by whenever you engaged in your creative project. When you finished your project you felt a sense of accomplishment, fulfillment and pride.

Creativity can take many forms. To refresh your memory I have listed a few examples.

Designing	Remodeling	Models
Knitting	Cross Stitch	Weaving
Macramé	Clay Sculptures	Puzzles
Cooking	Drawing	Photography
Gardening	Quilting	Redecorating
Sewing	Ceramics	Carpentry
Restoring a car	Needlepoint	Embroidery
Painting	Arts & Crafts	Pottery
Woodworking	Carpentry	Rug Hooking
Restoring Furniture		

If you want to be a completely healthy person it's time to bring creativity back into your life. You must allow yourself some mental pleasure and nourishment. Reading books is not being creative. Even though a fiction novel is an imaginary story, you are simply the *watcher* of someone else's creativity. You need to be the *doer*.

Creativity adds spice to your life. You will find joy and excitement in your new creation. We are all creators in the world. We create all the time. It's time to create for the shear enjoyment of it. Personal pleasure and self satisfaction come from creativity. It creates a mental escape from your problems and responsibilities. When you set aside your responsibilities and problems for awhile you feel refreshed. When you return to them later, you will find them easier to deal with.

Chapter 21

Remember that creativity engages the mind with purely pleasurable thought. The benefits are similar to those you get with positive affirmations. It brings balance to your mind and your thoughts. Your mind works very hard for you and deserves to have its own free time. When you balance your mind it becomes sharper, crisper and quicker. It will be recharged and fresh when you call it back to work on the intellectual level once again.

Chapter Twenty One Exercise
Decide on a creative project for yourself. Make your shopping list and pick up what you need today. Start doing it tonight. As soon as you start your creative project, you will feel the excitement and joy it brings you. Do it!

Chapter 22

Be Playful

*Allow yourself to play all day, every day.
It is through play that we discover
Joy, Creativity, Laughter and the
Love of life.
Play suppresses worry, stress and anxiety.*

Playing is as important as creativity yet the two are very different from each other. Creativity totally involves the mind in the activity. Play frees the mind because it can simply react and respond to the actions of your body. Play doesn't involve a goal or well thought out plan. Instead, it includes things like laughter, humor, and being silly. In play, the only desired outcome is pleasure and fun.

Making time for yourself to play is refreshing and lifts your mood. Playing is a magical form of meditation as it opens your heart charka and allows you to find fun, happiness, and joy. Happiness and joy create balance within you, which allows for miracles and manifestations to come to life.

I don't have to remind you of how well you were able to play as a child. A child's first priority of the day is to find playtime. In our hectic lives as adults, we often forget how to play. It becomes our last priority each day. All the necessities and responsibilities take first priority and often leave us no time at all for play.

When we are told to play it can seem like another stress for us because we've forgotten how. We have to search hard to find ways in which to play once again. Don't worry. You haven't forgotten how to play. In fact, you don't need to conjure up some big event or vacation in order to do so. Each and every minute of your life can be filled with play. Much of play is in our mental attitude about the activity we are doing. Think about it. Try approaching everything you do with a playful attitude.

Have you ever been doing something fairly serious when all of a sudden humor or laughter entered into the situation? The task didn't change, your attitude toward it did. When you add play to all you do, everything becomes fun and time flies by. Whether you're watering plants, balancing the checkbook or cleaning house, try to see the playful side of it. Stop being so serious all the time. See the world through the eyes of a child. They have no trouble turning whatever they're doing into playtime.

Making time for playful activities is very important as well. Planning and scheduling in periods of play for your self should be mandatory at least once a week. Make it as important as doing laundry or eating a meal. Think of it as cleansing and feeding your body, mind and soul. Play for the pure enjoyment of life.

We are supposed to enjoy our life. God wants us to feel happiness, not only in our accomplishments and work, but in play as well. He knows that if we allow ourselves time to play we become more productive when we work. Balance is the key once again. We must stay balanced in all that we do. Remember the saying, "All work and no play makes a man gray". A gray mood comes from lack of fun in your life. That gray mood will affect everything you do in life, including your job, relationships, and feelings about yourself.

Here are a few examples to get you thinking playfully in case you're still wondering how to do it.

Dancing	Fishing	Boating
Singing	Swimming	Playing with Children
Laughing	Hiking	Skiing
Bike riding	Any Sport	Horseback Riding
Skating	Bowling	Golfing
Going to the zoo	Museums	Camping

There are many different ways to play. Some take more physical activity than others. The important thing is to set no goal other than pure enjoyment. Shopping can be a form of play for some unless you have a list of things to buy or it's not in your budget and will cause a serious crunch to your finances. If you're just walking from store to store with a friend, laughing and talking, it's play. Going for an afternoon drive can be play if you have no planned destination and you simply go where wind blows you. Allow yourself to stop anywhere and everywhere you feel the desire, and a drive becomes playtime as well. Sharing a meal with friends or family is playtime if you are doing it for pure pleasure. Add in some laughter and silliness. Play is an attitude. There's no reason you can't add play into everything you do.

Chapter Twenty Two Exercise

If I gave a child this homework assignment they'd love it and have no trouble coming up with a way to play. Let the child in you come out and play. Force yourself to make the time. It's as important to your life and health as drinking water, sleeping, and eating. Plan something for this coming weekend. Be sure it fits the criteria for play. If camping is stressful for you because you have too much to do, that's not play. Be sure the activity makes you feel that old, childlike joy you once knew so well.

Part III

Your Emotions

The past had much to teach you,
Hurt and anger still reach you,
Heartache and pain still live,
And make it hard to forgive.

But letting it go, you must,
This method you need to trust.
It feels so good to release,
And it brings you inner peace.

The lessons forever last,
When you let go of the past,
But the pain cannot go on,
New love in you will soon dawn.

Forgive yourself and others,
Thank your sisters and brothers,
For teaching lessons of life,
And causing you all that strife.

Your emotional state affects your mental, physical and spiritual health. I've explained how you create thought and how thought creates a mental reality for you. You have learned ways to stay spiritually and mentally healthy. Even if you were able to hold nothing but positive thoughts and remain spiritually connected, an unavoidable event could trigger an emotional trauma. In the following chapters I will explain the emotional side of you.

Think back to a time in your life when you suffered severe emotional trauma. It could have been something like losing your job, divorce, the death of a loved one, moving away from loved ones, or having your first child. Emotionally you were put into shock. The event stirred emotions within you. Emotions can make you feel insecure, lonely, depressed, lacking in self esteem or confidence, financially insecure, abandoned, or unsafe. Looking back at just one of these instances, see if there was a new illness that followed. It could have been something like neck pain, back pain, headaches, the flu, an infection, a cold, migraines, stomach problems, or an injury. Your physical body and mind are directly related to your emotional frame of mind.

To understand this better, take a look at the opposite. Think back in your life to a time you felt on top of the world. You know the feeling. Nothing can get you down. No one can rain on your parade. You felt great! This often happens when a new love comes into your life. You feel as though you have a constant smile on your face. Your heart seems to beat faster just talking to them or thinking about them. You are happy, secure, content, and feel very loved. There's no problem finding the extra energy you need to get things done. Mentally and physically you are strong and confident. You're emotionally well. When we are emotionally healthy our body and mind is healthy too. When we are emotionally ill our body and mind become ill.

Anything less than perfection is created by your mind or body. Your soul sees everything as perfect. The only emotion your soul feels is love. When the mind and body experience anything other than love and perfection, we need to release it in order to connect to the truth of our soul once again.

Our lessons on earth often create many emotions that are aids to our learning and understanding. We can't avoid this, but we can choose to let go of anything that is no longer needed in the present. Carrying around old emotional baggage isn't necessary. The only things we need to carry from the past are the wisdom and understanding of the lessons themselves, not the pain.

Chapter 23

Love Yourself

Love your self, for only then can you love others.

Loving yourself means that you approve of yourself and accept yourself exactly as you are. Loving your self is the first step to being emotionally healthy. We are emotional beings and we all need love. Love is the essence of our soul and Creator. As we get older we continue to look to others to fulfill that emotion, yet we can feel loved by simply loving ourselves.

If you love yourself totally and completely you will not need the love and approval of others. You will never abandon yourself, and you will always be there for yourself. Your emotional well being can remain healthy by holding unconditional, sincere love for yourself. We need to start teaching our children this as soon as they are able to understand it. By teaching them self love we can protect them more than we can by loving them.

There is no human being better suited to love you completely, unconditionally and eternally than yourself. You are number one in your life. This is how it should be. There is nothing selfish or egotistical about feeling this way. When you love your self, you become the essence of love and everyone around you will feel your love. You will be able to love others as you love yourself. Love is created within. You can't love others if you don't love yourself first. Love is what we're all here to learn and understand, and every lesson we learn revolves around love in some form or fashion. Love is the basis for our life purpose and life path. It is also the culprit to most of our issues, phobias, illnesses, diseases and pain. Love heals more than a broken heart. It opens the door for miracles to happen. Love heals us spiritually, emotionally, mentally and physically.

As babies we know nothing but love because we are still so closely connected to our soul and our Creator. We love ourselves and others openly. No baby has been born thinking, "I'm bald', or 'Look at all the fat rolls on my body', or 'I can't do anything for myself'. Even though those things are true they still love themselves unconditionally.

As we grow into children we continue to love ourselves but begin placing more importance on how much we are loved by others. When Mom or Dad disciplines us we worry that they don't love us. We fight with our siblings and then think it means they don't love us anymore. We look for love and approval from our teachers and friends.

As teenagers we begin to seek out a different type of love. We begin to look for romantic love and a partnership with someone else. Young girls draw hearts around their notes and names. We become consumed with the need to be loved. We believe that if we have a boyfriend or girlfriend others will think we're lovable, and that if we don't there's something's wrong with us.

What happens when we place so much value on the love of others? Boom, someone comes along and breaks our heart. Over and over again we begin to feel unloved or unworthy of love because of someone else's lack of love toward us. The older we get the more it happens.

As a child, our friends can be ruthless and cruel. Our best friend today can abandon us tomorrow for a new best friend. Boyfriends and girlfriends drop each other like it's nothing and find a new partner as soon as they turn around. Our parent's negative reactions to our misbehaviors can make us feel as though they have pulled their love from us. Love becomes a game. Sometimes you win, sometimes you lose. It's no wonder that we get scared to fully love someone else. Through experience we have put up a guard to protect ourselves emotionally. We begin to think it would be better not to love than to be hurt again.

When you base your love on what you *receive* from others you set yourself up for heartaches. We need to base love on how much we love our self. This way, no matter what happens with others, we remain secure, content, and full of love with ourselves. We'll still be emotionally affected by others to a certain degree, but we'll always have the unconditional love, approval and acceptance of our self. Self love never has to die. We are the only one that can make it die, and as long as we love our self it never will. When we have love for our self we don't need the love of others to survive. It's wonderful to have a loving relationship with someone else but we need to love our self first.

The first step to loving self is to stop being so critical of yourself. If you've been doing your homework from Part II on creating positive thoughts, you're already taking the first step away from self criticism. Self criticism is a negative thought toward your self. Thought creates emotion. When you criticize yourself you are saying that you don't love your self. You are saying that you don't approve of and accept yourself as you are. This lack of love creates lack of self worth.

Soon we begin to feel unworthy of having what we want. We imagine that others will not love us because of our faults. After that, we roll into not feeling good enough and then the negative thought pattern begins self destruction. Our self criticizing words repeat themselves over and over again in our mind. Each time we repeat the word or thought, the wound gets deeper because the thought turns into our reality. The words become our perceived truth about who we are.

Thoughts and emotions are so closely intertwined that it's hard to separate the two sometimes. Positive thoughts and a healthy mental attitude keep us mentally healthy. Love keeps us emotionally healthy. Love involves being kind to our self, and nurturing to our emotions. Be patient and love your self unconditionally. If you are feeling sad, treat yourself as you would your own child. If you feel anger, don't react with anger toward your emotion. Be gentle as you heal the anger.

It amazes me how much easier it is to give our love and compassion to someone else than to ourselves. When we see someone hurt and crying our heart goes out to them. We are quick to hold them and comfort them. When we are hurt we become frustrated with ourselves and with those that hurt us instead of comforting ourselves from within. We believe we heal our emotions by justifying our actions or blaming others. We heal by loving our self.

If you have children, you know how easy it is to love them unconditionally. No matter what they say or do, you continue to love them. You feel like their body guard and it is your job to protect, nurture, and comfort them. We even believe that no one else can do this for them as well as we can. Why can't you be that way to yourself? Be your own loving parent. Give yourself a hug. Protect yourself and hold that same unconditional love for yourself. Become your own best friend when you need support and encouragement.

Remember, your soul is perfect. That perfection is within you and can never leave you. It is through your human mind, body and emotions that you feel anything less than perfect. Your body is simply the shell you chose for your soul in this lifetime. Your mind is thought that you create. Your emotions are strengthened by love. You may think your body is not perfect, you may have made some bad choices in life, or you may still hold negative thoughts at times, but none of this is a reflection of your true self.

Center yourself in your heart where love begins. Become the essence of your soul. Know that despite the imperfections of your mind and body, you are perfect in every way and you will always remain that way. That is the truth and you can always connect to it through your heart and soul. When you are trying your hardest, and doing the best you can, that *is* enough. You are perfect. Approve of and accept yourself as you are right now.

Chapter Twenty Three Exercise #1

Make a list of all the things you dislike about yourself. Don't hold back, let it all out. Now burn the list. As it burns repeat these words. "I now release all negative thoughts and emotions about myself. I promise to love myself totally and unconditionally from this day forward." Add these two sentences to the bottom of your affirmations and say them for at least thirty days. If you discover other things you dislike about yourself in the days to come, simply use this release for them as well.

Chapter 23

Chapter Twenty Three Exercise #2
Make a list of all the things you already love about yourself. This doesn't include loving the car or house you own. Material possessions don't count. It's about you. Are you a good student, parent, child, neighbor, or friend? Are you loving, giving, compassionate or supportive to others? Are you smart, strong, dependable, honest or kind? It could take you days or weeks to finish this list. Don't try to do it in ten minutes. As you go about your day pay attention to the qualities you love about yourself. You will find that the list will grow as you continue to recite the self-loving affirmations you wrote in Exercise #1.

Chapter Twenty Three Exercise #3
Start being your own best friend. Do something loving for your self each day. Teach your mind how to love yourself by staying centered in your heart. Love you!

Chapter Twenty Three Exercise #4
Stand in front of a full length mirror. Look at yourself in the mirror. Make a note of what you see. Where do your eyes go first, second and then after that? What are your thoughts about yourself? What do you think of what you see? Concentrate on your exact thoughts at this moment. Are you zooming in on fat or cellulite? Are you noticing the wrinkles that are beginning to appear on your face? Are you looking at your hair, your chest, your stomach or your hips? Are you looking at yourself and thinking negative thoughts about your physical appearance? Are there parts of your body you hate, or places you immediately focus on and wish you could change? While still looking in the mirror, recite the following affirmation. Be sure to look yourself in the eyes every now and then, just as you would if you were giving a speech. Repeat the affirmation daily until you feel the truth in it.

Mirror Affirmation
'The truth is that I am very perfect in this mirror. I am perfect in every way. The imperfections I noticed are only in my own mind. My mind is my worst enemy and the biggest cause of my

unhappiness with myself. I now release all the negative thoughts I have about myself. It is only in my own mind that I believe myself to be imperfect. I accept and approve of myself the way I am. I love myself for who, and what, I truly am. My body is just the shell in which I live. Everything about my body can be changed for it is not my true self. The true me is on the inside of this shell. The true me is perfect in everyway. I am beautiful, strong, fearless, and loving. I am perfect.'

Chapter 24

Be Love

*Life is short and we have not too much time
for gladdening the hearts of those
who are traveling the dark way with us.
Be swift to love. Make haste to be kind.*
Henri-Frederic Amiel, 1885

  I like to think of myself as *being love* rather than *giving love*. When we remove ourselves from the giving, we are taking away the thought of intent. For example, if I do this as a sign of my love, you will do that in return. If we are the essence of love, we also protect ourselves from giving too much of ourselves and draining our own resources.

  Think about it like this. You are love. Everything you do is out of love and is loving. Isn't that what life is really all about? When you choose to actually give your love, you are giving out pieces of yourself to others. These pieces get stuck out there, and in time you will end up missing pieces of yourself, while others will end up with fragments of you stuck to them.

  It may be easier to think of it in terms of a relationship with a spouse or partner. You pour out your love in thoughts, feelings, emotions and actions to this person. You give of yourself completely and constantly. You feel that if you give everything to them they will love you forever and never leave you. Soon you intertwine your love with them so much that you begin to identify yourself through them. One day, this other person decides your relationship is no longer what they want. The process of separation begins and you may be left wondering what happened. You begin to feel as though you gave the relationship everything you had, literally you did, and now you are left feeling used, confused, abandoned and scared. In your heart you felt that everything would be fine if you gave your love completely and constantly. Now your own heart is in need of repair because it didn't work out that way. As the two of you separate, you are left feeling like a piece of you is gone and that your partner is still holding that piece of you. The loss of these pieces, create feelings of distrust, betrayal, fear and resentment, not to mention the feeling of losing yourself and your own identity. Whether it's a romantic partnership or just a friendship, a separation is not an easy thing, but there is no need to loose a part of your self in the process.

If you adopt this new way of 'being' love instead of pouring it out by the bucket full, your relationships won't change. You won't be less loving of a person. Your partner won't feel unloved. You will still be loving to that person. They will know and feel the love you hold for them.

Most relationships create a 'give and take' to the love they share. This is true for all relationships, not just romantic ones. Have you ever felt betrayed or hurt emotionally by someone you loved? Your first reaction is revenge. You take on an 'I'll show him' attitude. Other reactions are 'See if I ever help you again', or 'I've done so much for her and this is how she treats me!' You have subconsciously put expectations on the relationship. Because of the love you gave to the relationship, you expected a certain reaction and it didn't happen that way. It's like saying, 'If I'm nice, they'll be nice'.

We do this all the time without even realizing it. We give, and because of that, we expect to receive. If you want to do something special for someone never use it to hold over their head until they return the favor. They don't have to do anything in return. It is only in your mind if you expect them to. Give because you want to give. Expect nothing in return. You can make the choice not to give if you're only doing it for a return of favor or if you really don't want to in the first place. Never feel guilty about choosing not to constantly give your love. If you are the essence of love all the time, you *are* always loving to your fullest capacity. When you

Chapter 24

sincerely can 'be love' in all that you do, that *is* sharing love. You can't feel guilty about not loving enough and you won't expect anything in return.

Even though life should be a balance of give and take, don't expect to receive from the same person you gave to. When I think back on my life there were many friends, and even some strangers, that helped me out when I needed it. One time, I locked my keys and my toddlers in the car with their seat belts on. My sons couldn't get out of their seat and unlock the doors. They started crying and then I started crying. To this day I have never forgotten the loving kindness of a complete stranger who came to my rescue. I'll never be able to repay that kindness to him. I never even knew his name. Therefore, I will balance the 'take' by 'giving' to someone else. If you give you will receive. No one ever said that you'd receive from the same person you gave to, so stop expecting it.

There were people in my life that helped me tremendously through rough times. Their love and support was what pulled me through. With many, I was never able to repay their kindness because for the duration of our relationship an opportunity never arose. To balance their giving I now give to others who need my support and love.

If I give to someone in hopes that they will give me something in return, the act of love isn't even involved. That would be more like a business transaction or a purchase. Love holds no intent. You do it because you want to.

I recently gave my neighbor $1,000 toward the purchase of some land they had for sale. They needed the money because they were having hard times. I needed a couple of months to get enough money together to buy the land. Knowing the money would help them, I made the choice to give them a portion of it 'as a down payment for the land'. They took the money and signed a paper stating that the money was a down payment. Someone else came along and was ready to buy the land for more than we wanted to spend. At that time, our neighbors told us they had no intention of paying us back. This situation is different from simply giving because we had a business agreement, stating that the money was to be used toward purchasing the land. Even though I gave them some money up front as an act of love because I wanted to help them out, I was not just giving without a reason. I gave out of love and compassion, but both parties knew it was for a business transaction.

A man once told me that he was very upset with his ex-secretary. He said he had given her a $700.00 wedding present, which I thought was extremely generous of him. When I asked why he was so upset he said that she 'had the nerve' to quit her job after that. He expected that she would remain his loyal employee because of his expensive wedding gift. Now he felt betrayed and used by her. The truth is, he made the choice to give that money. He didn't get a signed contract saying that if he gave her the money she would not quit. She never asked for that large of a gift. He made the choice, but he put expectations on it. Those were expectations that she was never aware of. It is important to clearly state that you hold expectations to your giving when that is the case. If you don't, you should expect nothing from giving.

Love is hard to explain in words or thoughts because it is an emotion. Emotions are something we feel. Love encompasses such feelings as compassion, respect, devotion, admiration and caring. These emotions come from the heart. We can feel these emotions toward anyone or anything. Love is not reserved for spouses, family and close friends. We should love all things. Once you love your self and start *being* love to all things, hate dissolves.

Love is not just an emotion you feel toward another living being, but a way of feeling toward your entire life. You can be loving toward your car by taking care of it properly. Try being loving to your home, plants, computer, job and everything else in your life. Be loving to your neighborhood, city, state, country and world. Be love always and everywhere. Be love before being anything else, and love will be showered back to you.

Chapter Twenty Four Exercise #1

Practice consciously being love all day long over the next few days. Be love by holding love in your heart toward everything you do and everyone you meet.

Chapter Twenty Four Exercise #2

Show the love within you toward others without expecting anything in return. Give because it feels good and that's all. *Give* to balance all the *taking* you've done.

Chapter 24

Open Your Heart

Love all things.
Give of your heart and soul.

Your inner Light shines brightly
when you open yourself to others.

Think not of yourself so much.
'Be' the miracle instead of looking for a miracle .

Serve God and all his creatures with unconditional love, compassion
and kindness.

Speak words of love to teach, heal and
comfort others.

Do not hold back, for your love is powerful
and the world needs to feel it.

Open your heart to help others,
for then you will be able to help yourself as well.

Chapter 25

Let Go of the Past

*If you always do what you've always done,
You'll always get what you've always gotten.*

The past is over and it holds no power over you. It's time to stop punishing yourself and others for things that happened long ago. Many times our current life events trigger the memory of past events in our mind. Our mind holds on to these memories long after they've happened and even after we think we've let them go.

For example, going through a divorce now can bring back memories of every relationship that ended. You may remember the pain, anger, rejection or abandonment you felt each and every time a relationship ended. The painful memory of losing your first love and every love since then can still be with you now. Even though years have passed and you no longer think about the past relationships, the emotions they stirred in you live on and are easily re-ignited. Since the emotional suffering is quite similar with each broken relationship, the old memories quickly surface once again. If you hadn't held on to the emotion of a prior memory your current situations would be easier to deal with.

This doesn't only happen with similar situations, just similar emotional distress. Let's say your best friend in grade school announced one day that she didn't like you anymore. The two of you had been inseparable and extremely close friends for a long time. You loved your friend very much. She tells you that you're just not cool anymore and that she has a new best friend. Instantly you react with emotions such as anger and jealousy. You feel abandoned and rejected by her. Subconsciously you begin to hold fear of future abandonment and rejection. Each time you see her with her new friend, your anger and jealously grow stronger. Eventually you find a new friend to take her place in your heart and you begin to feel better. The anger and jealousy diminish and become non-existent to you. Perhaps you still cringe every time you see her or think about her, but the pain has dissolved for the most part.

Now, twenty years later, you don't even remember that event. You are working for a large company. You've been there a while and you love your job. The company hasn't been doing well and there have been lay off's for some time. You prepare yourself for the possibility of losing your job by going on interviews and making tentative plans, just in case. One day your boss calls you in and says "We have to let you go."

Instantly you are flooded with emotions you can't explain. You thought you were prepared and you are shocked and surprised at your reaction. What happened? The words of your boss triggered the same emotions your grade school friend triggered. Even though the circumstances are very different, the emotions are similar. You feel anger, abandonment, and rejection toward your boss. You may feel jealously toward those who did not lose their job. Had you cleared yourself of the old emotional baggage you wouldn't have reacted as intensely. Yes, it would have still been difficult but it wouldn't involve past emotions.

Now imagine how many times you've experience this same sort of emotion with other friends, partners, and family members. No doubt there's more than one instance when a similar situation occurred. If you multiply your emotional reaction that many times, you can understand the magnitude of its effect on you. The past memories you continue to carry will hold all the emotions associated with the initial situations. The old emotions, even if we think we're unaware of them, mix with the emotions of the new situation and create an even larger issue to deal with because it increases and strengthens our current emotional distress.

In addition to carrying around emotional baggage from the past, we are also victims of constantly *comparing* current events with past events. Comparisons don't need a trigger and they seldom stir as

Chapter 25

much emotion, yet they keep us connected to the past. The events of the past are unrelated to the present. The only things important in the now are present and current issues. Allowing yourself to look back, compare, and even start to stack all the events together, will weaken your ability to survive and heal in the now. Constantly comparing everything we experience ties us to our past. It doesn't allow us to enjoy what we have in the now. Everything we say, do, feel and think can be compared to a prior experience. The past is over. Those experiences are over. They are 'thens' and we are living in the 'now' so they aren't relevant any more.

The past can't be identical to the future. There will always be differences because every moment of every day is a unique, new experience of its own. If you catch yourself saying things like, 'My old boss would have let me go home early', or 'My last dog would have never chewed my shoes', or 'My last partner never forgot my birthday', you are comparing. It's a waste of your energy and it robs you of enjoying the new in your life. You remain tied to the past. Why would you expect everyone and everything to be the same as in the past? That can never be and we wouldn't want it to be either.

Not only negative emotional baggage affects you. Positive past events do too. Positive past events are just as destructive because we use them to judge and compare new events. If you had the best vacation five years ago, you automatically compare every vacation since then to that one. You can find yourself saying things like 'This is a great vacation but that one we took five years ago was the best.' We compare jobs, holidays, outings, friendships, romantic partners, and every experience this way. You rob yourself of life's enjoyment and excitement when you constantly compare. Every moment of your life should be experienced and enjoyed for what it is and without comparison to the past. When you release the past you still keep the wisdom gained from the experience but it can not affect your enjoyment of the present. Look back at your past but realize that it is over and your life is happening in the now. Experience the now as it is and without judgment, comparison or old emotional attachment.

You also carry baggage from past lives. This type of baggage is locked in your cell memory. If you'll remember Part I, I talked about holding fears, emotions and thoughts that have no relevance to your current life. These negative issues still reside within your energy and must be released as well. If you continue to hold on to them, over time you will begin to identify more and more with them. Allowing ourselves to bring the emotions and thoughts of past lives to the surface in this life only solidifies their existence when, in fact, they do not really exist. The truth is, they hold no power or significance to your life now other than the wisdom and understanding they created for you. With past life events, you may not be aware of where these emotions came from. The important thing is to release them.

Do you have fears or phobias that you can't explain? For me, it's a fear of heights and falling. When I get to a high place I fear being sucked down to the ground against my will. I have never had an experience with falling in this life yet the fear is very powerful. There is no explanation for this fear. I have no conscious memory of falling so it most likely resides within my cell memory. If you have fears, negative thoughts, or negative emotions that are unexplainable, you may have carried them over from past lives. Everything we've ever experienced remains within our soul and therefore is a part of us. Carrying around the junk from past lives is even more ridiculous than the junk of this life. We don't even remember it, yet it continues to haunt and control us. We need to release those things.

To help you identify danger signals of patterns that need releasing, start paying attention to times you experience any of the following.

Guilt	Anger
Sorrow	Hopelessness
Pain	Jealousy
Resentment	Fear of illness
Fear of being alone	Fear of poverty
Fear of rejection	Fear of abandonment
Fear of losing your power	Fear of speaking your truth

Your body responds to every thought and emotion you have. Every negative thought and emotion stems from your ego mind. When the ego mind is allowed to act this way it directly affects you

Chapter 25

physically. This is because it creates a battle between your mind and soul.

Negative mental and emotional responses can also create illnesses and injury to your body. Let's say your feeling resentful of having to work so much. You work hard at your job all day and go home and work all evening for your home and family. Weekends are just more time for chores and duties around the house. You feel angry and resentful of this lifestyle but you have no choice... you have to earn money and take care of your personal life and family. The ego mind can slip in and create an illness or cause you an injury. Now you are forced to get the 'down time' you wanted in the first place. Even though the consequences seem far from desirable, you created exactly what you wanted.

Your ego mind will create it any way it can. This scenario can also be two fold in that others may show sympathy and compassion toward you in your weakened state. It's similar to saying, "I'll go ahead and punish myself (by being sick) so that the world can't punish me (by making me work too much). Louise Hay has two fantastic books that describe the mental cause of every illness you can imagine. She then gives you positive affirmations to help dissolve the issues related to those illnesses. Her books are *Heal Your Body,* and *You Can Heal Your Life*. I highly recommend these books as a medical reference guide.

We all carry around pieces of the past. Some of the pieces have been with us for hundreds or thousands of years. Even though you are not conscious of them, their weight is heavy upon you and can affect your well being immensely. There is a reason for everything that has ever happened to you, good and bad. It is important to remember the lessons you learned but you do not need to hold on to the emotions they created.

Life is about growth and learning. To properly grow and learn we need to let go of the past and live only in the now so our experiences aren't clouded by irrelevant issues. When you are able to see that every new event is a lesson and growth for your soul you can be thankful for the experience and then let it go. When you start doing this, the peace and understanding you feel will naturally dissolve and suppress any new emotional baggage before it locks into your memory.

One time I had my grandchildren for the weekend. I'd been cleansing and releasing for quite some time and I felt like I had let go of the majority of my current life's major issues. This weekend I was surprised when something popped up. I totally adore my grandchildren and we had a wonderful time, but off and on during the weekend I felt some familiar old emotions spring forth. It shocked me because I hadn't felt those emotions for a long time, and they weren't pleasant then and sure weren't pleasant now. It had to do with the years I spent as a single parent. Even if you've never been a single parent you can probably understand how frightening, frustrating and overwhelming it can be. Single parents also carry anger and resentment toward their ex-spouse for leaving them alone with this huge responsibility. They feel as though they have lost themselves to their new career as sole caregiver and parent. There's no one to share your pain, happiness, excitement or exhaustion with. It's lonely, scary and you continue to carry the pain of losing your marriage as well.

As soon as I realized old memories were surfacing I thanked God for bringing it to my attention. I realized and understood the underlying lesson of those years. I patted myself on the shoulder for doing such a good job. I thanked God for the wisdom it gave me, and quickly released all that I no longer needed to hang on to.

I have found that if there is something that needs releasing, it will be brought to our attention over and over again. My own experience that weekend wasn't all that happened. I received an e-mail the next day from my friend Jill in which she was telling me what a wonderful parent I had been because I had two great sons. The e-mail was so out of the blue. We hadn't been talking about it and I hadn't told her what I'd felt over the weekend. Her words were extremely comforting and powerful and came at the perfect time. She also talked about her own single-parent daughter and what she is going through.

At work the following day a single Dad approached me. He expressed to me his own frustrations and feelings about being a single parent. I quickly realized I could be a great help to him by simply listening and giving him words of encouragement. Pay attention. You will usually receive more than one heads up if something needs your attention. Remember to always be thankful

Chapter 25

and to always hold the same sympathy toward others who are going through similar situations.

It's a wonderful thing to release your own past and then help others through the same thing. Everything you've experienced qualifies you to be a teacher or guide for someone else going through something similar. Stay centered in your heart at all times. Pass on your wisdom and love to others and your releases will be much more fulfilling.

Now that you know why it's important to let go of the past, it's time to explore how to do it. Though it would be wonderful if saying "I release all positive and negative energy from my past" would take care of everything at one time, it doesn't work that way. Most of the time, you must bring the emotion or thought regarding an event into your conscious mind first. There are many professionals that can help you with this. Spiritual Healers, Hypnotists, Energy Workers, Psychic Healers and Regressionists are a few. Without the help of a professional you will need to release as new events occur or come into your conscious mind. This happens in your normal day to day experiences and often through dreams or meditation.

First, start paying attention to thoughts and emotions that don't seem relevant to the present. Notice times when you feel over emotional about something, fearful without just cause, or extremely negative without good reason. These sparks of awareness naturally begin to happen once you start paying attention and looking for problem areas. A spark can occur within you as a reaction to a new event or simply out of the blue and for no apparent reason. This signals a need for some releasing related to that event or emotion.

Holding a sincere desire and intent to clear and release is all there is to it. You don't have to have special words to say because it's your inner desire and intent that starts the release. Your willingness to let it go is most important. You can say something like,

'I release and surrender to God all fears,
thoughts and emotions related to this issue.
I willingly let go of this now'.

There are many ways to phrase your releases. Your words can be as dramatic, creative, or simple as you like. The release comes from within. The words are an affirmation, and intent, made verbal. Say what feels complete and fulfilling to you. Keep saying your release until you feel it's gone. Once can be enough. Be thankful for every release. Picture yourself surrounded by the white Light of God afterward. Know that the pure, white Light verifies that you are completely and eternally cleansed. When a new issue pops up, simply go through a release again.

Chapter Twenty Five Exercise
Pay attention to and release old baggage as soon as it surfaces. Ask God and your Guides to help you realize when there is a need to let go. It is good to ask for this help right before you go to sleep or during meditation. Ask that the wisdom and understanding remain but the negative emotions and thoughts dissolve. God does not want you to hold on to these negative things. He knows that it only gets in the way of your growth and learning now. Once you ask for help, and ask for the release, the process automatically begins.

Chapter 26

Everything is Perfect

*Be assured that all is perfect and time is of no use to your soul.
Trust in the natural flow and rhythms of life.
Know that all is balanced and divinely ordered.
All is well.
All is perfect.*

Everything is always perfect. We are to blame when we don't see the perfection of all things. You must remember that there is already a perfect plan with perfect timing for you. When we fight the natural flow and rhythms of life we create unnecessary hardship and frustration for our self.

It was very difficult for me to accept and digest this idea at first. Perhaps it's because it also involves the spiritual, mental and emotional side of us. I chose to place this chapter here because it is much easier to grasp the reality of it after you understand yourself spiritually, mentally and emotionally. The fact that everything is perfect is actually borne of our spiritually true self, our soul. The difficulties with accepting it come from our mind and emotions; two areas within us that create imperfections. Without understanding your spiritually true self and the power of your thoughts and emotions, it's difficult to completely understand that everything is perfect.

In the spirit world, free of the human body and mind, everything is perfect. Existence of your soul flows naturally with the energy and rhythm of the universe. There are no clocks to distract you from the natural rhythm. There's no mental chatter pulling you into negativity. Your soul feels only love, so you are not haunted with emotional baggage. One of the most valuable tools for life on earth is remembering the perfection of our soul and our real home, the spirit world. Imagining or visualizing that perfect state is a good start. Since we all have a soul, and our souls know this perfection, the knowledge is already within us. It's a memory, not a new idea. You just have to bring it into your consciousness again.

Knowing that everything is perfect doesn't mean you'll never experience undesirable things. It doesn't mean your life will be all happiness and no pain. Remember that you planned learning lessons for yourself in this life. Lessons can be learned in many ways and many of them involve going through rough times of some sort. As unpleasant as these times may feel, they are perfect for your intended lesson. Realizing the lesson at these times helps you understand why things happen as they do. You will begin to see the perfection in not only the good times, but the rough times as well.

Sometimes we think we want something to be as we wish, only to find out later that the way it worked out was actually much better for us. This happens a lot with divorce or the loss of a job. At the time it seems unfair, horrific or traumatic. When all is said and done you find yourself with a job or partner that seems better suited to you, is more fulfilling, or brings you more happiness. I'll share a personal experience.

My first big awakening to this idea was when we were selling our house. We thought we would have no room for our horses so we put them up for sale. A buyer came along, but when they arrived to pick up the horses we had some trouble. My younger horse wouldn't load in the trailer. We tried every trick in the book and I prayed and prayed for God to help us. It was no use and we eventually decided that was enough for one day. We agreed to give it a try the following weekend. The very next day we met with our realtor. She brought the land plat for our new home. What a shock it was to realize that we would own much more land than we originally thought. In fact, there was plenty of room to keep our horses and give them a wonderful pasture. It was as though the events of the day before were now a gift from above. Imagine how upset we would have been if the horses had loaded up and been sold, only for us to find out the next day, we could have kept them. When the day

Chapter 26

came for us to move the horses to their new home we were wondering if we'd have the same problems loading the young horse. No way, she loaded up like she was excited to go home.

Once you become aware of the constant perfection of life you begin to feel more peaceful and safe. You realize it's not your mind and body that creates this life of yours. The personal pressure of having total control over everything diminishes. Though you can still try to control situations you find that you don't have to. In fact, the road is much smoother if you just go with the flow.

Life isn't going to be perfect, but there is a perfect reason for everything that happens. Let go of the feeling that you are in the driver's seat. Allow the perfection that is already there, be your driver. Take your challenges in stride. Look at them from all points of view. See how they truly are a blessed gift for you. Stop trying to control your own rhythm. When you do this, your ego mind gets in the way and life becomes a struggle. Here's another example.

I was once again reminded of perfect timing while we were selling our house. This time we found a house that we wanted to buy. We had looked at house after house and were getting pretty tired it. One day we saw a house that outshined all the others. It had a beautiful pond and several acres of wooded, rolling hills. The house sat on a hill and had beautiful landscape. The interior, however, was not at all what we wanted. It was small, outdated, and we'd have to build on and renovate quite a bit. We made an offer on the house and waited anxiously to begin negotiations. I prayed that we'd get the house but we soon realized it wasn't going to happen. No matter what we did, the deal was not moving forward. We were heartbroken and thought it would be hard to find another home as good as that one. Well, within a month we found one that was. It had the same beautiful land but the house was three times bigger, and had everything we wanted. The price was about the same as the first house. We thanked God for *not* answering our prayers on the first house.

When the things you desire are not in your best interest you will not receive them. If your affirmations and prayers don't seem to be working, trust that there is a reason for it. When I feel myself struggling with something, I realize I am not trusting in the natural perfection and timing. I quickly let go of my power struggle. You can say, or think, such things as, 'What will be, will be', or

'Everything happens for a reason', or 'If it's meant to be it will be'. Everyone I know has heard those words roll out of my mouth many times. It's true. No matter what you do to make something happen, it won't if it is not meant to happen or if the timing is not right. Whatever words you choose to say will automatically switch off your need to control everything. It's an excellent way to reconnect to the natural flow and rhythms of your life.

When my father died I initially saw no perfection in it. I was so filled with sorrow and sadness. I felt angry and betrayed by God that he had to die. I wasn't ready. I wanted more time with him. How could he die so young and so quickly? Death is only difficult for those left behind. It is a blessing for those who pass. Knowing this, you can see how selfish it was for me to mourn his death. He got to go back home to complete peace, harmony, understanding, love and perfection.

When we lose a loved one, we should feel happy for them, not sad for ourselves. Oftentimes we feel like they left us here to suffer without them. There can be lessons for both parties in death. The lesson I learned from my father's passing was that it is only sad for the living. It must be hard to look down from the perfection of the spirit world and see our loved ones so sad and unhappy. I know they wish we could understand the happiness they feel. When we understand, it helps us heal from their death more quickly.

My father was diagnosed with cancer, suffered for six months and then passed. I started to realize that this wasn't a very long time to suffer. He never had to spend his last days in a hospital or institution. He didn't spend months bedridden or in a wheelchair. He always wished he'd never have to experience those things and he got what he wished for. He lived a successful life with many joys. When his job here on earth was done he got to go home. Though he had six months of suffering, it allowed him time to reflect on his life. This was also a time of reflection and healing between my mother and him. It gave everyone time to adjust and accept the possibility of his passing.

I know every death is different and his may seem better than one you are thinking about. Try to look at it as a positive thing for your loved one. If it was a quick death, don't dwell on not being able to say good bye or not having time to accept it. Think of it as the ultimate way to pass. No pain, no suffering, just go back home. If there were months or years of suffering, there were important reasons it happened that way. Perhaps that loved one chose their death in that manner as the last big lesson for their life. They may have chosen that method as a way to teach others their own life lessons.

Trust that everything is perfect. Next time you're stuck in traffic or a long line at the store, remind yourself that everything is perfect. Maybe you are getting an opportunity to work on a life lesson of patience. God isn't punishing you when things don't go your way or when something doesn't work out the way you wanted it to. God doesn't take your loved ones from you as a punishment. God can not save you from sorrow or pain because that may be part of the life you chose. He is always there for you and His love is eternal. He knows what is perfect for you. Trust is all you need. Let go and allow this beautifully orchestrated perfection of your life unfold as it is meant to.

Chapter Twenty Six Exercise #1
Write down some of the times you had a desire that did not come true as you had wished. Think through that time period and beyond to see if you can find a reason why things happened the way they did.

Chapter Twenty Six Exercise #2
As you go about your life, pay attention to the perfection in all things. Become aware that this is true. Don't struggle so much with living. Let the natural flow and rhythm be your driver.

Chapter 27

Be Thankful

Gratitude is the best attitude.

When you are thankful for the gifts and blessings in your life, your heart opens and love pours out. Keeping an open heart allows you to receive more gifts, love, and blessings in return. What you give you will receive ten fold and so the cycle begins.

We've all heard the phrase, 'You must give to receive'. Did you know that one way to give is to be thankful? Think about this. If you are showered with gifts from the spirit world, how do you give back to them? Not with money or material gifts, for they are earthly possessions and mean nothing in the spirit world. It is through love and thanks that you repay the Divine gifts. Just because these dear friends aren't of this earthly plane doesn't mean they don't desire to know the joy and happiness you receive from their unconditional love.

Whenever your prayers are answered you need to give thanks. If you receive Divine guidance you need to feel gratitude. When you've asked for a short line at the post office and you get it, be thankful. Let nothing go without giving thanks. You know how good it feels when someone thanks you for something you've done. It's no different in the spirit world. As you become more aware of all the little blessings in your life remember to always be thankful.

Gratitude is an emotion from the heart. It's the ultimate expression of love. You can not be the essence of love without sharing the ultimate expression of love. From the moment you wake up and start your day there are many reasons to be thankful. To begin with, you can be thankful for the wonderful hours of slumber you just gave your body. Be thankful for the cozy bed you slept in and the helpful alarm clock that woke you up. Thanks can be given for the running water you use to wash yourself and brush your teeth. Give thanks for the sewer or septic system that's *so* convenient. The coffee pot, electricity, your car, your job, your loved ones are all reasons to be thankful before you even leave your house in the morning.

Some people forget to be thankful until they have to do without. We take things for granted until one day those things break down or we no longer have them. Without them we quickly realize how wonderful they were. Take your car for example. You drive it everyday. It takes you everywhere you want to go. You *expect* it to work and you forget to be thankful that it does. One day it doesn't start. You have to tow it in to the service center, find another ride to and from your destination, and spend the next day or two without a car. It requires money to fix it and it's a major hassle and inconvenience until you get it back. You get upset that it broke down and you realize how important it was for you. When it's repaired you feel thankful to have it back. Doing without made you realize what a blessing it truly is.

We shouldn't have to be reminded of our gifts and blessings this way. Though days go by and we may not specifically say 'thank you' for our car, give your thanks whenever you think of it. Every time it starts and gets you somewhere is an opportunity to be thankful.

If I see someone broke down on the road I quickly give thanks that I am not. Don't wait until you go without to remember your blessings. The more consciously thankful you become, the more reason you'll have to give thanks. The last thing before going to sleep at night and the first thing in the morning are excellent times to give thanks. God gives us many things to be thankful for. It's time to start acknowledging His gifts. He is not so high and mighty that He doesn't need or want to be thanked. It's precisely the opposite. He loves to hear about your gratitude and happiness. While God already knows when you are happy, you still need to express it.

If you have trouble feeling thankful, begin to imagine waking up to no food, water or air. These are three simple things we take for granted yet we couldn't survive without them. Visualize having no electricity for the next week. Most of us have experienced how inconvenient that is. On a smaller scale, imagine if your microwave, stove, refrigerator, blow dryer or washing machine stopped running. Imagine life without these things. Be thankful for the gifts you already have before you have to experience being without in order to appreciate them. The gifts from above are many and when we feel sincere love and gratitude for them, we receive even more gifts in return.

Thanking those on this earthly plane is easier for us. When someone gives you a gift or does something nice for you, it's easier to remember to thank them. You should be thankful for their friendship and presence in your life as well. All living things deserve to receive our gratitude and love. Let nothing go without thanks, including human beings, insects, animals and plants. Your pets give you security, devotion and companionship. Plants give us beauty, food, herbs and medicines. Flowers give us joy with their beauty. The birds control our insects, pollinate our world, and sing sweet songs for us. Bees supply us with honey, the grass provides us with a lush green lawn, and trees give us shade from the sun's harsh rays. The rain sustains life and keeps our rivers, lakes, animals, plants and us alive. Lightening, wind, sun, clouds are all gifts. Everything is a gift worth being thankful for.

Sometimes there are people that hurt us or cause us pain. They should be thanked too for the lesson they taught us. The parent who pushes you to learn independence by not being there for you is a teacher. Thank your ruthless neighbor who taught you how to set boundaries by trying to take advantage of you. Give thanks to the boss that degraded you all the time and taught you how to stand up for yourself and speak your truth. Be grateful for the friend that taught you self confidence by not helping you out when you wanted them to.

Become the essence of love by remembering the ultimate expression of love. Be thankful for everything and everyone in your life. They are all a part of the plan you made for yourself. Each one is important in their own way, therefore they all deserve your gratitude. Thank God, your Guides, your deceased loved ones and all who help you along your path from the spirit world. Thank all living things for the gifts they bring you. Thank all nonliving things for what they add to your life. Give thanks every morning when you wake up and every night when you go to sleep.

When you become thankful for everything in your life, you begin to receive more gifts in return. You will be amazed at how many gifts begin to come your way. It is true that whatever you give you will receive back ten fold, and it doesn't take long before you begin to experience this. Open your heart not only to love but to gratitude.

Chapter Twenty Seven Exercise
Begin to be more thankful and appreciative of all that you have. Before you get out of bed in the morning, be thankful for the gifts you will receive that day. When you go to bed give thanks again for all the gifts of the day. Thank people for even the little things they do. *Feel* gratitude even if you can't express it.

Chapter 28

Forgiveness

Be at peace with all and see beauty, love and Light in all.

Forgiveness is another emotion that begins in the heart. Like gratitude, it is a reaction to an action. When someone does something nice for us we thank them. When someone hurts or angers us we can choose to forgive or be unforgiving. When you are unforgiving it closes your heart and you cease to hold love. Love is borne of forgiveness. Hatred and anger are borne from being unforgiving. When you can not forgive, you can not hold love in your heart.

Unforgiving means that you are unable to stop making judgments of good versus bad. The dualities of good/bad, right/wrong, acceptable/unacceptable and so on, cause us to judge and condemn. God loves us all. There are no dualities in His being. He knows only love. It is your ego mind that creates dualities. First, let go of the thought that something is either right or wrong. Once we let go of dualities we can forgive in an instant. If we see ourselves or others as doing something wrong we create a reason, or need, for forgiveness. If we hadn't seen it as wrong in the first place there would be no need for forgiveness.

When someone does something we consider bad, we immediately begin to judge and condemn the guilty party. We also impress upon them that they are guilty of being bad because we can not forgive them. Once this happens we are unable to freely forgive them. We also create an unforgiving attitude within that person. They feel bad, so they will have difficulty forgiving themselves.

When you see your life and its experiences as the way it was meant to be, you can't judge wrong from right. Knowing that our life must include lessons, some of which include the darker side of us, it becomes important that we experience it all. When you're learning a lesson about love and it stirs a response in you of hate, how can that be judged? It may have been important for you to feel and act in that manner. Therefore, rather than judge yourself as being a terrible person, realize that it was for love that you did it. Whatever happens to us happens for a reason. There is no need to blame ourselves or others for anything.

Many people blame themselves and feel guilty for things they did in the past. Some things we've done may not seem good. If you feel you've done something bad or wrong, it's hard to forgive yourself. If you aren't forgiving of all the events of your past you will be unable to truly love yourself. Unconditional loves means always finding forgiveness in your heart. You must stop condemning, blaming, judging and criticizing yourself or your life so that you can love yourself completely. The only reality is that things happen for a reason and our entire existence on earth is a sequence of different lessons based on love. How we learn is irrelevant.

The fact that we learn is the important thing. Being able to accept and love ourselves for all we've been through is holding unconditional love for ourselves. Stop beating yourself up over and over again for the wrongs you've done. The past is over and holds no power over you. Past events aren't a reflection of who you are, just what you've had to go through to get where you are. The present is where you are living. Look at your past as one experience or lesson after another that got you to the present moment.

We do the same thing with others. Quickly we pass judgment on their actions when we have no right to do so. Being unforgiving makes us feel powerful, in that we control our love, or lack of love, as a response to their behavior. In truth, we are not here to judge and we certainly shouldn't push our love around like a power tool. If someone does something that hurts you greatly, you need to forgive them as quickly as possible. Forgiveness doesn't mean you accept their actions. It means you forgive them for their actions. There was a reason they did what they did. Rather than keeping yourself from experiencing all the joys of love by building hate over

Chapter 28

their actions, let it go and forgive. We are the ones who suffer most when we are unable to forgive. It does *us* more damage than *them*.

If you can't forgive you create hate, anger, jealousy, and resentment in yourself. You continually feed these negative responses if you choose never to forgive. In the same way, love feeds love. If you begin to forgive and accept yourself and others, you will receive more love. I remember one time when my husband lost his keys. I was thinking, 'How could he be so irresponsible'? It irritated me that he lost his keys and now I had to spend my time getting the spare key to him. I held the thought that he was totally irresponsible and I continued to check on whether or not he had his keys for days after that. A couple of weeks later I lost my keys. I couldn't find them. I began to get angry with myself that I did such a stupid thing. I was angry with myself because I found it hard to forgive my husband for doing the same thing. Once I realized I had been unforgiving toward him, it helped me understand why I was beating myself up for losing my own keys. We both found our keys and I learned a great lesson from it.

The best way to start being a forgiving person is to look at your past. Find out if there's someone you may be having trouble forgiving. See if there were things you did that you still don't forgive yourself for. Cleaning up all the unforgiving you still carry around from your past is necessary even if you begin forgiving everyone from this point on. As soon as you feel yourself holding a grudge or bad feeling about someone, go out and make things right with them. If you can't actually contact the person you hold anger toward, you can still forgive them within yourself.

When you catch yourself blaming or judging someone, stop it immediately. Remind yourself that you are not the judge. Everyone, including your self, needs to be forgiven. When you decide not to forgive someone of their actions you are confirming that they are bad. Whether it's within ourselves or toward others, we should never raise the feeling of not being good. Accept the reality of life. It won't always be perfect in your ego eyes. Surrender to life's reality by being forgiving.

The more you forgive, the more love you hold in your heart. The more love in your heart the more you will love life. Forgiving opens our heart so that love pours forth. Forgiving ourselves allows us to completely love ourselves. When you forgive someone else, their heart also opens and sends love back to you. It's similar to being thankful and receiving more gifts. Forgiveness creates more love. Your heart will be pure once again and you will be able to love all people and yourself. The burden and weight of those negative feelings will leave you permanently. When you forgive and release, you find happiness, peace and love within your self and within others.

Chapter Twenty Eight Exercise #1

Take a look at your heart. Do not look at it as an organ right now. Look at it as a storage bin for all the anger, resentment, and heartache you've ever stored in it. Look closely and see what you have stored in your heart. Make a list of everyone in your *past* that has caused you anger, resentment or heartache. Write down everyone you can think of. Now make a list of anyone *currently* in your life, who causes you anger, resentment or heartache. Name everyone you can think of. Forgive them all now. See if you have already forgiven some of them. Why did you forgive some and not all?

Chapter Twenty Eight Exercise #2

Now I want you to look deeper in your heart and see if you have ever been the cause of any anger, resentment or heartache within yourself. Do you hold resentment over something you did in the past? Do you blame others for their actions when you knew you had total control over the situation and may have even created the situation? Do you hold anger toward someone for their actions toward you, even though you could have protected yourself from their actions? Did you suffer heartache from someone that you could have avoided and did not? Forgive yourself now.

PART IV

Your Body

*We are all one,
and are connected through waves of energy
and the Light of our Creator.
Existence is through the natural flow
and rhythm of our energies;
connecting, passing, and surrounding us.*

*Simple, eternal, and powerful.
Use your energy to heal, balance,
and create more energy.
Share your energy in exchange for peace,
love and understanding.*

*Let God's message flow through your energy
and out into the world.
Know that all is perfect and balanced
through energy and love.
Open yourself to receive,
then open yourself to share.*

Chapter 29

Energy

*Energy is your life force.
It connects your body, mind and soul.
Sustaining a vibrant and flowing
energy system is the key to a healthy life.*

You are energy. It is energy that sustains and maintains your entire existence. Many people believe that life is given by our heart, lungs and other organs alone. While our organs and physical body do keep us up and running, it is our energy body that gives life to them. Our energy body sustains our physical body.

Think back to Part I, when I explained how our soul lives eternally and continues to live in the spirit world. What makes our soul live eternally? Energy. Our soul is energy, and that energy is the part of us that lives forever. The physical body we are given in each lifetime is simply the shell for our energy body, or soul. Since our true self is our soul, we must take care of its energy. That means we must nourish and maintain our energy body in order to have a healthy life inside our physical body.

When a soul enters a human body it gives the body life. When the soul leaves the human body it no longer has life. Every living thing is sustained and given life by the energy of a soul. Plants, trees, animals, insects and humans are alive because of their energy. The unique energy that makes you, shapes the way you think, feel, react and live. It affects everything about you.

Now think back to Part II, when I explained how we carry subconscious thoughts over from past life events and how negative thoughts patterns of this life or past lives can become lodged in our cell memory. Since we are born into each life on earth with a different mind and body, where do these cell memories of past lives come from? They are stored in the energy of your soul, the part of you that is eternal and continues to be your life force in each and every human form.

In Part III, I explained that emotional baggage from past lives is also stored in your cell memory. This is the same thing. These unexplainable emotions, phobias and feelings are carried from one life to another within the energy of your soul. Your conscious mind does not make sense of them because they were not formed from events of your current life. Your soul holds all the positive and negative memories of every life it ever had.

The soul is simply energy. When you think of yourself as only what you see, matter or your body, you neglect to give attention to the most important part of your existence, the part that is your true self and that will continue on for all eternity.

Although I waited until now to teach you about energy in this book, the truth is that energy is the common medium of your mind, emotions, body and soul. It is everything about you. It is easier to understand the vastness and importance of your energy body after you see the whole picture of who you are and how the body, mind and soul operate. Once you understand how these parts operate, it makes sense that there must be a common medium to connect each of them.

Since energy gives life to your entire existence, it is extremely important to maintain and balance it. Unfortunately, most people aren't even aware of their energy body. They have no idea that it exists, much less an understanding of the relationship between their good health from a vibrant energy or their illness from depletion in their energy. When you don't treat your energy body, you never really get to the core of the illness and therefore it may never be completely healed. Drugs can suppress and treat the symptoms but you must address your illness at the energy level as well. When you maintain a healthy energy level, your body will be able to release anything negative that could create illness. Clearing, releasing and increasing your energy also allows the body to constantly heal itself. With regular maintenance, your energy body will naturally keep you mentally, spiritually, psychologically and physically healthy. It's

Chapter 29

that simple. Sustaining a vibrant and flowing energy system is the key to a healthy life.

There are many ways to increase or decrease your energy. You can have blocks in your energy that severely affect its natural flow. When your soul was first created its energy was strong, pure and vibrantly flowing. With each lifetime, your energy was affected by your environments, mental and emotional experiences, and contact with others. Everything you've experienced has been stored in your energy, or soul. After many lives the negative influences begin to build up and this can cause problems within your energy system today. The natural you is the energy of your soul, therefore all the influences that affect your energy become who you are.

When your energy system is running at its peak performance it naturally maintains constant healing within your body. Energy is what heals you and it does it very well when it is vibrant and flowing. In the same way, it causes pain and illness when it gets blocked, depleted or out of balance. No matter what the cause of the energy breakdown, it will eventually affect your physical body if left un-repaired.

For example, if you experience emotional distress or trauma from a partner who breaks your heart by leaving you, it would create an energy disorder in your body. You may feel that closing your heart would protect you from further heartache, so you close off the energy in that area. Different emotional responses affect different parts of your body. In time, any closure or decrease in energy to a certain part of the body will cause a physical reaction of pain or illness. The physical reaction is directly related to the mental and emotional distress you feel.

If you feel that you have lost the *joy of love* in your life you may create things like angina, anemia, heart problems or even heart attack. If you continue to hold *anger* over the heartache you can create bladder problems, vaginitis, sexual dysfunctions, or prostate problems. If the heartache causes you to feel as though you are no longer *supported* by a loved one it can cause back problems. If you become *afraid*, you may begin to have stomach problems. Deep *resentment* can create cancer. *Anger* in general can create things like boils, burns, cuts, fevers, sores and inflammations. If you feel *guilty* about the relationship's breakup you can create pain. All of these symptoms are created by decreases in our energy body.

Anytime we alter the naturally healthy flow of energy in our body and neglect to address it, a physical ailment develops. I have listed some excellent books in the Suggested Reading Material section of this book that describe the relationships and causes of every illness and pain. As I stated earlier, my favorite reference book is *You Can Heal Your Life*, by Louise Hay. Her book makes a wonderful medical reference guide because it helps you diagnose the underlying issues of your illnesses and pains.

Most people go to the doctor when they are ill. The doctor gives them medicine to treat their condition. While medicine can treat and suppress the symptoms, it doesn't heal the underlying issue itself. If we don't heal ourselves at the energy body level we will never be completely and truly freed of that illness because we have not eliminated the underlying cause. Since we haven't addressed the true issue, we will also continue to carry the cause of that illness within our soul's energy forever and it will become a recurring issue lifetime after lifetime.

Although medicine can fix you up, the problem will resurface over and over again until you repair the energy system. This explains why so many people must take daily medications for the rest of their life. The medicines have become mandatory for their health and survival because they haven't diagnosed and healed themselves of the underlying issue, which lives in their energy system.

Self healing is the natural you. When your energy is vibrant and healthy it automatically maintains the health of your physical body, mind and spirit. That's how it's supposed to work. The only thing you need to do is maintain your energy. When you have a healthy energy system you are guaranteed the greatest possible health and well being of your entire existence.

Maintaining a healthy energy system improves every part of your life. Being aware of things that can negatively affect your energy is a powerful start to maintaining your energy health. In the following chapters I will be teaching you ways to increase your energy. I will also explain what can deplete your energy. You will absolutely love the fantastic feeling that floods your entire body as you raise yourself to a higher energy frequency.

Chapter 29

Chapter Twenty Nine Exercise
Think back in your life to a time you felt depleted of your natural energy. Analyze what mental or emotional issue may have depleted your energy during that time.

Chapter 30

Chakras, Meridians & Auras

*Your energy emanates from various
points within your body.
It then circulates throughout and
around your body.
The energy body consists of chakras,
meridians and several layers in your
auric field.*

Chakras & Meridians

Chakras are spinning vortex's that send and receive energy to or from your environment and body. The word chakra means wheel, disk or vortex. There are seven chakras in your body. Each one has its own relationship to your body, mind and soul and must be kept open, balanced and spinning properly in order to be energetically healthy.

For the most part a chakra that spins clockwise is considered to be healthy and open. When a chakra spins counterclockwise it is considered to be blocked, closed or unhealthy. Many layers of energy are formed from these vortex's and each layer can spin differently depending on your current situation. As the chakras produce energy it is carried throughout the body in the meridian system.

The meridians are energy lines or paths that run up and down throughout your body. The meridians feed the chakras and the chakras feed the meridians. Meridians also help remove toxins from our energy system. Without open, flowing meridians we are susceptible to toxic overload, illness and disease. The meridians are to your chakras what your arteries and blood vessels are to your heart. Both need to be working well for the other to do its job.

There are fourteen meridians in your body. Two meridians open directly to the environment, and energy can enter or exit the body through them. The other twelve are all connected but branch off to their own specific areas of the body. Meridians carry energy throughout your body like arteries carry blood throughout your body. Proper or improper function of the meridians can affect your immune, endocrine, digestive, circulatory, nervous, respiratory, lymphatic, skeletal and muscular systems. When energy is flowing properly in a meridian, the area it corresponds to will be healthy. Therefore, meridians are similar to chakras in that they directly relate to certain physical body functions and parts. In addition to keeping your chakras open and balanced, it is essential that the meridians remain open and flowing as well.

I like to think of the body's energy system as a mass transit system. There are stations (chakras) and there are transit ways (meridians). If any of these shut down or malfunction we have problems with the transport or production of our energy. When the energy stations and transit ways are unobstructed, energy flows efficiently and smoothly throughout your body.

Each of the seven chakras have their own specific location and regulate certain parts of your body. They each have a basic color. The colors can be light, dark, or even change, depending on your current situation. Energy healers often see the color of your chakra when working with your energy. This helps them determine what is influencing it and what its overall condition is. Chakras 1, 2 and 3 relate to your physical and external power while chakras 4 through 7 relate to your nonphysical and internal power. The following is a brief description of where each chakra is located and what it influences.

Chapter 30

Chakra 1
Name: Root or Base Chakra
Location: Base of the spine
Color: Red
Element: Earth
Sense: Smell

Body Relationship: Physical support, base of spine, legs, bones, feet, rectum and immune system.

Malfunction:
(mental/emotional) Fear of survival or abandonment by tribe, family, or group, or not fitting in with the group. It creates fear of rejection by the group, fear of the future or of death, loss of the will to survive, insecurity, loss of honor, integrity and ethics. It can also create anger, stress, anxiety, and the feeling of being over-worked, overwhelmed, out of control and powerless.

Malfunction:
(physical) Low back pain, sciatica, depression, hemorrhoids, rectal tumors, rectal cancer, varicose veins, and immune related disorders.

Healthy: Strong family bonding, safety, and feeling connected to, and part of, the physical world. Strong basic survival instincts and the will to live in the physical world. Tribal/family identity and security, feelings of sexuality, ethics, loyalty, honor, integrity and unity of all people. It also creates a strong will, a take-charge personality, the ability to stay grounded and live in the moment.

Chakra 2
Name:	Sacral Chakra
Location:	Just below the navel (womb area)
Color:	Orange
Element:	Water
Sense:	Taste

Body Relationship: Sexual organs, large intestines, hips, appendix, pelvis, bladder, lower back, reproductive organs and gonads.

Malfunction *(mental/emotional)*: Fear of losing control, being controlled by others or loss of power. Fear of not having enough money, loss of creativity, lack of ethics and morals, emotional instability, negativity, laziness, sadness, moodiness, apathy, guilt, addictions to food, drugs, alcohol, sugar or nicotine.

Malfunction *(physical)*: Low back pain, sciatica, bladder and urinary tract problems, pelvic problems, sexual impotence, uterus, ovary and vaginal disorders, prostate problems, hip disorders, appendicitis.

Healthy: Self empowerment, being in control of yourself, financial security, sexual connection to self and others, nurturing, creativity, emotions rather than thought, sociability, intuitive gut feelings, independence, and the ability to sense the energy of others.

Chakra 3

Name:	Solar Plexus
Location:	Belly Button to lower rib cage
Color	Yellow
Element:	Fire
Sense:	Sight

Body Relationship: Abdomen, stomach, upper intestines, spleen, liver, gall bladder, kidneys, pancreas, middle back and adrenal glands.

Malfunction:
(mental/emotional)
Fear of rejection, over-sensitivity to criticism, feeling physical appearance isn't good enough, low self esteem and self confidence, lack of self respect and honor, poor decision making, unable to care for yourself and others, feeling intimidated by others, lack of trust in others, fear of failure, acting timid, and feeling no direction in life.

Malfunction:
(physical)
Liver dysfunction, gastric or duodenal ulcers, arthritis, colon and intestinal problems, pancreas problems, indigestion, diabetes, anorexia, bulimia, hepatitis, adrenal dysfunctions, and middle back pain.

Healthy: Personal identity and power, ego, self esteem, self confidence, self respect, solid relationship to our self, courage, ambition, ethics, logic, responsibility, cunning and rationalization, mental will, the ability to be analytical, intellectual, focused and confident. Fun loving, hopeful, optimistic, enthusiastic, and self disciplined. This chakra is the vibration of your being.

Chakra 4

Name:	**Heart**
Location:	Over the heart
Color	Green
Element:	Air
Sense:	Touch
Body Relationship:	Lungs, heart, circulatory system, shoulders, arms, ribs, breasts, diaphragm, thymus gland and hands.
Malfunction: *(mental/emotional)*	Fear of loneliness, emotionally vulnerable or weak, issues with commitment, jealousy, sorrow, anger, hatred, unforgiving, lack of love in life, resentment, hatred, grief, envy, impatience, selfishness, unworthiness, loss of hope and trust, lack of self love and being self centered.
Malfunction *(physical)*	Lung problems, bronchial pneumonia, upper back and shoulder pain, breast cancer, asthma, allergies, cardiomegaly, mitral valve prolapse, heart attack and congestive heart failure.
Healthy:	LOVE, forgiveness, hope, trust, joy, compassion, thinking of others as well as self, connection, affinity, love of self, love of others, balance in relationships, giving, patience, perseverance, dedicated, helpful to others, high ideals and aspirations, and natural healers or teachers.

Chapter 30

Chakra 5
Name: Throat
Location: Throat area
Color: Light Blue
Element: Sound
Sense: Hearing

Body Relationship: Trachea, throat, thyroid, parathyroid, mouth, teeth, jaw, neck, esophagus, hypothalamus and shoulders.

Malfunction: Suppressed willpower, not being
(mental/emotional) able to express oneself or be in control of oneself, being emotionally controlled by others, not listening to others, being over-talkative or not communicating, not able to follow your dreams, addictions, judgments and criticisms, inability to make decisions or be flexible, dishonesty, disloyalty, depressed and feeling as though there's not enough time for self.

Malfunction: Laryngitis, raspy throat, sore throat,
(physical) swollen glands, thyroid dysfunctions, scoliosis, TMJ, gum and mouth problems.

Healthy: Power of choice and expression of will, faith, personal authority, decision making, keeping your word, speaking your truth, hearing others speak their truth, following your dreams, using your power, strength of will, good communicator, expressive and receptive, artistic, intuitive listeners, truthful, loyal, honest, non-competitive, and desiring peace, calm and quiet for self.

Chakra 6
Name:	Third Eye
Location:	Between the eyebrows
Color	Indigo Blue
Element:	Light
Sense:	Third Eye or Second Sight
Body Relationship:	Brain, ears, eyes, nose, pineal gland, pituitary gland, and neurological system.
Malfunction: *(mental/emotional)*	Fear of the truth, lack of good judgment, fear of discipline, fear of looking within self to see fears and weaknesses, closing off intuitiveness and psychic abilities, feeling inadequate, not open to the ideas of others, lack of emotional and intellectual abilities, lack of discernment and not able to be grounded.
Malfunction: *(physical)*	Blindness, seizures, deafness, brain tumor, strokes, brain hemorrhage, learning disabilities, and neurological disorders.
Healthy:	Connects us mentally, psychologically, consciously and unconsciously. Intuitiveness, intellectual and emotional intelligence, psychic abilities, telepathic, premonitions, spiritual vision, imaginative, deeply spiritual, seekers of truth and the meaning of life.

Chakra 7

Name:	**Crown**
Location:	Top of the head
Color	Violet or White
Element:	Thought
Sense:	Knowing

Body Relationship: Skin, skeletal and muscular systems, summarizes your total energy state and resonant color.

Malfunction:
(mental/emotional)
Spiritual fears, crisis, abandonment, loss of identity and disconnection with our life and other people, loss of values, ethics and courage, selfishness, narrow mindedness, lack of faith and inspiration, indecisive, and overly attached to people and things.

Malfunction:
(physical)
Sensitivities to light and sound, mystical depression, energy disorders, unwarranted chronic exhaustion, and sensitivity to the environment.

Healthy: Allows for entry of universal energy to our body, faith in God, inner guidance and insight, deepened awareness and connection to the universal consciousness, unconventional, open minded, decisive, filled with thoughts and ideas, non-judgmental, tolerant of others, playful, childlike personality, excellent channeling abilities and having a sense of knowing.

A malfunction of any chakra first creates an emotional or mental disorder, but in time it also affects the physical body. Since I've been as brief as possible in explaining how the chakras work, I recommend purchasing a book specifically about chakras if you'd like to pursue this topic in more detail.

The next time you experience pain or illness, put some thought into what current life issues may be affecting, or creating it. If you pulled your back lifting something heavy, ask yourself why your body decided to create the pain. When you take your self healing to this level, you will be amazed at how quickly your body will heal and mend itself. Next time you get a stiff neck, perhaps you aren't being flexible to the advice of others, you're not speaking your truth, or you're not expressing your will. If you experience stomach problems you may be feeling low in self-esteem, self-confidence, self-respect, or it could be you feel rejected in some way.

Anytime I have pain or illness, the first thing I do is evaluate my self and my current life situations at the chakra level. If you can diagnose and cure the mental or emotional problem, there may be no need to heal your self at the physical level. Of course, taking the necessary steps to avoid the emotional and mental issues from arising in the first place will, in itself, maintain your health. When I first became aware of the mental and emotional association of pain and illness I would get irritated with myself when I did get sick. I would think, "How could I allow my mental or emotional state to collapse and create this illness"? Thinking this way is self abusive. Don't beat yourself up over feeling pain or illness. Think of illness and pain as a wonderful opportunity to work on self improvement issues. The signals you get from pain and illness are a way your body communicates with you.

That amazing communication *is* the ultimate healer within you. Be thankful for the warning signal and listen to your body, mind and soul. Healing is a natural process. Illness and pain are signals that healing is needed. Be a loving, nurturing and compassionate caregiver to yourself.

If you know your ill health is because of a certain emotion or thought, but you are unable to deal with it or release it, don't forget to ask God for help. Some emotional issues may have been caused from severe trauma many years, or even lifetimes ago. For example, physical, emotional or sexual abuse may involve much more than a desire to forgive and release. When you ask God or your Guides to help you, they quickly come to your aid.

During the release process you may experience a feeling of being set back, or you may feel as though you are reliving your initial trauma. This is normal and necessary. It does not mean that the situation will recur or become worse. Oftentimes we must allow the feelings to resurface temporarily in order to release them. Trust in the love and healing Light of God. Hold the intent, and be willing to release. God will help with the rest. Working on the lessons of Parts I, III and III of this book also help you to release.

If you have an illness or pain you simply can not diagnose, an Energy Worker can help you unravel the cause and release it. I will introduce you to the fascinating world of Energy Workers in Chapter 40. Once again, awareness of a problem is your first step to healing it.

Auras

Your aura is energy that emanates from your chakras and surrounds your body. It is an exterior energy field that holds your energies in layers outside of the body. I like to think of the aura as a cocoon of energy that surrounds the body. There are seven layers to your aura. Each of the layers connects to and corresponds with the seven chakras in your body. The aura color that corresponds with the different chakras, reflects your current thoughts, emotions and health. Each of the seven layers of the aura can have different colors with lighter and deeper tones to the color. Even though there are seven layers, they interpenetrate with each layer under them and connect to the physical body.

The aura can be thin or dense, reflecting the strength of your energy and the quality of your vibrations. Your aura can pull inward and becomes dense as a means of protection. When you are sick your aura pulls in to keep your energy field protected, supported and to protect others from your illness. When your energies are open and healthy, the aura is loose and extends out from the body. Holes or tears in the aura signal problems in that area. Blocks in the aura show as dark colors. The aura also reflects the frequency and volume of your energy. The higher your energy frequency the more distance your aura projects outward. Volume indicates the strength of your aura, the amount of protection your energy is giving you, and the intensity of your auric influence.

Your aura also protects your energy from external toxins such as pollution, electromagnetic energy and people with negative energy. When your energy and aura are healthy, it's like wearing a suit of armor at all times.

It's possible for everyone to see auras and you can begin to see them with a little practice. Animals and plants also have auras you can see. Plants are a wonderful way to practice seeing auras because they don't move as much as people or animals. It also helps to have a light colored background when you first start practicing and the sky behind the trees is perfect. The first time I saw the aura around trees I realized that I'd been seeing it all my life, I just didn't know it was an aura. Chances are, you have already seen the aura of trees and plants.

To begin, look at the area around the tree or plant. Allow your eyes to soften and go into more of a stare or gaze than a direct focus. When you begin to see the aura, do not allow your eyes to directly focus or it may disappear. The more you practice softening your eyes and gazing the more natural it will feel for you and the more aura you will begin to see.

People see auras differently. Some people see them all the time, while others have to work at seeing them. I met a woman who has been seeing auras around everyone since she was born. The amazing thing is that she has no idea of the body's energy system or what an aura is. She has lived twenty six years with a gift of seeing auras and never appreciated it. To her, it was a big distraction and irritation. Although she continues to be uninterested in the aura, I believe that one day she will be able to use her gift to find and follow her life path. Your own life path may not require you to see auras and therefore you may never feel fluent with it, but you certainly can train your eyes to see it to a certain degree.

While everyone sees differently, you may only see waves of non-colored air moving off the object. You could see a closely attached, thin layer of color or color that extends far beyond the object. A puffy light colored cloud or a dense light cloud is the aura as well. I found it easiest to practice seeing the auras of people on airplanes or sitting in waiting rooms. Their bodies are basically still and there's usually a light background. Don't worry if you can't see auras right

Chapter 30

away. It may not be important for you at this time. Keep practicing whenever you get the chance and you will begin to see them when the time is right.

If you can't see an aura yet, chances are you have felt one. Have you ever experienced someone walking into the room you're in and felt their energy? You could have felt a strong, overpowering energy, or their lack of energy. Perhaps you felt their anger or rage as soon as they came near you. You can also feel sadness, sorrow, love or compassion in an energy field. Some people seem to suck the energy out of you. Even small amounts of time with them, drain you of your own energy. The energy of these individuals may be spinning counterclockwise and drawing inward rather than extending out. They actually feed off our energy. Other people you come in contact with seem to excite you and make you want to be around them more. When this happens your energies are blending, feeding, or feeling familiar to one another.

One way people describe feeling another person's aura is, 'I felt their vib'. You can pick up on the energy vibration of someone you've never met before as soon as they come near you. This is why you can feel attracted to someone's energy, or adverse to their energy, without knowing them well. When someone invades your aura, you experience a feeling that they are in your space. You instantly feel they are too close and you want to back away from them a bit more. At these times, your auras have come so close that they actually cross each other and merged together. Depending on whether your energies want that merge or not, it may feel good or it may make you want to run the other direction. When we fall in love we blend and merge our energies with our loved one all the time. This allows us to give, take, and feel each others love even more so.

Some people are so tuned in to the energy of other people, they can actually feel what the other person is feeling. For most people, it is much easier to *feel* the aura than to *see* it. When I do energy work I can feel the aura with my hands and I know and sense how dense it is. Practice feeling energy by walking around your yard with your hand open, palm facing down. As you walk past plants, concrete, animals, benches and whatever else you come across, pay attention to the temperature changes in your hand. See if you can feel the difference between light and dense air. Notice if some objects feel hot, warm or cold to your hands.

Next, try walking around inside your home from room to room and feel the energy differences with your palm. You should notice differences between chairs, beds, countertops, desks, couches, tables, etc. Many times energy from the body is left in cushions and mattresses long after someone has left them. Objects that don't pick up and hold energy will have a different feeling. It won't take long before your hands become sensitive to the subtle changes in energy around you. Different rooms will hold different energies in general too. You may notice the energy in your child's room as being similar to your child's energy. When people come into your house and visit, they can leave their energy in your home after their physical body has left. Every living thing has its own unique energy system that, with practice, can be seen or felt.

Another excellent way to practice feeling energy is between your own two hands. Hold them about three or four inches apart, palm to palm. You may feel warmth as well as a pressure as you move them slightly closer and farther apart. Once you can feel the energy, imagine projecting energy out of your hands and see if you feel the difference. You can even project energy out of one hand toward the other hand. This time you should feel the energy in the receiving hand. Try doing this exercise with another person and see how it feels. Have them project their energy to you and visa versa. Gaze at the space between your hands and you may even see the energy exchange between the two.

You can also have a partner close their eyes and hold their hands up, palms toward you. Point your index finger at their palm and keep it about an inch away from their skin. Ask them if they can feel the energy of your finger. Move your finger to a new spot and see if they can tell that you moved and where you are pointing. Now move your finger slowly around their palm, making sure you never touch them. If they can feel it, try drawing different shapes slowly and see if they can feel what shape it is. Start with a circle and if they feel that, make a square and so on. Take turns and have them draw on your hand.

Aura Imaging Systems are amazing ways to see your aura and chakras. They use a plate with contact points to pick up on your energy. By placing your hands directly on the plate, a computer program displays your aura and reads your chakras. Some systems even provide a DVD of your session. With this, you are able to see the colors of your aura, the spin and size of your chakras, the yin and yang balance, energy frequency and volume of your energy. Normally you receive a narrated DVD and a complete printed report as well. This is a fantastic way to see your energy and understand what your particular energy says about you.

Chapter Thirty Exercise
Practice seeing and feeling energy by using the examples given in this chapter. Don't give up just because it doesn't work the first few times. Keep working at it and you will become more and more sensitive to seeing and feeling.

Chapter 31

Checking your Chakras

*Keeping your chakras open, spinning
and healthy
is 'preventative maintenance'.*

Even if you still can't see or feel your energy, you can easily check the condition of your chakras using a pendulum. When a chakra begins to clog or get out of whack it triggers a reaction mentally, emotionally and then physically. If you keep the energy of all your chakras balanced and flowing you avoid those triggers. An unhealthy chakra energy station creates illness and pain, so if you keep an eye on your chakras and make sure they remain healthy, you can avoid pain and illness. With regular chakra check ups you will be able to nip an illness in the bud.

Test your chakra energy by holding your pendulum over the first chakra. Be sure you don't support the arm that is holding the pendulum. You can dangle it the full length of the chain or drape it over your finger. Use the method that seems right for you. When I drape my pendulum over my finger I can feel the direction it is going to swing before it even starts to move. The movement then verifies my feeling. Most people like to dangle it with three to six inches of chain between their finger and the chakra.

Keep your arm steady and hold no expectations of how it will move. Take your mind off the diagnosis and just *allow* the pendulum to do the work for you. If the pendulum moves in a clockwise circle, the chakra is open and healthy. If there is no movement, it may be closed. To be sure that it isn't just the way you are holding the pendulum, give your pendulum a little swing in any direction and then take your mind off of it and see what happens. If it becomes completely still again it is a good diagnosis. No movement or a counterclockwise swing means the chakra is closed. A closed chakra needs to be opened because it's already at the point of creating problems for you. The pendulum can swing in a straight line or move in any direction. Anything other than a perfect clockwise circle indicates work is needed on the chakra. Continue checking each of the seven chakras and write down any that need repair. Now you are ready to start doing your chakra energy work.

To fix chakras that are not open and harmonious, place your dominant hand (the one you write with) over the chakra. Keep your palm down and your fingers and thumb together. Hold the hand about five to six inches above the skin surface. It may help you tune in to their energy by closing your eyes and taking a few deep, belly breaths at this time. Hold your hand there and try to feel the chakra energy. Ask God and your Guides to help you feel its energy in order to keep yourself healthy. Move your hand in closer and then farther away to determine where you can feel its energy the best.

Once you feel a slight pressure and/or warmth on your palm you are in contact with the energy. Don't worry if you can't feel anything. You can still work on it even if you can't feel its energy. Keeping your hand where you feel the energy best, or about five to six inches above the body if you feel nothing, begin to make slow, clockwise circles over the chakra. Keep your hand open, fingers and thumb together, and continue circling the entire area until you feel the chakra is open and spinning well. Trust your intuition if you don't feel the sensation in your palm. Check it again with your pendulum. If it's still not making a clockwise circle go back and work on it a little more.

If some time goes by and you're still not having any success, try holding a clear quartz crystal in your hand. A crystal with a point is especially powerful. Aim the point of the crystal toward the body and start making slow, clockwise circles again. The crystal will help you connect to the chakra energy because it carries an energy of its own. That energy, combined with your own energy and movement, should do the trick.

Chapter 30

Once you have all the chakras spinning correctly, run your hand from the bottom chakra to the top chakra, about five to six inches above the body. Then run it back down from the top to bottom. Visualize each of the chakra energies blending with the others. Although we want each individual chakra running well, they need to blend with each other as well. Now make fluffy, loose circles up and down the chakras in a clockwise motion. This is just another way of blending their energies.

At this time, I like to extend the aura out from the body by placing both hands close to the skin surface and slowly lifting them up, away from the body. It feels like you're pulling and stretching the energy outward. Pull it out two to three feet, arms length, or whatever you feel guided to do. Be sure to pull the energy of all your chakras up and out. To finish, I fluff and blend the energies again at a distance of two to three feet away from the body. Make loose circular motions in all the space between body and outside edge of the extended aura. Run up and down all the chakras as you feel guided. I always feel like an Orchestra Director when I do this, only I'm directing a perfectly orchestrated mix of energy instruments rather than musical instruments.

Chapter Thirty One Exercise

Practice working on your chakras and using your pendulum. Ask others if they will let you check and work on their chakras too. It's a wonderful experience working on your own or other people's chakras. Anytime you feel a little off, check your chakras. The more often you practice this method of testing, the more confident you will become.

Self diagnose your current mental or emotional condition prior to testing your chakras. Using the chakra descriptions in Chapter 30, see if you can pick out which chakras will be running well and which will need some work. In time you will be able to instinctively and intuitively *feel* which chakra needs your attention. The pendulum is always a good way to check your accuracy.

Chapter 32

Energy Influences

Be your own Energy Body Guard.

Our bodies are extremely sensitive to the energies around us. We've been living with, and experiencing, energetic influences all our life yet most of us have lost touch with how we can manipulate our own increases and decreases. Your body has some built in protective devices. There are some things you do automatically when your energy is low. Raising your awareness of how and when to help boost your energy level will improve your mood, thought, emotions and overall energy level. This chapter will explain ways you can increase, protect, and project your energy.

Projecting
You project energy to others even if you're quiet and simply in the same room with them. As soon as you engage in communication, your energy is projected outward even more so. The energy of other people is projected toward you in the same way. With so much energy exchange occurring constantly, wouldn't it be wonderful to consciously control the energy you take in and give out while communicating?

Think back on a class you attended where the speaker captivated your attention. You were mentally tuned in to every word and time flew by. Afterward, you felt charged and excited by their lecture. You loved the teacher. The truth is, the teacher was excellent at projecting their energy to the group. You felt the teacher's energy, thought they were a good teacher, and therefore enjoyed the class. Words are an expression of our energy. The tones you use and the passion behind them can grab the attention of your audience, whether you're talking to one person or a group. As we speak we are sharing energy.

Now remember a class that practically lulled you to sleep. The topic may have been something you were very interested in but because of how it was presented, you just couldn't get into it. The teacher most likely had poor energy projection and was unable to passionately express the energy of the lesson to you. Even though you were excited about the class, you left feeling let down. You didn't feel the teacher's energy, thought they weren't a good teacher, and therefore didn't enjoy the class.

When you feel drained and tired, your energy will be down and others will pick up on that. When you're energy is strong and vibrant, you project it outward to others that way. The people you come in contact with feel the energy you project, even if they aren't consciously aware of it. I have been teaching for fifteen years and I am extremely sensitive to the energy levels of my students. I can walk in the classroom and feel the overall energy level of the class immediately. If the class is sluggish and low on energy, I can raise their energy level with my own energy. If I sense stress and tension I can relax the class with my energy. I can pick up on the individual energy of each student and literally bring everyone to a higher frequency by projecting the energy they need toward them. Within five minutes of walking into my classroom I can create the best energy atmosphere for each student's peak performance.

No one ever taught me how to do this. I was doing it long before I was aware of the body's energy system. In fact, I am sure you have done this many times in your life. We constantly share, blend and mix energies with other people. I became more aware of the process because it was important for me to captivate my students and give them a good class.

Selectively combining *tones* to your words, enhances their energetic qualities as well. Words are sound and tone is sound, and each carry an energy of their own. It's not so much the words themselves but the energy behind the word. Tone is another expression of the energy behind your words. For example, words of encour-

Chapter 32

agement toward someone who's feeling inadequate or low in self esteem would carry a tone and energy that's supportive and nurturing in quality. A person who's feeling tired and drained, needs words and tones of encouragement that carry a motivating and re-charging quality.

My son Josh and my husband Johnny teach the martial art of Tae Kwon Do. I have watched them pick up a group of one hundred kids through the use of tone and words. They can capture the attention of an audience of three year olds or adults in the way they communicate the lesson.

My son Jason works in sales. His job involves working with people who want to know about his product or service. Tone is extremely important when speaking to people who are not completely sold on an idea. Projecting words and tones of caring, honesty, true concern and confidence are mandatory for his job. Would you be as willing to try something new if the person didn't project honesty in what they said, or if they made you feel like your concerns weren't important? Of course you wouldn't. Salespeople, doctors, public relations, politicians, speakers, teachers and everyone else, use their tones and the emotions of their words when communicating. Some are better at it, but their ability to express themselves is evident in their personal success or failure.

We constantly communicate with people all day long. Why not create the atmosphere of energy you want by consciously projecting yours. You don't need an audience or classroom to practice using your energy, do it with everyone you talk to. If someone is upset with you and expresses anger toward you, don't waste your energy by feeding their anger. Anger feeds anger so you won't get anywhere by giving them back what they gave you. Instead, try projecting the opposite energy. In this case it would be best to project love or kindness back to them. When you project kindness, they will have a hard time holding on to their anger. Your kind energy will soften their angry energy. This doesn't mean you have to succumb to their angry rage or agree with them. Your response just needs to carry a lovingly kind energy. Here's an example.

Your neighbor storms over to your house in a furry. You can tell he's extremely angry and upset by the way he's walking. He says, "If I catch your dog in my yard one more time I'm going to shoot it!" His words cause you to become defensive because you feel his anger so you blurt out, "You better not touch my dog or I'll shoot your dog". You fed his anger with anger and created war. We tend to pick up on other people's energy and respond in a similar way. If you were to respond with lovingly kind energy you could say something like, "I understand how upset you are but I'm having trouble keeping him in the yard. Could you please bear with me a little longer while I figure out a way to keep him in the yard?" This way you soften his angry energy without giving in completely.

As soon as you feel negative energy in someone, consciously react with the opposite energy. It works every time if you are sincere about it. When you can use your energy through words as well as projection, you enhance everything you say and maintain control of the energies around you.

Have you ever been around someone who's down in the dumps and before you know it you are too? Even if you are having a great day these people rob you of your energy in no time. Because we are very energy sensitive, it's natural for us to feel the energy of those around us. A miserable person can make you feel miserable. A depressed person can make you feel depressed. An angry person makes you angry. A nervous person makes you feel nervous. This is because you are picking up on their energy and allowing yourself to become the same. If you were to respond to them with the opposite energy, you could help them out and protect yourself at the same time. If you do not allow yourself to be dragged into their negative energy, by responding with happy, positive energy instead, they will begin to pick up on it. Negative people carry negative energy. Positive people carry positive energy. Both project their energy outward to others. Let your positive energy influence others and you will see how healing it becomes. Protect yourself from negative people by staying aware of your own energy in this way and using it to create balance, instead of fuel for the fire.

Giving and projecting your energy are two different things. Projecting is good. Giving is not. In addition to falling victim to another person's negative energy, you can also get caught up in giving too much of your energy away. When I project my energy I do not give it away. I am expressing and sharing the feelings my own energy gives me. I project the way I feel through my thoughts, words

Chapter 32

and actions without giving my energy away. This way I do not deplete my own energy level or allow others to suck energy out of me.

If you allow others to take your energy, you will be left feeling drained and exhausted. I'm sure you have met people who take your energy. They take your positive energy to increase their own. This isn't necessary, but they don't know that. People do not need to take your actual energy, they just need to feel the essence of your energy. Since we are *all* quite sensitive to the energy around us, others will pick up on your energy by simply being around you. They will begin to mimic what they see, hear and feel in you. It's a subconscious thing most of the time. When you are around someone excited, happy and vibrant, it reminds you of how great it feels to be that way. You don't need to take their energy because just being around them begins to create the same feeling in you.

Actions

Actions also carry energy. I'm sure you've heard the phrase, 'Actions speak louder than words'. While this is not completely true, because words carry their own energy, actions are definitely energy carriers as well. Combining an action with your words intensifies the energy of the words themselves. Therefore, a kind, loving action is another way to amplify the expression of positive energy. It's nice to hear your loved ones tell you they love you, but if they express their love through an action such as helping with chores, buying you flowers, or giving you a card, you feel their loving energy even more.

Physical *exercise* is an action that dramatically enhances and increases your energy. Doing something *creative* is an action that elevates your mood and recharges your energy. *Playing* is an action that makes you happy, and increased happiness creates increased energy. A smile or hug behind kind words helps to express and share your energy with others.

Any action is an outward projection of our energy, even if it only triggers an emotional or mental response that affects your energy. This would be the case in the use of actions such as waving to someone versus flipping them off, or a nod of approval versus a look of disapproval. When this is the case, actions are relayed through sight. Without saying a word, we can send an energy affecting action toward someone.

We are also influenced by the energy actions of others toward us. This is extremely important when we are relating to children. They pick up on the smallest action and internalize it immediately. Imagine someone, child or adult, talking to you. If your body actions indicate that you are not listening or are too busy to give them your full attention, you are sending negative energy through your actions. If on the other hand, you look them in the eye and give them your full attention, you are creating an action that tells them you care and are interested in what they are saying.

Actions can encourage or discourage. They can approve or disapprove. They can show love or lack of love. Every action creates a reaction.

Emotions and Thoughts

Expressing our emotions allows our energy to flow out of us as well. When we open our self in that way, we project the energy behind the emotion, be it positive or negative. While thought alone expresses energy, the emotion created by that thought enhances it even more. Anything you do, think, feel or say, projects your energy. The same goes for everyone you come in contact with. Everything they do, think, feel or say, is projected toward you. This is why we must be extremely careful not to allow others with negative energy to affect us. A day full of negative people can do a lot of damage to your own energy level.

In Part II of this book, I explained how important it is for you to hold positive thoughts. Your positive thoughts become a part of your energy. Whether you hold negative or positive thoughts, they are transferred out to the world through your energy field. For this reason, the thought behind our words is important. We can say the words but if we don't believe in them, by holding the same inner thought, they won't carry the same energy. If you are apologizing to someone because you know you should, yet deep down you are thinking "I'm not really sorry', the words won't carry positive energy because they are not sincere. Be careful using words that go against your thought. The words will not carry the energy without the proper thought behind them.

Chapter 32

In my early twenties I suffered a severe depression. I wallowed in my misery for nearly a year. My therapist told me to 'up my attitude', a common phrase back then. He said that if I started putting on a happy face I would feel happier. I tried being perky and happy on the outside but inside I was still thinking, "I wish I were dead". One day my Mom told me "No one else is going to get you out of this depression. You have to do it all by yourself". At first I was mortified and outraged with what she said. How could I do this myself? I didn't care anymore. I lost hope. She then added "You have to stop thinking negatively and start getting out more, doing positive things, whether you want to or not".

After fuming for a few days and thinking that she was a really cold, ruthless person to say that to me, it started to make more sense. No matter how perky I was on the outside, my thoughts were still creating negative energy. I started writing poetry to express and release my negative energy. Then I *forced* myself to go out with happy people, even though their happiness sometimes made my skin crawl. I also *forced* myself to start thinking about all the good in my life. I woke up each day and said, "This is a new day and it's going to be better than yesterday. I will get through this. I want to be a happy person again." When I said the words I tried to remember and feel the joy and happiness I once knew.

Even though I was still very depressed, I used my memories to visualize how it felt before I was depressed. Although I couldn't hold on to positive mental thoughts just yet, I was able to hold the feeling by remembering the past. These feelings served as my emotional and mental backup. Even though I didn't want to, I started making myself attend the after work get-togethers and social events. I started sitting in the employee lounge during lunch instead of hiding in my car. I sat outside my apartment in an effort to meet more people.

It doesn't sound like much, but it worked. Within a month I was a whole new person. I had friends, dates, goals for my future, and social events on my calendar again. The actions of making myself get out and be around happy people helped me greatly. I was exposing myself to the positive energy of others. I began to feel their energy and I started to like what I felt... positive energy!

The moment you hold a negative thought it instantaneously depletes your energy level. If you think about, or are exposed to, things that create negative thoughts, your energy body suffers immediately. The more exposure or time you give it, the more energy you deplete. That is why stressed out people often suffer many stress related illnesses. Because of, and due to, their stressful mental anguish they are unable to stop their mind from repetitious negative thought patterns. If they were to engage their mind in something pleasant as often as they could, it would balance the negativity. We have seen the effects of positive thought in prisoners of war and our military servicemen. While each person is subject to the same horrific conditions, some of them amazingly pull through while others lose it, or crack in time.

Senator John McCain wrote a book on his amazing experience. During the Vietnam war, Senator McCain was placed in a POW camp. The prisoners were kept in cages near the water. The constant wet conditions made the skin of their feet extremely sensitive and thin. Even if they could escape, the skin on their feet would open as soon as they began walking. Senator McCain relates that he spent much of his time actively engaging his mind in make-believe golf games. This had always been something pleasant for him and it now allowed his mind to experience the same pleasure despite his horrific and abusive reality. Mentally projecting himself to an activity, and place, that he enjoys so much balanced the negativity of his reality. Many of our military personnel carry photos, letters, and other memories of their loved ones back home. These mementos have the same effect on their will to survive and their ability to pull through their own situation.

Positive thoughts and emotions carry positive energy. Negative thoughts and emotions carry negative energy. When you maintain both positive thoughts and emotions, you maintain, increase, and strengthen your energy level.

Next time you're feeling exhausted and stressed out, close your eyes and hold the thought of something pleasant to you. Perhaps it is a place you once visited, a person you love, an activity you find enjoyable, or an image that is beautiful. Even if you can't close your eyes, the thought and emotion alone will lift your energy level. You can keep a photo or postcard of a pleasant place in your wallet, purse, or on your desk, and look at it frequently. The image will instantly create a positive reaction and therefore increase your energy level.

The following are five sensory ways to increase or decrease your energy level. We experience much of life through our five senses of sight, sound, taste, touch and smell. Each one affects and influences our energy level because they trigger a mental or emotional response in us. We are all unique, which means that each of us can react differently to the same experience. I will give you two examples.

Roses create a negative response for me. The smell and sight of them remind me of funerals and I do not like them. To others, a rose may be positive because they love its beauty, scent, or it reminds them of expressing love.

The song *Amazing Grace* is loved by many, however it reminds me of funerals and therefore hearing it does not create a positive feeling for me. Each time I hear it I feel a deep sadness. I have created a list of different stimuli for each of the five senses. Looking at the list, identify which things are positive and which are negative for you. Do the same for someone else. See how many of your answers differ.

Sight
Photos of war scenes	A waterfall
An angry person	Someone smiling
Scenes of violence	A murderer or criminal
A lake with trees around	A lake next to a power plant
Mother and newborn baby	Mountains
Two people fighting	The deep woods
A brightly lit room	A dimly lit room

Smell
Roses	Bread baking
Cookies baking	Liver being cooked
Wood smoke	Cigarette smoke
New car	Cut grass
Mildew	Musty, damp basement
Leather	Plastic
Rain	Bacon sizzling

Sound
Sirens	Classical music
Rock and Roll	A baby crying
Laughter	Screaming
Birds singing	Waterfall or bubbling water
Yelling & arguing	A ringing telephone
The words "I love you"	The words "I hate you"

Taste
Medicine	Chocolate
Apple Pie	Salt water
Chemically treated water	Pure spring water
Milk	Sour milk
Green peas	Blue cheese dressing
Sour foods	Liver and onions
Sugar	Peppermint

Touch
Engine grease	Soft blanket
Thorns	Suede
Furry kitten	Snake skin
Dry, chapped skin	Soft, velvety skin
Water	Dirt
Rocks	Silk
Satin	Tree bark

We all experience and react to our environment in our own unique way. It is important for you to become aware of what makes you happy and joyful, and what makes you feel sad or disgusted. Every reaction you have affects your energy level. We can't remove all negativity from our life but we can increase the positive stimuli and avoid the negative as much as possible.

Toxins

Aside from the *internal* negative thoughts, emotions and feelings that can cause energy disorders or malfunctions, there are many *external* toxins that deplete and affect your energy as well. Although it may not be possible to eliminate all of them from your life, you can be more conscious of avoiding them whenever possible. By avoiding what you can and limited others as much as possible, you will greatly improve your energy system. Some of the external toxins that deplete your energy are:

- Chemical food preservatives and additives
- Hormones in our meat (injected in the animal for improved growth)
- Radiation in fresh produce to preserve its shelf life
- Pesticides, Fertilizer and Herbacides added to food during its growth
- Air pollution, including cigarette smoke
- Prescription Drugs
- Non-Prescription Drugs
- Alcohol
- Electromagnetic energy (televisions, computers, power lines, cell phones)
- Negative energy from other people
- Negative television programs, including the news
- Cleaning products
- Microwaves
- Fuel and gas
- Fluorescent lights (incandescent is better)

Limiting your exposure to these things whenever possible will help you tremendously. You can cut back on processed foods and buy more fresh foods. Even if you can't always buy organic, fresh is much better than processed. Many grocery stores have organic meats now too. Drink spring water instead of purified or filtered water in which chemicals are used to make it drinkable and purified. It may cost you a little more time and money, but what good is more time and money if you can't live a long and healthy life to enjoy them.

Try cutting back on drinking alcohol and smoking if you can't stop completely. Limit your time in front of the television and computer or look into purchasing electromagnetic blockers. Turn off your electronics whenever you are not using them so they don't continue to emit electromagnetic energy into your environment. Never sleep with the TV on. Be aware of negative influences transmitted by certain television shows and the news. Try not to watch negative shows or hold negative conversations while eating.

The negativity you are exposed to at the time you are consuming food enters through your digestive tract. Avoid negativity of any kind right before bed. Watch a comedy or positive television show or turn off the TV and read a few pages of a motivational, uplifting book right before sleeping. Say your affirmations as often as possible, especially before going to bed and the first thing in the morning.

In the following chapters I will teach you about alternative products you can use to treat illnesses, maintain your energy body, and increase your energy level. I will also give you some easy exercises to do in order to increase and balance your own energy. Chapter 40 will introduce you to a variety of Energy Workers who can help you maintain, diagnose and remove energy problems created by spiritual, emotional and mental issues.

Chapter Thirty Two Exercise

Now that you know how many ways you can be energetically influenced by your environment, your thoughts, your actions, and other people, start paying attention to these things. Be aware of toxic overloads in your day to day activities. Create a balance to the negative energy you *must* be exposed to by adding as much positive energy as possible.

Be your own energy body guard. Manipulate and create the energies that best serve you and your life. Don't sit back and allow yourself to be drained of your energy life force.

Take action!

Take charge!

Do something whenever you can!

Chapter 33

Increasing and Protecting Your Energy

If you don't take the time to do what's necessary to stay well you will have to take the time to be sick.

This chapter will teach you some quick and simple exercises to recharge and protect your energy throughout the day so you can maintain your energy body to a level that creates constant self healing. You've learned how energy works and what influences can rob you of your natural energy. Aside from working on your meridians, chakras, spiritual, mental and emotional states, and limiting exposure to negative energy, there are short, effective exercises you can do on a daily basis as well. Since there's no way we can protect ourselves one hundred percent of the day, every day of our life, these exercises are extremely beneficial to your energy maintenance program.

While it would be wonderful to do all of them everyday it may be difficult to find, or make, the time each day. For that reason I will suggest certain exercises as daily, and others will be at your own discretion. The daily exercises are ones you should try your hardest to make time for every day. The others would be great if used daily, but if time does not allow it, use them as a quick pick-me-up. Once you learn them, you will naturally be drawn back to them when you need them most. Let your body guide you.

There are no specific rules or guidelines to doing any of them. You can personalize any of them by changing them to what feels right to you. Your energy body may have a more effective way, or preferred method of doing the same thing. When I began to learn the different exercises it occurred to me that I was already doing some of them naturally. This helped me understand the amazing power that is already within each of us. Remember, the energy you is the natural you. Therefore, it will, and has been, naturally taking care of you and your body all your life. Due to the circumstances in our lifestyle and environment, we sometimes overload ourselves with energy robbers. That is when we can support our energy body by doing the following exercises. It helps tremendously if you can hold the conscious intent of raising or protecting your energy as you perform the exercises. Your intent intensifies your results.

The biggest challenge is going to be *doing* the daily exercises even when you feel great. When your energy level is high it's easy to feel as though you don't need to do them. Remember how many negative influences affect you each day and how quickly you can get zapped of your energy. These exercises are not just to increase your energy but to protect your energy too.

You can leave your house in the morning feeling vibrant and energized from a good night's sleep but by noon your energy level can drop significantly because of your environmental influences. Protecting your energy before you start the day is insurance that you'll feel just as energized at the end of the day as you did when you left the house that morning.

You may be wondering how you can find time for these exercises in your already too busy life. When I first started hearing about all of them I felt overwhelmed and stressed because they seemed like just another thing on my to-do list. My days were already so hectic and packed. Now I had to add even more duties. The amazing reality is that if you spend the extra few minutes doing them, you will feel more relaxed, calm, and in the moment. They greatly decrease your stress level too. Your busy days will glide smoothly along and you'll begin to feel there are plenty of minutes in your day. This is partly due to the fact that your energy level has become high enough and protected enough to easily sustain all your activities. The rest is because you gave yourself time to be in the moment and get tuned in to the natural you. Staying in the moment slows down time as we have come to know it. Tuning in helps you stay in the natural rhythm and flow of your soul and energy body. Staying in the rhythm removes the pressures and demands of time and schedules.

If you can't get the exercises done before you leave your house in the morning, don't think you can't find the time or place to do them later. There is one private place you go many times a day... the restroom. Most of these exercises can be done behind the closed door of the bathroom. No one will ever know you're doing them, and your bladder will guarantee you have plenty of opportunities to optimize your energy level all day long.

Creating Your Sacred Space   **Daily**

This exercise can be done just about anywhere. I usually do this before I get out of bed in the morning. If I've had an especially draining day I will do it again later or just before falling asleep at night.

To begin, imagine your energy aura radiating out from your body. Push it out three to four feet in every direction until it encompasses you like a big cocoon. Now ask God to add His loving and healing Light to your cocoon. Next, ask for the universal energy force to brighten it with its energy. See yourself basking in this light and feel it surrounding you completely, creating a cushion of vibrant, dense energy. Now seal it by visualizing a thin layer of color around the outside edges. Make sure you completely seal it. The outer edge can be any color or texture you feel suits you and protects you best that day. Once you're sealed add words of intent into your cocoon.

You will have different words each day depending on the challenges of the day. I generally put 'love' and 'forgiveness' in every day, adding other words that directly relate to the activities of the coming day. When I know my daily activities will challenge my patience, I add that. If I have to do something brave I may add 'power', 'bravery', or 'determination'. If I anticipate a confrontation with someone, I may add 'speaking my truth', 'self confidence' or 'compassion'. When I know I'll be around someone aggressive or angry, it could be 'understanding', 'wisdom', or extra amounts of 'love'. Dot your cocoon with as many helpful words as you feel will be needed for that day. You can visualize each word as a different color if you wish. Sometimes I do that but most of the time I do not. That's it. Now you are protected from outside energies attacking your own energy body.

You can also do the same thing, visualizing the cocoon around things like your home, work place, property, animals, community, and even the entire world. While I do my own body every day, I occasionally create sacred space around larger areas. If serious weather threatens, I like to do my home, property, animals and our business. It is a generous and loving act when you create sacred space that includes others. While it is best that each person create their own sacred space, placing them in the area of your sacred space is a gift to them. Always create your own sacred space first and then move outward encompassing more area. This way you are still held safe within your own energy field.

Grounding   **Daily**

This exercise feels best to me if I do it standing up but I have done it sitting and lying down too. Grounding helps us connect to Mother Earth's energies and all that sustains our human life form on earth. Energy is not only in the universe, but in our earth as well. Think of the magnitude of energy this earth holds for us. It keeps us connected to this planet through gravity and gives life to all living things. While universal energy is important, we must not forget to connect to Mother Earth as well. If we only connect to the universe we won't have balance to our energy. Even though the universal connection is powerful and spiritual, we must remember that we are here on earth in human form and we very much need to appreciate and connect to Her as well.

Begin by standing with feet shoulder width apart. Closing your eyes may help you stay focused and visualize. Stand there for a few moments and begin to take deep belly breaths as you become aware of the earth beneath you. Know that the energy of Mother Earth is always there for you. Now picture roots coming out of the bottom of your feet. These strong roots move down easily through the floor, the foundation, and the first layer of dirt. Keep pushing further through the layers of dirt and rock, moving toward the core of Mother Earth. Feel the warmth of Her energy as your roots go deeper and deeper. Notice the warmth rise into your feet and up your legs. Keep pushing the roots deeper and deeper and feel the energy increase more and more until you reach the core. You are now fully connected to Mother Earth's energy source. Stand there as long as you'd like and simply enjoy Her warm energy.

Take deep breaths. Give thanks to the earth for giving you so much energy, freely and constantly, every minute of every day. When you are ready, slowly pull your roots back through all the layers until they come back into your feet. Open your eyes and wiggle your toes and feet. Know that the energy you connected to will stay with you forever and is always there for you.

Connecting to Universal Energy   **Daily**

You can do this one standing, bathing, sitting, lying down or meditating. It can even be added to the last exercise of grounding. Begin by closing your eyes and taking a few deep belly breaths. Now visualize a beam of pure, white light coming down from the universe. See the beautiful beam of light surround your entire body. Pause for a few moments and feel its warmth, love and peace permeating every cell of your body. Now visualize your crown chakra opening up. See the top of your head as a vessel for this pure light to enter your body. As the beam of light enters your crown chakra, feel its warmth and energy begin to fill your head, chest, arms, torso, legs and feet. Slowly fill your entire body with the Light.

Breathe and give thanks as you enjoy feeling filled with the Light and energy of the universe. When you feel ready, slowly open your eyes. Remember, the universal light that has filled your body will remain with you, and you always have this beam of light and energy shining down upon you.

Meditation   **Daily**

Meditating is always recharging even though you may feel relaxed and even a little sleepy directly after doing it. As I told you earlier in the book, it is the closest you get to the spirit world while fully conscious and awake. After you meditate, the sleepiness you feel will stay with you if you do not engage in anymore physical activities or go to bed soon afterward. If you begin to get active you will soon feel more energized from it. Your energy will have a calmer nature to it, but you will not feel sleepy all day as some people think.

Meditating for ten minutes is like taking a four hour nap. I have meditated in my car at the park over lunch hour. This refreshes and recharges me for the rest of the day. There are many ways to guide yourself through meditation if you find it difficult to clear your mind and relax. You can buy tapes or CD's where someone else guides you along. I feel irritated and bothered by listening to guided meditation but my husband finds it much more effective. Do whatever you feel gives you the best meditation.

The following are examples of different guided meditations I have used in my classes. Do them for yourself or read them aloud for others. You can even tape record a guided meditation for yourself so you don't have to talk yourself through it during meditation.

Be sure to begin each meditation with the general relaxation process I described in Chapter 19.

Darkness and Light

Begin by appreciating the darkness that you see. Instead of darkness being isolating and cold, this darkness makes you feel warm, safe, secure and relaxed. As you enjoy the darkness, feel how it relaxes your muscles and soothes your eyes. It completely surrounds you and comforts you. Now, see a tiny dot of light in the darkness. Allow the light to come closer and closer to you. As it gets closer, begin to feel the energy that it holds. Energy that is just for you to enjoy. Allow the light to enter your body. Feel the warmth of the energy quickly spread to every part of your body. Enjoy that warm feeling of energy filling up your entire body and energizing every tissue, fiber, and organ in your body.

Now release all your worries, fears, illnesses and anxieties to this light. Know that the energy light will absorb and disperse those things instantaneously and permanently. Let go and release everything. Notice the warmth and soothing comfort you get from your releases. They are gone. They are gone for good. Relax and enjoy this moment as long as you'd like.

Chapter 33

When you feel ready, slowly open your eyes and know that this energy will remain with you, constantly cleansing your body and giving you energy at all times. It can not leave your body now. It is yours and it is very powerful.

<u>The Woods</u>
Picture yourself in the deep woods. See the massive trees tower above you and shelter you from the hot sun. Visualize yourself following a trail through the woods. As you walk, you see squirrels, rabbits and birds cross your path. Stop now and enjoy the trees. Take a deep breath of the clean, fresh air they create for you. Notice how strong each tree is, with their roots deeply implanted in the earth. Stand there for a moment and picture your own roots coming out of your feet. Let your roots dig down deeper and deeper in the earth, through the sand, clay, rock, and then even deeper, reaching for the very core of Mother Earth. Notice how you feel the warmth of the earth's core as your roots drive deeper and deeper. Now push your roots down to the very core and feel the energy that Mother Earth supplies you. Energy that is always there for you and that she will gladly share with you.

Next, picture a ray of sunlight shining down upon your head. With your roots still planted in the core of the earth, I want you to picture this sunray flooding your body with energy from the universe. This energy is also warm, as it washes through your entire body and then goes out through your roots. Enjoy the feeling of energy running up and down your body. Energy from the universe and from the earth, flowing freely through every part of your body and giving you the energy you need to allow yourself to heal, cleanse and refresh your body.

Take deep breaths now and just enjoy this feeling. Stay connected to the warm energy from above and below. Breathe and relax. Fully filled with your new energy, allow your roots to slowly come back up. Bring them up through all the layers of earth and back into your feet. The sun now moves slightly in the sky and the ray of light to your head has been covered by the leaves of the trees. Silently thank Mother Earth and the universe for this new energy. Take one more deep breath and slowly open your eyes when you are ready.

The Mountain

Picture yourself standing in a forest on the side of a huge mountain. The air smells crisp and clean. A cool breeze brushes over you, and you feel the warmth of the sun on your face. The trees sway slowly and rhythmically with each breeze and it calms you even more. You hear birds singing their sweet songs, and see them flying to and fro around you. Slowly and easily you begin to walk up the mountain, and toward the top.

Walking through the forest you hear the crunch of leaves beneath your feet with each step. Except for the songs of the birds, it is quiet and peaceful here. Soon you come to the edge of the forest and see an open, grassy, meadow that extends up to the top of the mountain. In the distance you see deer grazing in the tall, green grasses. They look up and see you but do not run away.

You continue to walk toward the top of the mountain and notice how easy it is to make your way up, up, up. When you reach the top you pause a moment to look out at the most beautiful view you have ever seen. Mountains, streams, meadows and valleys surround you. Slowly you turn yourself in a circle, noticing the beauty is all around you.

Now look up toward the sun and feel its warm rays upon your skin. Close your eyes and stretch your arms up toward the sky, taking a couple deep breaths of the crisp, clear air. When you open your eyes, the sun seems to be closer. It is very bright now and you squint your eyes to keep looking at it. It moves closer and closer to you until it seems to be right above your head. Feel the warmth and energy of the sun come down through the top of your head. It moves through your head and continues down your neck and spine, into your hips and then down your legs to your feet, filling your entire body. It soothes you and energizes you.

As you bask in the energy from above, become aware of the earth beneath your feet. Begin to feel the warm energy of the earth rising up through the soles of your shoes. It moves up your legs, through your stomach and continues on to the top of your head. Stand there for a while and let the energy rise up from the earth and stream down from the universe, soothing you and relaxing you. The energy becomes stronger and stronger and you begin to feel an inner strength like you've never felt before. Your heart beats faster and

Chapter 33

your breathing gets deeper. You absorb the energy quickly and freely. Take a few moments now to breathe the crisp air, and absorb the warm energy of Mother Earth and the universe.

Becoming completely filled with energy, your body begins to release all negativity. It quickly and easily releases all the fears, worries, anxiety, neglect, illness, rejection, and pain that you have ever felt. Free of all negativity, thank Mother Earth and the universe for their healing energy. Energy that is always available to you and will always cleanse your body, mind and spirit anytime you ask for it. Take one more deep breath and slowly open your eyes when you feel ready.

The Beach & Sparkling Light

Begin by picturing yourself on a sandy cliff overlooking the ocean. Feel the sunshine warm upon your face and feel the soft breeze as it passes over your body. Looking down, you see a beach of beautiful, white sand. Walk down the cliff to the beach. Feel the warmth of the sand on your feet. Stop for a moment to take off your shoes and wiggle your toes in the warm sand.

You are alone on the beach and it feels good to have the beauty, peace and quiet all to yourself. Ahead, you see a chair near the water. You walk over to the chair and sit down on the big, soft cushions. The cushions feel warm from the suns rays and it relaxes you even more. Relax and enjoy watching the waves wash over the white sand in their own natural rhythm. Take a few moments to visualize the waves washing in and out, relaxing you more and more.

In the distance you see a brilliant, sparkling light, just above the water. As you watch, it moves closer and closer to you, becoming bigger and stronger. You feel the energy of the light more and more as it moves right in front of your body. Allow this light to enter your body and feel it's soothing warmth fill you completely. It flows through you freely and quickly, spreading to every tissue, cell and organ. Feel the energy building more and more within you. Now, release any heartbreaks, illnesses, injuries, stress, fears and worries to this new light within you. Let go of everything that is robbing you of your natural energy. Know that the light will absorb all of it and will instantly and permanently disperse it. Notice how wonderfully soothing it feels to let go of all these things… how it gives your body a surge of energy each time you release more to the energy light.

Relax and release for as long as you want. Know that this energy will remain with you forever, constantly cleansing your body and giving you energy at all times. It will not leave your body. Its power belongs to you now. Realize that fears worries, stress, and physical or emotional illnesses only deplete your energy, and you have the ability to release those things and gather more energy for yourself anytime you want. When you feel ready, slowly open your eyes and remember the energy will remain with you.

Nature   **Whenever Possible**

There is no easier way to recharge your energy while holding no intent than to take a walk in the woods, a park or sit amidst nature. Plants and trees emit a tremendous amount of energy. When you share their space it is passed on to you. It is so simple, refreshing and recharging. As you spend time in nature, be sure to admire at the beauty around you. See the leaves and branches of the trees and the soft grasses or dirt beneath your feet. Take many deep belly breaths to inhale that sweet oxygen into your lungs. Be thankful for the trees and plants. They give you oxygen, beauty and an endless source of energy.

While working years at an extremely stressful job, I often spent my lunch hour at the park. Its natural beauty soothes the eyes from the effects of the fluorescent lights in the office. The heavy oxygen you breathe gives your body a break from the controlled and recycled air indoors. The birds create a diversion from the constant chaos of phones and voices at work.

I am extremely sensitive to the energies of nature. It was hard to keep me inside as a kid and still now as an adult. I prefer being outdoors more than indoors. In fact, most of this book has been written while sitting outside in nature. My home is snuggled in the woods and I find it to be most energizing and recharging when I'm home. After long periods away from home I can feel the difference as soon as I pull up in the driveway. You can have the same energetic affects of nature by spending time in your garden or yard. As long as you're around trees and plants, you will receive their energy.

Protecting Your Energy **Whenever Needed**

Sometimes we are exposed to the energies of negative people or people who seem to suck the energy out of us. When you feel this situation you can quickly protect yourself by doing one of the following exercises.

<u>Arms Over Midsection</u>
In this exercise you simply place your arms across your midsection. The arms do not have to be crossed over each other but they can. When you cover your solar plexus and sacral chakras you protect yourself in these two areas. It's like closing the door to attacking negative energies.

<u>Legs and Arms Crossed</u>
Another way to hold and protect your energy is to cross your legs or ankles and cross your arms or wrists. This will protect you and hold your energy in. You can do this quite nonchalantly and loosely so that it's not noticeable. Cross your legs or cross just at your ankles. Your arms can cross or you can cross your wrists and lay them in your lap.
People have asked me if I'm cold when I cross my arms. Other people, who are aware of body language, may think you are closing them off and being rude. In a way, you are closing yourself, just energetically instead of mentally or emotionally. Don't worry about what you look like or what others will think. If you feel you need protection, do it.

Increasing Energy **Whenever Needed**

Sometimes, you may be feeling drained and in need of a quick charge of energy. It may not be possible to ground, make your sacred space, or work on your chakras. The following four exercises are easy and don't call much attention to what you're really doing.

Laying of Hands

This first exercise is simply a matter of placing your hand or hands over different chakras. We see people do this over their heart chakra when something shocks them or stirs them emotionally. You catch people putting their hand to their forehead (third eye) when they feel mentally exhausted, confused or are thinking deeply. Quite often you see people put their hand over their upper (solar plexus) or lower (sacral) abdomen when they feel upset or fearful. When you place your hand over a chakra for energy, keep your fingers and thumb together for increased effectiveness. Ask for universal energy or for help from your Guides or God. You need to hold an intent, or ask for help, so it is known exactly what you want. The energy will flow through your hands and into your body. If you only use one hand, and can choose which one, use your dominant hand (the one you write with). Generally, your dominant hand 'gives' and the other hand 'pulls'. If you can't use your dominant hand don't worry. Your intent will allow the other hand to be an adequate sender. Sometimes I put my left (puller) hand on my heart and my right hand (sender) somewhere I feel energy is needed. This helps pull the loving energy of my heart to the other area.

Finger and Thumb Shooter

This exercise shoots energy directly in to your body by joining the fingers and thumb of one hand. The hand cups in order to make all of the fingers and thumb join together. Now point the tip of the connection toward your body at either the second, third or fourth chakra. If you have another area you know needs an energy boost, point it toward that one. If you don't feel guided to a certain area, use the second chakra, just below the belly button. If you use both hands put one on the second chakra and the other on the third chakra, a few inches above the belly button. I use the heart chakra when I need to add more love or compassion to my energy.

Finger Cross Over Head

This one stabilizes, increases and holds your energy. For this exercise you interconnect your hands by crossing the fingers on the 'inside' or 'palm' side of the hands. Bring your hands together back to back and intertwine the fingers. Keeping the fingers joined this way, place them palm down on your crown chakra, the top of your head. Again, hold the intent and be consciously aware that you are stabilizing and increasing your energy level.

<u>Triangle Hands</u>

This exercise also brings a tremendous amount of energy in to your body. Interestingly, it is used at the beginning of a Tae Kwon Do form. In the form, the triangle is held over the third eye chakra for increased mental focus, concentration and alertness. Begin by holding both hands open palms facing away from you and thumbs touching. Keep your fingers together and turn your hands in toward each other until the fingers touch. You should have made a triangle. Now hold this triangle in front of you at any point you wish to send more energy. When in doubt, hold it in front of the second or third chakra point. It doesn't matter if you turn the triangle upside down while working on the lower chakras, as long as you are making a triangle. Try using it in different areas and see if you can feel the energy it produces.

There are many exercises you can do to maintain, balance and increase your energy level. Play around with all of them and pick the ones that feel most effective. With the exception of meditating, most of these exercises can be done just about anywhere and don't require you to hold it for a specific period of time. Any amount of time is better than nothing. Reading or watching television are also great times for sending extra energy to your body. Do them at your desk, while you're waiting to get your food at a restaurant, or at a red light. Use them when you feel personally attacked by negative energies from other people or your environment. They really work and are quick and easy to do.

Chapter 34

Rocks and Crystals

Rocks and Crystals are healing jewels from Mother Earth.

Rocks and crystals are powerful energy transmitters and absorbers. Each one has a uniquely different vibration and carries its own distinct healing properties. In ancient cultures they were used for healing and were also considered to have sacred meanings. The rocks and crystals today are no different. They haven't lost their amazing power. We are the ones who have lost touch with how to use them for those purposes.

People have been attracted to gem stones like Diamonds, Emeralds, Rubies and Sapphires for thousands of years. Semiprecious stones like Garnet, Carnelian and Lapis have also adorned mankind for thousands of years. Crystals like Amethyst, Obsidian and Malachite have been equally loved and worn for many years. I love my rocks and crystals. They are scattered throughout my home and I often carry some in my purse. I have acquired many over the years. Some were bought for a specific reason, some I felt guided to buy for their healing qualities, and others just caught my eye.

There are hundreds of wonderful rocks and crystals to choose from. I will give a little information about a few of my favorites so you can get an idea of their amazing properties, but I would suggest buying a good rock and crystal book. I use my crystal book like you would use a medical reference guide. The more acquainted you become with the benefits of each, the more you will be able to know when and how to use them. When I am stumped over which rock to use, I fan through my book and open it when it feels right. It always opens to a rock that carries the qualities I'm looking for. Occasionally, the page that opens reveals a rock that carries a different quality, but one that I should also be considering.

If fanning the book doesn't work for you, use your pendulum by touching the name of a rock and asking for a yes or no. You can always go to a rock shop and use your intuition or pendulum. If a certain rock catches your eye, feel it, hold it and if you just have to have it, it's a keeper. If, for instance, you know you want a Tiger's Eye but they have a whole bucket of them, put your hand in the bucket and play with all the rocks until one seems to stick to your hand or feels like the right one. You will be drawn to rocks you need and they will draw themselves toward you.

This happened to me when I was on vacation in Arkansas. My husband and I went to a rock shop. I wanted to buy one of the large crystals but we were on a tight budget so I didn't. Instead, I picked out a few small rocks. When we returned home I pulled out the rock bag and dumped it out. Along with the rocks I'd bought, out fell a huge quartz crystal like the one I wanted. I ran to my husband and thanked him for surprising me with the massive crystal. He quickly confessed that he didn't buy it. That crystal later became my most powerful healing stone for doing energy work. I was supposed to get it and did not, yet it still ended up in my bag.

If my pendulum or intuition guide me to a specific rock that I'm not familiar with, I look it up in my book for two reasons. One, for confirmation that it is going to do what I'd hoped it would do and two, to get familiar with all of its qualities.

An important step in buying your rocks and crystals is to cleanse them shortly after you get them home. Since they transmit and absorb energy, you want to be sure to remove all the negative energy it may be carrying so as not to absorb it yourself. It's also important to clean your rocks and crystals occasionally, after you own them. I clean my rocks every month or two. If I use them for energy work I clean them after each session. Your rocks and crystals will be constantly cleansing and transmitting negative energy for you, no matter where you have them. Whether they sit on a shelf untouched, are carried with you, or you use them for healing, they will get dirty with negative energies. Aside from the possibility that they can transmit negative energy back to you, their healing properties won't be as effective when they are dirty.

There are many beliefs in how to cleanse your rocks and crystals. I've heard all sorts of different methods. Personally, I believe the best method is to soak them for a few hours in sea salt water. I put them in salt water in the morning and take them out when I get home that night. After they have soaked, rinse them off well. As you are running the fresh water over them, hold the intent that they become clean and pure. When time permits, I follow that procedure up with a few hours of letting them sit in the sunlight, moonlight or both. The sunlight and moonlight recharge them and the sea salt cleanses them.

Another method of cleansing is to simply hold your hands over the rocks, and ask God to cleanse them. I will do this if it's not possible to soak them. Other people tell me they run them through the flame of a candle to cleanse them. Still others blow the smoke from burning sage over them. While I believe in salt water, sunlight and moonlight, I also believe that the important thing is to hold the *intent* of cleansing your rocks. Use your intuition with your own rocks.

Since there are so many different rocks and crystals to choose from, it would be impossible for me to briefly introduce you to all of them in this book. I have decided to introduce you to a few of them by describing the ailments they can be used for. I've tried to use the same rocks over again, whenever possible, to help you choose one or two rocks that may serve more than one purpose for you. In no way am I advocating that the rocks listed below are the best or that they are better than others. This list simply gives you an idea of the magnitude of healing properties each rock can have.

<u>Self Cleaning</u>
These three clean themselves so they are maintenance free. They *do not* need cleaning.

        Citrine   Kyanite   Azeztulite

These two will clean other rocks if you place them together in a bowl or bag, or if you place the other rocks on top of them, but they *do need* regular cleaning themselves.

Clear Quartz   Carnelian

Mental Enhancement
Green Tourmaline   Amethyst
Aventurine   Beryl
Bloodstone   Calcite
Carnelian   Citrine
Emerald   Iolite
Jasper   Sodalite

Electro Magnetic Blockers
These clean up and/or block electromagnetic debris. Place them in front of the computer, television, throughout your home, or near your cell phone.

Smoky Quartz   Black Tourmaline
Amethyst Geode   Fluorite Cluster
Aventurine   Sodalite
Turquoise

Energy Boosters
Selenite (Angelic energy)   Orange Carnelian
Calcite   Chrysocolla

Increase Intuition and Spirituality
Amethyst   Sodalite
Turquoise   Azurite
Apophyllite   Bloodstone
Iolite   Citrine
Emerald   Chrysoprase
Chrysocolla   Lapis Lazuli

Chakra/Aura Cleaning and Protection
Amber   Jasper
Smoky Quartz   Agate
Amethyst   Tourmaline

Chapter 34

    Garnet   Kunzite
    Calcite   Chrysocolla

For Love or to Mend a Broken Heart
    Rose Quartz   Aventurine
    Beryl   Emerald
    Garnet   Iolite
    Jade   Kunzite
    Lapis Lazuli   Turquoise

Stress Reduction
    Amethyst   Azurite
    Beryl   Lapis Lazuli
    Topaz   Turquoise
    Calcite   Sodalite
    Chrysoprase   Chrysocolla
    Citrine

Insomnia
Place these on your nightstand near bed or under your pillow.

    Amethyst   Topaz

Emotional Balance
    Aventurine   Emerald
    Topaz   Quartz

Fear and Worry
    Azurite   Beryl
    Bloodstone   Carnelian
    Garnet   Sodalite

Sadness
    Azurite   Garnet
    Tiger's Eye   Topaz

Illness (Immune System Builders)
    Bloodstone   Jasper
    Clear Quartz   Topaz

Clearing Negative Energies
    Chrysocolla   Calcite
    Chrysoprase   Citrine
    Garnet   Jade
    Quartz   Turquoise

Chakra Work
When you want to heal or balance your chakras, place a stone on the front or back of the body in the area of that chakra. Leave it there for fifteen minutes.

Root/Base Chakra
Red or Black   or   Garnet, Ruby, Red Jasper,
                               Azurite, Obsidian, Bloodstone,
                               Smoky Quartz, Black Tourmaline

Sacral Chakra
Orange Stone or   Amber, Orange Carnelian, Citrine,
                               Topaz, Orange Calcite

Solar Plexus Chakra
Yellow Stone or   Yellow Jasper, Citrine,
                               Golden Topaz, Tiger's Eye,
                               Golden Beryl

Heart Chakra
Pink Stone   or   Rose Quartz, Aventurine, Peridot,
                               Kunzite, Emerald, Pink Danburite

Throat Chakra
Blue Stone   or   Azurite, Lepidolite, Turquoise,
                               Sodalite, Kunzite, Aquamarine,
                               Chrysocolla, Lapis Lazuli,

<u>Third Eye Chakra</u>
Indigo Stone   or   Sodalite, Amethyst, Lapis Lazuli, Royal Sapphire, Azeztulite

<u>Crown Chakra</u>
Purple Stone   or   Amethyst, Citrine, Selenite, Clear Quartz, Clear Tourmaline, Purple Jasper, Lepidolite

A brown stone may be placed below the feet, representing the earth.

A clear quartz crystal can be placed above the head, representing your higher crown chakra.

Rocks and crystals also have healing qualities for physical ailments. Since each physical ailment stems from the mind or emotions, I don't feel comfortable telling you about rocks for specific illnesses. For instance, if you have a headache it could be from stress, allergy or an emotional issue. The type of rock you choose to heal your headache would need to be chosen according to the underlying issue that is creating your headache. Get acquainted with rocks and crystals in general and you will be guided to which ones are important for you.

Chapter 35

Essential Oils, Aroma Therapy, Rock & Flower Essences

*Health is our heritage, our right.
It is the complete and full union
between soul, mind and body.*
        Dr. Edward Bach 1884-1936

In addition to rocks and crystals, there are many healing benefits from Essential Oils, Flower Essences and Rock Essences. They are easy to use, easy to find and quite affordable. I enjoy using them because they are completely natural, gentle and effective.

Essential Oils and Aroma Therapy
Essential oils can be used to heal the body, mind and spirit. The oils are extracted from leaves, flowers, bark and peels. They emit powerful aromas that heal us through our sense of smell. Essential oils also carry the energy of the living plant or tree it came from and that energy creates a response within our body as well. Our body is an energy body and it responds to outside energies. Oils, like rocks, carry energy but they also provide a bouquet of tantalizing scents for our enjoyment. The moment we catch a whiff of something we find pleasurable, our energy body responds positively.

We can use essential oils as aromas or rub them directly on the skin. It may be hard to believe that an aroma could be healing for us when we're so used to taking a pill to get well. Nature and Mother Earth provide us with so many natural medicines to heal ourselves. Natural medicines were used long before chemical drugs were introduced to us.

When essential oils are extracted they become 70% more concentrated than if we used the plant itself. That is why they are so affordable. A couple of drops go a long way. The aroma produced from the oil is purely natural. With aromas, the scent alone can trigger healing but it is also absorbed through the nasal tissues.

Every essential oil has its own scent and can be used on the body instead of perfume. Imagine getting natural healing properties from your perfume instead of spraying on a bunch of manmade chemicals. Since I've come to love essential oils, I no longer buy expensive cologne. I choose my essential oil *perfume* each day, according to what I feel I need emotionally, mentally or spiritually. You only need one drop to rub on both wrists and behind each ear. The fragrance stays with you much longer than perfumes and colognes, and essential oils are a lot less offensive to others who are forced to smell you all day. I have received so many compliments on my perfume since I've been using oils. When I tell people the scent is an essential oil they get curious, check them out, and many end up switching over to oils instead of perfume.

The process of extracting the oil is simple but it takes many leaves or flowers to fill a small bottle of oil. Some oils are processed through steam distillation, where the steam forces the oil-bearing glands to rupture and expel the oil. Oils can also be extracted using solvents or by cold compresses. Rose, Jasmine, Chamomile, Neroli and Sandalwood are expensive because it takes many plants to make a little oil. Because of this, there are some company's that try to bulk up their oils so they will go a little farther or cost less.

Don't be fooled by low prices. This is probably an indication the oils are not totally pure. You want only pure, natural oil with nothing else added. Your nose will get good at telling the difference between pure and impure oil after a while. For that reason, I believe the best way to pick an oil is with your nose. Purchasing them at a store where you can smell them is important. Buying them over the internet can be risky. You wouldn't want to spend a lot of money on

Chapter 35

oils that were not pure and natural, yet most companies make the claim that theirs are. I have tried buying over the internet for convenience but each time I was dissatisfied with the quality I received.

Another reason to smell your oils first is because you want them to be pleasing to your nose if you're going to smell them all the time. When I first got interested in oils I bought a book on them. After reading the healing properties of each oil, I made a list of which ones would be good for me to use. I took my list to the computer and ordered all of them over the internet.

I was so disappointed when I got my oils. Almost half of them had aromas I disliked so much I never used them. The others smelled good but I later found out they were not very pure. When I smelled totally pure oils they were very different. The aromas I disliked in the other brand smelled fairly good when they were pure. Be sure you like the smell and are willing to smell it often before you buy an essential oil. Using your intuition and pendulum are great ways to choose oils, but your nose really knows. If someone wants to try my oils or I am using them to heal another person, I often choose two or three different oils that would be appropriate for their needs. I ask them to smell each one and choose their own. Their nose will guide them to the best oil for their needs.

Rose oil has many healing properties that I could have benefited from on numerous occasions however I can't stand the smell of roses. Even though it would seem to be good for me, I would be miserable smelling it, so I don't use it.

One time my daughter-in-law Erica was reading through the properties of each oil. Without smelling it first, she chose Rosemary for its healing benefits and applied it to her skin. Instantly she disliked the smell of it. We were both shocked moments later she developed a serious allergic reaction to it. For her, the reaction was a severe headache and sinus misery. Had Erica allowed herself to smell the oil first, she would have never picked Rosemary because she didn't like the smell of it. The nose knows!

There are many ways to use oils. You can use them directly on your body, add them to your bath, or use just the aroma. For aroma you can put the oil on a body part that will allow you to smell it often. The neck, back of the hands, wrists, or chin work well. You can even put a drop or two on a tissue, cotton ball or small cloth and wave it in front of your nose every now and then.

Buying a diffuser allows the scent to fill the entire room. A diffuser is a small basin or cup with a candle area underneath it. Put 3 to 8 drops of oil in the basin with a little water. Remember, the fragrances are powerful and a little goes a long way. As the candle burns, it warms up the basin and the oils scent is dispersed into the air. Diffusers are inexpensive and easy to find. The smaller they are the better they work. You don't need a huge basin for eight drops of oil. The farther the candle is from the basin the harder it will be for the warmth to reach the basin and maintain enough heat to keep the oil burning. You can also put a few drops of oil in a small pan of water and heat the pan on the stove. Don't use too much water and be sure to turn off the stove before the water is gone. I like small diffusers with little tea candles best. The candle and water seem to run out at the same time.

I also love soaking in a bath of oils. You can use just one oil or a blend of two or three different oils. If using just one oil, add 3 to 8 drops. I would suggest starting with 3 drops to see how powerful the aroma is. You can always add more. When I use three different oils I use two or three drops of each one. The bath is soothing but your whole house will smell wonderful from it as well.

You can also make a compress and apply it directly to the affected area by adding 5 drops of oil to a large bowl of water. Soak a small towel in the water and then squeeze out the excess water. Apply the damp towel to your skin.

If you want to use oils for massage you can add 1 or 2 drops to your regular massage lotion or make your own massage lotion using base oil. When blending essential oils to base oil, use a ratio of 2 parts base oil to 1 part essential oil.

Whenever you blend oils try not to use more than three different oils at a time. Using too many different oils can create an aroma overload. If you have sensitive skin, start with the minimum amount of oil and gradually increase it to be sure your skin won't have an allergic reaction to it.

One time I was wearing lemon oil and a friend of mine smelled it and asked if she could put some on herself. She put a drop on each wrist and then a drop on both sides of her neck. Within minutes she said her neck was burning. Her skin got red and she was very miserable. Her wrists never bothered her. Then she told me that she can't eat lemons because they irritate her mouth and throat. Instantly, we realized that her reaction on the neck was related to her inability to eat them. She was able to use the oil on any other body part with no reaction.

The following is a list of some of my favorite oils and their uses. Because I love and use so many different oils, it is difficult to choose just a few to write about. Again, please do not think that all the other oils are not as good as these. I want to give you a small selection in order to see the many healing properties in each essential oil. The best way to know if they will work for you is to try them. You will have your own favorites. Your body will decide which oil carries the best energy vibration for you, and which ones are most effective and pleasurable for you to use.

A Soul's Guide to Abundance, Health And Happiness

Essential Oils for Physical Healing

Physical Ailments

Acne	Frankincense, Geranium, Lavender, Petitgrain, Sandalwood
Aggression	Sandalwood
Allergies	Lavender
Anger	Petitgrain
Anxiety	Clary Sage, Ylang Ylang, Orange, Frankincense, Jasmine
Arthritis	Petitgrain
Asthma	Clary Sage, Fennel, Frankincense, Lavender, Myrrh
Awareness (Sharpened)	Lemon
Baby Blues	Geranium
Bad Breath	Cardamom
Bladder/Kidney	Jasmine, Clary Sage, Sandalwood
Bloating	Fennel, Sage
Blood Cells	Myrrh
Boils	Petitgrain
Boredom	Orange, Frankincense, Jasmine

Chapter 35

Bronchitis	Cinnamon, Lavender, Myrrh, Neroli, Rosemary, Sage
Bruises	Lavender
Burns	Lavender
Butterflies Stomach	Bergamot
Capillaries broken	Neroli
Cardiac System	Cinnamon, Sandalwood
Cell Stimulation	Lavender
Cellulite	Rosemary, Orange
Chills	Cardamom
Cholesterol	Clary Sage
Circulatory System	Cinnamon, Clary Sage, Neroli, Frankincense, Lemon, Rosemary
Colds/Sinus	Frankincense, Myrrh, Rosemary, Cinnamon, Lemon
Colic	Neroli
Colitis	Cinnamon
Comfort	Geranium
Concentration	Rosemary
Confusion	Lemon
Congestion	Lemon, Eucalyptus, Rosemary, Sage

Constipation	Orange, Fennel
Cough	Sandalwood (dry), Sage (loose/fluid), Neroli, Rosemary, Lavender, Myrrh, Frankincense, Jasmine, Cinnamon, Lemon
Cramps	Clary Sage, Fennel, Geranium
Dehydration	Orange
Depression	Sandalwood, Bergamot, Neroli
Despondency	Bergamot, Cardamom, Cinnamon
Dermatitis	Bergamot, Geranium, Sage
Diarrhea	Neroli, Myrrh, Peppermint, Sandalwood, Cardamom, Cinnamon
Dyspepsia	Cardamom, Cinnamon
Edema	Orange, Rosemary
Emotional Fatigue	Sage, Lavender, Frankincense
Emotional Instability	Jasmine, Myrrh, Clary Sage, Frankincense, Geranium
Emotional Weakness	Myrrh
Emotional Wounds	Myrrh
Energy (low)	Cinnamon
Eczema	Geranium, Lavender
Exhaustion	Lavender (mental, physical),

Chapter 35

                    Petitgrain (nervous), Sage (physical)
                    Rosemary (nervous, mental and over tired)

Fatigue	Lavender, Petitgrain
Fear	Frankincense, Jasmine
Fertility	Jasmine
Fever	Ylang Ylang
Focus (Lack of)	Rosemary, Lemon
Frigidity	Clary Sage
Frustration	Lavender, Petitgrain
Fungal (Anti)	Cinnamon
Gas	Jasmine, Peppermint, Fennel
Genito-Urinary	Bergamot, Clary Sage, Jasmine
Giddiness	Lavender
Grief	Frankincense, Sandalwood
Hair Loss	Rosemary
Headache	Rosemary, Lavender (stress)
Healing of the Body	Geranium
High Blood Pressure	Lavender, Ylang Ylang, Clary Sage
Hormone balance	Sandalwood, Ylang Ylang

Hysteria	Lavender
Immune	Sage
Impotency	Cinnamon, Neroli, Ylang Ylang
Indigestion	Neroli (discomfort), Peppermint, Jasmine (gas), Bergamot, Cardamom, Fennel (digestive tract), Petitgrain (painful), Sage (upset stomach)
Infections	Sandalwood, Bergamot, Cinnamon, (skin), Lemon (skin & general) Rosemary (respiratory), Ylang Ylang (intestinal)
Inflammation	Geranium, Petitgrain
Inner Strength	Myrrh
Insomnia	Neroli, Orange, Petitgrain, Sandalwood, Ylang Ylang
Intestinal Discomfort	Neroli
Intestinal Infection	Ylang Ylang
Irritability	Lavender
Kidney/Bladder	Sandalwood (inflammation), Clary Sage, Jasmine
Labor	Geranium
Laryngitis	Sandalwood, Myrrh
Lethargy	Cardamom, Cinnamon, Rosemary

Chapter 35

Lightheadedness	Lavender
Liver	Orange (detox), Rosemary, Jasmine (cleanser), Peppermint, Sage (disorders)
Low Blood Pressure	Sage, Rosemary, Lemon
Lungs	Peppermint, Frankincense (congestion)
Lymphatic System	Cinnamon, Lemon
Memory (poor)	Rosemary, Sage
Menopause	Clary Sage, Ylang Ylang, Sandalwood
Menstruation	Fennel
Mental Fatigue	Peppermint, Lavender, Rosemary, Sage
Mental Strain	Sage
Migraines	Sage
Mobility	Cinnamon
Mood Swings	Clary Sage
Mosquito Bites	Geranium
Muscles Aches	Cardamom, Rosemary, Jasmine, Frankincense, Clary Sage, Orange, Sage
Muscles Slackened	Neroli, Lemon, Petitgrain

Muscle Spasms	Lavender, Jasmine, Clary Sage, Petitgrain, Sandalwood
Muscle Sprains	Jasmine
Nervous Disorders	Bergamot, Petitgrain (nervous exhaustion), Rosemary (exhaustion)
Nightmares	Frankincense, Jasmine
Nosebleeds	Lemon
Obesity	Clary Sage, Orange, Rosemary, Fennel, Lemon
Palpitations	Lavender, Petitgrain, Ylang Ylang
Panic	Frankincense
Parasites (intestinal)	Cinnamon
Perspiration (excessive)	Bergamot, Petitgrain
Physical Exhaustion	Sandalwood, Rosemary, Sage, Myrrh, Lavender, Peppermint
PMS	Neroli, Sandalwood
Post Natal	Geranium
Post Op Care	Lavender, Neroli
Purifying	Fennel
Relaxation	Petitgrain
Reproductive System	Clary Sage, Sandalwood

Chapter 35

Respiratory Disorders	Lemon, Petitgrain, Rosemary (infections), Sage (fluid)
Restlessness	Jasmine
Revive Body/Mind	Petitgrain
Rheumatism	Geranium
Scar Tissue	Lavender
Shock/Trauma	Neroli
Sinusitis	Rosemary
Skin, dry	Petitgrain, Sandalwood, Ylang Ylang
Skin, dull/congested	Orange, Frankincense
Skin, oily	Geranium, Sandalwood, Ylang Ylang
Skin, scars	Neroli
Skin, sensitive	Neroli, Ylang Ylang
Skin, stretch marks	Neroli
Skin, wrinkles	Myrrh
Slackened Muscles	Lemon, Neroli
Sore Throat	Sandalwood, Myrrh, Cinnamon
Stomach Acid	Lemon
Stress	Sandalwood, Lavender,

	Frankincense
Tension, Mental	Frankincense, Cardamom,
Tension, Nervous	Ylang Ylang, Frankincense, Jasmine, Clary Sage, Orange
Thread Veins	Lavender
Trauma	Neroli, Lavender
Ulcers	Bergamot, Myrrh, Sage
Urinary Disorders	Bergamot, Jasmine, Clary Sage, Sandalwood (infections)
Vigor	Lemon
Virus (viral infection)	Sage
Visualizations	Myrrh (improves)
Vitality loss	Cinnamon, Lemon
Vomiting	Peppermint
Water Retention	Fennel, Sage
Wounds	Bergamot, Cinnamon, Frankincense, Geranium

Chapter 35

Essential Oils for Emotional *Healing*

Emotional Ailments

Acceptance	Frankincense
Aggression	Sandalwood
Anger	Petitgrain, Ylang Ylang
Anxiety	Clary Sage, Ylang Ylang, Orange, Frankincense, Jasmine
Aura Cleansing	Sage
Awareness	Lemon (sharpened awareness)
Balance	Geranium
Boredom	Orange, Frankincense, Jasmine
Certainty	Geranium
Clarity	Lemon
Comfort	Geranium
Compassion	Lavender
Concentration	Rosemary
Confusion	Lemon
Creativity	Fennel, Orange
Depression	Sandalwood, Bergamot, Neroli
Despondency	Bergamot, Cardamom, Cinnamon

Direction	Lemon
Disappointment	Neroli
Emotional Fatigue	Sage, Lavender, Frankincense
Emotional Instability	Jasmine, Myrrh, Clary Sage, Frankincense, Geranium, Sage (imbalance)
Emotional Weakness	Myrrh
Emotional Wounds	Myrrh
Enthusiasm	Fennel
Fear	Frankincense, Jasmine, Sandalwood
Focus	Lemon
Grief	Sage, Sandalwood
Harmony	Geranium
Helplessness	Sage
Higher Self	Frankincense (connect to)
Hysteria	Lavender
Inner Coldness	Ylang Ylang
Inner Peace	Myrrh
Inner Strength	Myrrh
Insecurity	Lavender, Fennel, Geranium

Chapter 35

Insight to Move Forward	Frankincense, Petitgrain
Isolation	Myrrh
Joy (lack of)	Jasmine
Loneliness	Sandalwood
Love (lack of)	Jasmine
Memory	Rosemary
Mood Swings	Clary Sage
New Ideas	Jasmine
New Possibilities	Fennel
Obsessive Behavior	Orange
Overwhelmed	Clary Sage, Lavender, Rosemary
Panic	Frankincense
Paranoia	Frankincense, Jasmine
Pessimism	Fennel
Psychic Abilities	Myrrh
Purpose	Lemon
Rigidity	Orange, Sandalwood
Sadness	Bergamot, Orange, Frankincense, Jasmine, Neroli, Sage,

	Sandalwood
Self Esteem	Ylang Ylang, Neroli
Self Expression	Fennel, Lavender
Self Worth	Neroli
Spirit Revived	Lavender
Spirituality (lack)	Lavender, Myrrh
Stability	Petitgrain
Stagnation	Frankincense
Trust	Lemon
Vigor (loss of)	Lemon
Visualizations	Myrrh (improved)
Weepy	Sage
Wisdom expanded	Sage

Chapter 35

Essential Oils For Healing

Bergamot
Wounds
Ulcers
Dermatitis
Infections
Sadness
Depression
Nervous Butterflies
Infections in Body
Indigestion
Excessive Perspiration
Poor Appetite
Genito-urinary infections
Despondency
Acute Nervous Disorders

Cardamom
Lethargy
Bad Breath
Dyspepsia
Low Energy
Tension in Mind
Despondency
Sore/Tired Muscles
Digestive Disorder
Diarrhea
Tension in Body
Winter Chills

Cinnamon
Bronchitis
Colds
Skin Infections
Colitis
Lymphatic System
Dyspepsia
Impotency
Despondency
Mobility
Anti-fungal
Coughs
Sore Throats
Wounds
Diarrhea
Circulatory/Cardiac System
Parasites
Lethargy
Lack of Vitality
Increases Energy
Anti-infectious

Clary Sage
Genito-Urinary
Cramps
Menopause
Frigidity
Spasms
Reproductive System
Uterine Contractions
Mood Swings
Asthma
High Blood Pressure

Obesity
Cholesterol control
Anxiety
Nervous Tension

Muscle Aches & Pain
Emotional Instability
Circulatory System
Feeling Overwhelmed

Fennel
Digestive Tract
Gas
Asthma
Cramps
Obesity
Cellulite
Lack of Enthusiasm
Purifying
New Possibilities
Creativity

Bloating
Constipation
Menstruation
Childbirth
Water Retention
Insecurity
Pessimism
Cleansing
Self Expression

Frankincense
Panic
Anxiety
Acne
Asthma
Nightmares
Fear
Acceptance
Stress
Skin Conditions

Insight to move forward
Cuts/Open Wounds
Circulation
Paranoia
Lung Congestion
Grief
Emotional Fatigue
Tension
Connect to Higher Self

Geranium
Acne
Dermatitis
Oily Skin
Rheumatism
Mosquito Bites
Certainty
Balance
Menstrual Cramps
Balances Emotions

Eczema
Wounds
Inflammations
Prebirth labor
Postnatal Blues
Comfort
Security
Harmony
Healing of the Body

Chapter 35

Jasmine
Liver Cleanser
Gas
Muscle Sprains
Fear
Restlessness
Fertility
Promotes new ideas
Nightmares
Emotional Suffering
Lung Congestion
Muscle Spasms
Nervous Tension
Lack of Love
Lack of Joy
Lack of Creativity
Urinary-Genito
Paranoia
Opens to New Ideas

Lavendar
Acne
Bruises
Thread Veins
Burns
Hysteria
Lightheadedness
Giddiness
Exhaustion
Trauma
Irritability
Self Expression
Compassion
Bronchitis
Muscle Spasms
Eczema
Scar Tissue
Skin Wounds
Allergies
Palpitations
Revives Spirit
Post Op Care
Fatigue
Cell Stimulation
Frustration
Lack of Spirituality
Insecurity
High Blood Pressure
Asthma

Lemon
Congestion
Infection
Infected Skin
Poor Circulation
Obesity
Low Blood Pressure
Stomach Acidity
Certainty
Direction
Respiratory Disorders
Nosebleeds
Slackened Muscle Tissue
Coughs
Sluggish Lymphatic system
Confusion
Lack of Purpose & Direction
Clarity
Sharpened Awareness

Vigor   Vitality
Trust   Purpose
Focus

Myrrh
Ulcers   Aged Skin (wrinkles)
Sore Throat   Asthma
Bronchitis   Colds & Coughs
Diarrhea   Isolation
Emotional Weakness   Loss of Spirituality
Emotional Wounds   Blood Cells
Inner Strength   Improved Visualizations
Psychic Abilities   Inner Peace

Neroli
Colic   Intestinal Discomfort
Depression   Impotency
PMS Symptoms   Stretch Marks
Scars   Sadness
Sensitive Skin   Bronchitis
Broken Capillaries   Post Op
Slackened Muscles   Circulatory Disorders
Diarrhea   Insomnia
Shock   Disappointment
Low Self Worth

Orange, Sweet
Dehydration   Dry, Dull, Congested Skin
Cellulite   Obesity
Edema   Constipation
Toxic Liver   Sore Muscles
Nervous Tension   Insomnia
Boredom   Rigidity
Sadness   Lack of Creativity
Obsessive Behavior

Peppermint
Gas, Flatulence   Indigestion

Vomiting
Bronchitis
Sciatica
Arthritis
Colic
Liver Fatigue
Toothache
Mental Fatigue
Physical Exhaustion

Asthma
Chest Infections
Neuralgia
Muscle Aches & Pains
Diarrhea
Menstrual Cramps
Apathy
Low Vitality

Petitgrain
Acne
Dry Skin
Inflammation
Palpitations
Frustration
Painful Digestion
Sound Sleep
Stability
Respiratory Infections
Muscle Spasms
Nervous Exhaustion
Revives the Mind & Body

Boils
Insomnia
Arthritis
Anger
Fatigue
Relaxation
Insight
Excessive Perspiration
Nervous Asthma
Inflammation
Slackened Muscles

Rosemary
Hair Loss
Obesity
Congestion
Sinusitis
Circulation
Low Blood Pressure
Edema
Lethargy
Overwhelmed

Lack of Concentration
Poor Memory
Respiratory Infections
Bronchitis
Muscle Aches & Pains
Sluggish Liver
Nervous Exhaustion
Over Tired

Sage
Bronchitis
Digestive System

Congestion from colds
Ulcers

Respiratory Fluid
Arthritis
Muscle Aches
Sluggish Immune
Viral Infections
Grief
Weepy
Aura Cleanser
Expands Wisdom
Liver Disorders
Upset Stomach

Dermatitis
Migraines
Low Blood Pressure
Mental Strain
Physical Exhaustion
Helplessness
Emotional Imbalance
Poor Memory
Balances Mind & Body
Fluid Flush
Poor Immune System

Sandalwood
Hormone Balance
Infections
Chafed & Oily Skin
Dry Coughs
Sore Throat
Diarrhea
Grief
Kidney Inflammation
Rigidity
Fear

Reproductive Functions
Acne
Congestion
Laryngitis
Muscle Spasms
Insomnia
Urinary Tract Infections
Aggression
Heart Health
Loneliness

Ylang Ylang
Irritated or Oily Skin
Palpitations
Intestinal Infections
Impotence
Nervous Tension
Low Self Esteem

High Blood Pressure
Fever
Hormone Imbalance
Insomnia
Inner Coldness
Anger

If you are interested in Essential Oils I suggest finding an Aromatherapist to teach you more about them. There are many classes available now. Our local community college even offers one. The Aromatherapist will be able to show you proper dosages and blending. Of course, you will want to have a good essential oil book to keep on hand as well. Experiment with your oils and have fun using them.

Flower and Rock Essences

Flower and rock essences are amazing ways to transfer natural energy. Their healing qualities are highly effective and extremely safe. They connect our physical healing with the wellness of body, mind and soul.

The rocks or flowers used in essences are placed in water and then set in sunlight for several hours. Through this process the energy vibration (or essence) of the flower or rock is released into the water. Apple cider vinegar, vegetable glycerin, brandy or vodka is then added to the essence as a preservative. Since you only use two to four drops of the essence, the alcohol isn't sufficient enough to have any affect on you.

Rock and flower essences are usually taken orally but can be applied topically or added to your bath for direct absorption through the skin. When using them orally add only two to four drops to your drinking water. Taking more will do you no good. It is the frequency of your dosages that increases the potency. If you are using more than one essence it would be best to use two drops of each essence. Don't worry about overdosing or using the wrong essence. It is suggested that you do not mix more than six different essences at one time. In general, the fewer you use the better. Your body will use what it needs and it will not absorb or disperse the essence if it is not needed. It isn't dangerous to use more than four drops, it's just wasteful.

Essences can also be used orally by directly dropping them under the tongue. Again, only use two to four drops. I enjoy adding them to my water much more. I believe that by drinking them in your water you are fed smaller amounts of the essence over a longer period of time.

You can also use the essences topically. Add a couple of drops to your bath or to lotions or base oil and rub it directly onto the skin. It will be quickly absorbed. While I do not regularly use them topically, there are times when I feel it is the most effective way to do it.

I suggest experimenting with all the methods to see which ones work best for you.

Essences can affect everyone differently. Some people feel their energetic vibrations immediately and others may feel as if nothing has changed. Typically, the effect of essences is subtle, gentle and gradual. You may be thinking it isn't working and then all of sudden one day you notice a big change in yourself. Essences can be helpful with things like stress, relationships, self esteem, attitudes toward life and states of emotional, mental and physical well being.

When using rock essences, choose the essence according to the energetic properties of the rock, as explained in the last chapter. Using your rock and crystal reference book will help you choose which essence is best to use.

You will have to get acquainted with the different flower essences. Most stores that sell them also have free pamphlets to help guide you in your selection process. There are many different brands of flower essences available although it was Dr. Edward Bach that first discovered this method of healing. Dr. Bach was an English Physician and Scientist. In the early 1930's he realized that in order to treat people's physical ailments it was necessary to treat them at an emotional level as well. He was a firm believer that drugs tend to mask or worsen the symptoms, so he wanted to develop something completely natural. Dr. Bach spent years in research before he discovered thirty eight natural remedies using tree and flower essences to address emotional issues and thus heal physical ailments. Dr. Bach only discovered thirty eight essences, but since then other people have developed and created many more.

To help you understand the healing properties of essences I will give you a brief explanation of what some of them can do for you.

Aspen
If you feel troubled by anxiety, apprehension or vague fear.

Beech
If you are often critical or intolerant of other people.

Chapter 35

<u>Centaury</u>
If you are unable to say 'no'.

<u>Clematis</u>
If you find it hard to concentrate or stay mentally focused.

<u>Elm</u>
If you feel overwhelmed by your responsibilities.

<u>Gorse</u>
If you feel despair or hopelessness.

<u>Honeysuckle</u>
If you tend to dwell in the past too much.

<u>Impatiens</u>
If you are impatient.

<u>Larch</u>
If you lack self confidence.

<u>Oak</u>
If you are a workaholic.

<u>Pine</u>
If you are a perfectionist.

<u>Star of Bethlehem</u>
If you suffered a trauma, surgery, accident or loss.

<u>Walnut</u>
If you are undergoing change or transition.

<u>Water Violet</u>
If you are introverted and have trouble developing relationships.

<u>White Chestnut</u>
If you are distracted with too much mental chatter or sleeplessness. This one is a great aid in channeling or meditation.

If you are interested in flower essences I would suggest getting at least one book by Dr. Edward Bach. There are many wonderful books available but I believe Dr. Bach is our Master Teacher and his theories and practices should be understood. You will also want to buy a book to use as a guide or reference in selecting and using your essences. Most health food stores now carry a wide variety of essences. You can also order Bach Flower Essences over the internet. Again, you need to use your intuition when choosing a brand of essence. Some may be better than others.

Chapter 36

Vitamins and Minerals

A nutritionally healthy physical body supports your energy body.

Vitamins and minerals greatly enhance your spiritual, mental, emotional and physical performance as well as your energy level and overall well being. Providing the body with sufficient amounts of each helps support all body functions. Even if you follow all the previous methods in this book for self healing, you must also maintain the nutritional health of your physical body. This chapter and the following chapter will address your health at a more physical level. When you maintain a nutritionally healthy physical body your energy body is also maintained because it has the support it needs to keep your energy level high.

Nutritional supplements are well known to the general population. More and more people are taking them now. Even with this rise in nutritional awareness and health, most Americans are still deficient in their vitamin and mineral levels. Most of these deficiencies are not serious enough to create obvious problems, but even slight deficiencies can cause feelings of fatigue, lethargy, difficulty concentrating, lack of well being, and other vague symptoms.

I am not a nutritionist and everyone has there own unique nutritional needs, but there are some basic supplements that everyone can benefit from. For a more personalized program I would suggest seeing a Nutritionist or Naturopath.

In general, we should all be taking the following:

- High quality multiple vitamin and mineral supplement
- Extra antioxidants (vitamins C & E)
- Flaxseed Oil

Vitamin and mineral supplements ensure that your body is getting all it needs to prevent possible deficiencies from occurring. There is no need to take mega doses unless a nutritionist or doctor prescribes it. The recommended dosage should be adequate enough.

Antioxidants are extremely important in breaking down free radicals in our body. Free radicals have been proven to be responsible for initiating many diseases such as cancer, heart disease, and chronic degenerative diseases. They are also believed to aid in slowing down the aging process. Vitamins C and E are two primary antioxidants found in the body. In addition to your vitamin and mineral supplement it would be safe and helpful to add an extra 500-800 IU of Vitamin E and 1,000-1,500 IU of Vitamin C. There are many premixed antioxidant formulas available also. If you feel you are getting sick you can add more Vitamin C and include Echinacea to help build your immune system.

Organic, unrefined Flax Seed can be purchased and used in pill or oil form. Pill form is much easier. Flax Seed helps restore the proper level of essential fatty acids to our body by providing us with Omega 3 and Omega 6 fatty acids. In fact, Flaxseed is the richest source of Omega 3 fatty acid. A deficiency of these essential fatty acids can create a serious health threat to our energy levels and can create things like cardiovascular disease, cancer, skin disease, allergies, inflammation, and auto immune deficiencies like multiple sclerosis and rheumatoid arthritis.

Eating a healthy diet and taking your vitamins and minerals will ensure that your body is getting the nutrition it needs. Don't overdo it but don't discount the potential of a simple vitamin and mineral supplement.

Chapter 37

Herbs and Homeopathy

Adopt a user friendly approach to your healthcare.

Herbs

Herbs are plants. You already know that plants carry their own energy. Using herbs instead of chemical drugs is a more natural way to heal your self. The more natural your healing modality, the more 'user friendly' it is. Your body will respond significantly better to natural remedies, but can become significantly worse from taking chemical drugs because they are synthetic. I'm not saying you should stop taking your prescription drugs, but be open minded to the world of natural medicine such as herbs and homeopathy. Natural remedies can even be taken in conjunction with synthetic drugs.

Just because herbs are natural doesn't mean you can take as much as you want. Herbs are strong medicine and you should never take more than the recommended dosage. It isn't too likely that you could have serious medical problems from overdosing on herbs but taking too many can create a toxic or allergic reaction.

Growing your own herbs is enjoyable and fun but it would be much safer to buy your herbal supplements over the counter. Choose organically grown herbal products from reliable and reputable sources. Follow the directions on the bottle. Most health food stores offer a wide selection, and good advice, on choosing which ones to use. Aside from pill form, herbs can be purchased in teas, extracts, tinctures, powder, juices, lotions and many skin and hair products.

There are literally hundreds of herbs available. Except for a few I am very familiar with, I let my doctor choose which ones are best for me. I've known many people who overdo it with herb consumption. I suggest using herbs as you would medicine. If you aren't showing symptoms of an illness or problem, don't use them. In other words, if you feel fine there's no need to take mega doses of herbs 'just in case'.

An herbal reference guide can help you get acquainted with the different herbs and what they address. Again, you can use your pendulum to determine which one you need by touching the name of the herb and asking for a yes or no. I take no herbs on a regular basis. They are my medicine and I use them only when I need them. To give you an idea of how and when to use herbs I've created a list of things herbs can be used for.

Skin irritations	Breath Freshener
Earache	Insomnia
Deodorant	Energy
Headaches	Motion Sickness
Arthritis	Muscle Aches
Rheumatism	Diarrhea
Bloating/water weight	Sunburn
Toothache	Constipation
Fever	Allergies
Gas/Indigestion	Vomiting
Nausea	Colds
Flu	Sore Throat
Coughs	Athletes foot
Menstrual cramps	Hemorrhoids
Osteoporosis	Anemia
Enlarged Prostate	Infections
Liver Disease	Dry hair
Vision	Strong nails
Skin care	Stress
Lowering cholesterol	Circulatory problems
Alzheimer's	Mental alertness

Chapter 37

Vertigo
Weight loss
Blood sugar regulator
Concentration
Joint pain
Parasites

Since herbs are medicine, children and pregnant women should consult their doctor before taking herbal supplements. Try to find a doctor that uses natural medicine to guide and consult you as you explore the world of herbs. My doctor uses only herbs, vitamins, minerals and homeopathic medicine and I feel totally confident, happy and healthy with that.

Homeopathy
Homeopathy believes that 'like treats like'. Don't worry about taking more of the same thing that's making you sick. Homeopathic remedies are extremely diluted so you are only taking minute amounts. The dilution is around 1 part remedy to 1,000,000,000,000 parts water. If you have a bacterial infection you would take a remedy that uses the same bacteria. It doesn't matter if the bacterial infection causes multiple symptoms like chest congestion, sinus pressure and earache; there is still only one remedy to take. That one homeopathic remedy will treat all the symptoms associated with the bacterial infection. Homeopathic remedies are quite amazing. They are easy to use, extremely effective, and work very quickly.

One of the reasons I love homeopathic medicine is because the results are usually permanent. Throughout my life I was overcome with poison ivy once or twice a year. There were a couple of times when it spread all over my body, into my ears, nose, eyelids and over my scalp. The first time I took a homeopathic remedy for poison ivy the symptoms disappeared in a couple of days. The amazing thing is that I've never had poison ivy since then and it's been ten years. With the help of my homeopathic doctor, I have eliminated nearly thirty other allergies over the last ten years. Homeopathy is not only quick, easy, and effective, but permanent many times as well.

Homeopathy is completely safe for children and pregnant women too. My grandchildren have been taking homeopathic and herbal remedies since the day they were born. They are two and four years old and have never been to a doctor of western medicine. There are no side affects to homeopathic remedies. It's completely natural and based on purely natural ingredients; therefore it works in harmony with your body. As I've explained earlier in this book, western medicine generally only suppresses the symptoms and does not address the underlying cause of the illness. For example, western medicine will treat a cough with a cough suppressant rather than treating the cause of the cough. Coughing is your body's way of cleaning the lungs. Suppressing the cough without treating the cause means your body will not be able to remove the toxins from your lungs.

Homeopathy can be used alone or with other medications. It is not addicting and there are no side effects. The remedies are used for a shorter period of time than prescription drugs. Once your symptoms are gone you can quit taking the remedy. If the symptoms persist, you know you're taking the wrong remedy.

It is best to have a knowledgeable homeopathic doctor diagnose and treat you. Since homeopathy addresses the underlying cause, it can be difficult for us to determine what that is. A headache must be explored to find out what is causing it. It could be caused from stress, allergies or a number of other things. Cold symptoms could be caused by bacteria, staph, virus, strep or yeast infections. You can use your pendulum to self treat, but without knowing all the different possibilities, it may be difficult for you to find the correct diagnosis without the help of a professional.

Homeopathic doctors have their own remedies to sell you, but if you know the cause of your illness or allergy you can buy remedies in most health food stores. The remedy is taken from a dropper bottle. Generally you only need to take six drops, three times a day until the symptoms disappear. The drops are taken directly under the tongue for immediate absorption. You should avoid food or beverages, other than water, ten minutes before and after you take the drops.

If you don't already have a doctor of natural medicine I suggest you seriously consider finding one. It is very comforting knowing you are taking purely natural medication. Your energy body will thank you for the change. You will experience more complete recoveries and the possibility of recurrence will be much less than with western medicine.

Chapter 38

Diet and Exercise

Diet and exercise are the easiest things to control, yet most people are out of control.

Your body is a temple and your soul is the inner sanctuary. Despite the fact that your true self is your soul, your soul dwells in the body you have. An unhealthy body robs you of your energy and therefore affects your soul. Your body can not be neglected because it houses and services your soul. It also directly relates to your emotional, mental and physical well being. Just as pollutants, chemicals, electromagnetic waves and toxic people deplete your energy body, a lack of exercise and an unhealthy diet depletes your energy as well.

Diet
Your body is very sensitive to what you eat and drink. Everything you put into your body is important to your energy level and overall health. Foods and beverages can carry energy, or rob you of energy. There are many fad diets and beliefs about good versus bad foods today. We have people telling us to stay away from certain foods because they are high in fat, cholesterol, carbohydrates, proteins, etc. I would rather talk about the energetic qualities of food. The healthy functioning of our body is directly related to our energy body so it's time to start thinking about the energy in your foods and beverages. When you look at food as either energy producing or energy depleting, it makes a healthy diet seem simple.

Eating energetically doesn't involve measuring and weighing amounts of food. Its benefits are to raise and sustain your energy level. If your energy level is high, you will feel terrific, lose weight, look younger, and keep your entire health system strong and naturally self healing.

As soon as you place restrictions and rules on your diet, you create a huge emotional and mental crisis. Your mind instantly says, 'Oh no, I can't have this and that anymore', therefore you start craving it even more. Knowing you can't have something you want creates mental stress and negativity because your mind continually fights you by holding cravings. Rather than approach your new energy diet guidelines with a 'do or die' attitude, be gentle with yourself. Let your body and mind adjust slowly and make it a nutritional goal to eat more energetically.

If you give your body time to start feeling the energetic increases, your body and mind will start to work *with* you instead of *against* you. Since your body is extremely sensitive to energy increases and decreases, you will soon feel drawn to energy foods more than others. Place no time frames on when you will be 100% switched over to only energy foods. It can take weeks, months or years to keep your energy robbing foods and beverages to a minimum. However long it takes is okay. Be happy knowing you are making a difference by improving even slightly. Any amount of improvement is still improvement.

If you just have to indulge in too many non-energetic foods once in a while, try to feel what they do to you. Become more aware of when you feel energized by your food and when you feel bogged down. When you become aware of those differences, your mind will make sense of why you should and should not consume different things. In time, your mind and body will work in harmony. When you can create harmony, you will no longer feel punished or deprived by not eating the junk you now crave. It's the negative emotional and mental involvement that makes you want to cheat on diets and go back to your old way of eating.

A healthy diet should become a way of life, not an unnatural restriction you place on yourself for a few weeks in order to quickly drop a few pounds. How many people have you known that went on a diet, lost weight, and then gained it all back shortly after they quit dieting? They mentally and emotionally endured the diet but they knew it would be over one day. Once they served their time, and were free to eat as they chose once again, their mind quickly returned to thinking they had to have junk food.

Be aware, be patient, and try to eat as energetically as you can. Don't panic or feel bad about yourself if you slip up and devour a candy bar or eat a big hamburger every now and then. With the energy diet it's okay to have energy robbing foods occasionally. It's all about balance. As long as you primarily eat energy building foods your body will be able to handle splurges of non-energetic foods.

Remember that making even slight improvements will enhance your diet, health and energy level. You can always ask God and your Guides to help you release cravings and improve your diet. They are always willing to help you, if you are willing to change. Love yourself, your soul, your body and your energy body and everything will come together naturally and in its own time. The more energy food you consume the better you will feel and look.

Energy foods also help keep you connected to your spiritual self by opening up the communication lines between you and the spirit world. Eating foods that continually rob you of your energy makes it more difficult for you to hear the guidance of your higher self, God and your Guides.

Alkaline versus Acid

Akaline foods create energy and acid foods deplete it. Certain foods create an Alkaline state in your body while others create an Acid state.

Eating too many acidic foods lowers your body's ability to fight off viruses, disease, infection, and bacteria. An alkaline body creates a pH balance that naturally wards off those things. When your body maintains its alkalinity those things can not enter, much less grow and mutate within your body. Your immune system is supported by alkaline foods and it is broken down by acid foods.

If your diet includes mostly acid foods, any alkaline reserves you have stored become depleted. This is because your body uses alkaline to neutralize the excess acids. Without alkaline, your body becomes weakened and susceptible to disease, bacteria, infection and viruses.

Symptoms of too much acid in the body can include such things as:

Acne	Fungi
Parasites	Colds
Diarrhea	Ulcers
Acid Reflux	Migraine Headaches
Rheumatoid Arthritis	Flu
Water Retention	Insomnia
Constipation	Weight Gain
Obesity	Diabetes
Hormone Imbalance	Osteoporosis
Joint Pain	Cardiovascular Damage
Fatigue	Yeast Overgrowth
Slow Digestion	Low Energy
Premature Aging	Bladder Problems
Kidney Problems	Mouth Burning
Difficulty Swallowing	Bumps on Tongue
Immune Deficiency	

There are many delicious alkaline foods so don't start to panic. Your goal should be to eat 80% alkaline foods and 20% acid foods. It's all about balance. This means you *can* eat the acid foods, just keep them to a minimum. For instance, all meat is acidic. If you love meat you can still eat it, but choose alkaline forming foods for your side dishes. If you crave sweets, eat them. Just make sure the acid foods you choose to eat do not make up more than 20% of your diet.

It's not difficult to follow this diet if you take the time to become consciously aware of which foods are which. I keep a copy of the food chart on my refrigerator. If I notice my food intake for the day has included too many acidic foods, I will have an alkaline based dinner.

If you're good about drinking adequate amounts of water, squeeze fresh lemon juice in each serving. Lemon water is an excellent alkaline builder. Although lemons are acidic, they create an alkaline reaction in your body. Freshly squeezed lemon is better to use than lemon juice from a bottle.

It's easy to follow the alkaline/acid diet. You won't feel deprived because you can still eat your acid foods. Take steps toward creating an 80/20 balance. Chances are you've been eating predominantly acidic foods. Most Americans do. If this is the case with you, then even the slightest improvement will be a huge step toward eating healthier.

As soon as you raise your alkaline and decrease your acid, you will notice a major improvement in your well being. Every body function benefits greatly with even the slightest improvement and your body won't have to waste its precious energy in order to maintain your health. Imagine having extra energy, versus always using your energy to keep your body healthy. Because an alkaline body maintains a higher state of consciousness, it improves your spiritual, mental, emotional and physical well being. You will find that energy work, channeling, and your psychic abilities will improve dramatically.

The following is a chart of alkaline and acid foods to use as a dietary guideline.

A Soul's Guide to Abundance, Health And Happiness

Alkaline vs. Acid Forming Food Chart

Alkaline should be 80% of Diet

Most Alkaline	Alkaline	Low Alkaline
SWEETENERS		
Stevia	Maple Syrup	Raw Honey
Agave	Rice Syrup	Raw Sugar
FRUITS		
Lemons	Dates	Oranges
Limes	Grapes	Unripe Banana
Mangoes	Kiwi	Peaches
Watermelon	Apples	Cherries
Grapefruit	Raisins	Coconut
Papaya	Melon	Avocado
	Papaya	Pineapple
	Berries	
	Pears	
	Figs	
VEGETABLES BEANS AND LEGUMES		
Asparagus	Okra	Carrots
Onions	Squash	Tomatoes
Parsley	Green Beans	Fresh Corn
Raw Spinach	Beets	Chives
Broccoli	Celery	Mushrooms
Garlic	Lettuce	Cabbage
Cucumber	Zucchini	Peas
Red Radish	Sweet Potato	Potato Skins
Most Vegetable Juices	Endive	Olives
	Cayenne	Fresh Soybeans
	Sorrel	Artichokes
	Carob	Cauliflower
		Tofu
		Rutabaga

Chapter 38

Acid should be 20% of Diet

Lowest Acid	Acid	Most Acid
Processed Honey Molasses	White Sugar Brown Sugar	Equal Sweet n Low NutraSweet Aspartame
Plums Processed fruit juices	Sour Cherries Rhubarb	Blueberries Cranberries Prunes
Cooked Spinach Kidney Beans String Beans	Skinless Potato Navy Beans Pinto Beans Lima Beans	Chocolate

A Soul's Guide to Abundance, Health And Happiness

Alkaline vs. Acid Forming Food Chart (cont.)

Most Alkaline	Alkaline	Low Alkaline
NUTS AND SEEDS		
Soy Nuts soaked & air dried	Almonds	Chestnuts
	Hazelnuts	Sesame
		Caraway
		Fennel
OILS		
Olive Oil	Flax Seed Oil	Canola Oil
	Borage oil	
GRAINS, CEREALS AND HERBS		
Barley	Mung Bean	Wild Rice
Alfalfa	Wheat, broccoli	Millet
Kamut Grasses	& other sprouts	Amaranth
Oat Straw		Quinoa
Horsetail		
Soy & Radish Sprouts		
Dandelion		
MEATS		
EGGS AND DAIRY		
	Breast Milk	Soy Milk/Cheese
		Goat Milk
		Buttermilk
		Goat Cheese
BEVERAGES		
Herb Teas	Green Tea	Ginger Tea
Lemon Water	Some Herb Coffees	

Chapter 38

Lowest Acid	**Acid**	**Most Acid**
Pumpkin Seeds Sunflower Seeds Filberts Brazil Nuts Flax	Pecans Cashews	Peanuts Walnuts Pistachios
Butter Corn Oil	All heated oils	All fried oils
Brown Rice Sprouted Wheat Bread Spelt	White Rice Corn Oats Rye Buckwheat	Wheat Bread White Bread Pastries Pasta
Cold Water Fish Venison	Turkey Chicken Lamb	Beef Port Shellfish
Eggs Butter Yogurt	Raw Milk	Cheese Ice Cream Homogenized Milk
Black Tea	Coffee	Beer Soft Drinks

Alkaline vs. Acid Forming Food Chart (cont.)

Most Alkaline	Alkaline	Low Alkaline
COOKING		
Raw	Steamed	Boiled
ADDITIVES		

Chapter 38

Lowest Acid	**Acid**	**Most Acid**
Frozen	Smoked Canned	Fried Foods Processed Food Food Chemicals Preservatives
Semi Processed	Additives Colorants	

A few foods are not energy foods but are significantly better to use than their alternative.

- Use butter instead of margarine.
- Use sugar instead of artificial sweeteners.
- Use organic meat whenever possible.
- Cook fresh meals instead of buying prepackaged, processed foods.

There are two ways to confirm that your body is healthy and balanced. Your urine should run as clear as water with no aroma, and your bowel movements should be light in color and float.

Before concluding this section, I want to talk a little about children and diet. It disturbs me greatly to see the growing number of overweight and/or obese children today. Children eat what their parents buy. They can't drive to the store, or even walk to a store, and buy junk without money from their parents. We feed them what they eat. The only one to blame for obesity in children is the parent. Plain and simple, we can not blame children for their weight problems.

Even if we adults can't control our own junk food intake, it's time to start teaching our children how to eat well. Set the stage for a lifetime of healthy living, not an instant replay of the terrible eating habits we've picked up in the last thirty years of fast foods. If you refuse to buy junk food they can not eat it. Adults are in complete control of their child's dietary intake.

While some schools now have snack and coke machines, you can avoid giving them extra money to use in the machines. Most school lunches don't include energy foods. The vegetables are over cooked and have no flavor. The fruits are generally canned and full of sugar. The rest of the foods are high in starch (sugar), fat and cholesterol. The best thing to do is pack your child's lunch. Sure, they can look for someone to give them money for the coke machine or to trade food with, but you will still make a great improvement in their diet. Be sure to give them lots of food and plenty of choices. Keep the portions reasonably small but have lots of variety to choose from.

Chapter 38

When I was a child, we weren't allowed to eat anything but fruits and vegetables between meals. We never had soda, chips or candy in the house unless we were having a party or company. Kids will adjust, and are healthier and happier when they have a good diet. Who knows, their friends may start wanting their healthy foods instead of the junk they eat for lunch.

Exercise

Exercise is a vital part of your spiritual, mental, emotional, energetic and physical health. Through exercise, every aspect of your being is nourished, revitalized and cleansed. It saddens me to hear that most Americans, including children, don't get enough exercise. As a teacher of Cardio Karate for ten years, I've heard all the excuses. The most common excuses are, 'I don't have time', 'I can't afford it', and 'I'm too tired to exercise'. Being too tired to exercise is contradictory in itself because exercise dramatically increases your energy level. Time and money aren't very important once you get sick or God forbid, have a stroke, heart attack or serious illness. What could be more important and beneficial to spend your time and money on than your body's well being?

An out of shape body is the exterior sign of lack of exercise, but it's the invisible, internal damage that we should be more concerned with. The interior damage often eludes us until it's too late and serious complications are already taking place. Some of the hidden, internal damages include heart disease, circulatory problems, high cholesterol, hormonal imbalances, hardening of the arteries, high toxicity levels throughout the tissues, organs and bloodstream, osteoporosis, high blood pressure, lowered immune system, and decreases in lung capacity. On the outside we see things like decreased flexibility, muscle loss, joint pain, arthritis, low metabolism, lack of energy, stress, physical fatigue, mental exhaustion and confusion, depression and decreased self esteem.

Three hours a week is the minimum amount of exercise you need. There are a total of 168 hours in a week. Surely you can find three or four of those hours to exercise. You must make time to exercise just like you make time to eat and sleep. I have always said, 'I'd rather exercise more, than restrict my diet or calorie intake.'

I believe the real reason most people don't exercise is because they don't like the method they've chosen. They begin to feel like its torture to exercise instead of looking forward to it as something fun and exciting. It's important to find a form of exercise that you enjoy. If you enjoy it, you will want to do it. Enjoyment is the key to sticking with a regular exercise program. In this day and age we have so many different physical fitness avenues to choose from. Going to a gym only works for a few people, yet most people think that they have to join a gym to start working out.

Try different things and see which one you like the best. If you loved gymnastics or cheerleading as a child, you might like taking a martial arts class. If you loved dance as a child, take a dance class. If you enjoyed team sports as a child, get on an adult sports team. If you really don't like working out, you might look into Tai Chi or Yoga. If you love meeting new people, choose an activity where you'll have other people around so you can socialize before, after or during class. Choose not only your exercise program, but your instructor and the place of business as well. When it all clicks you have a winner.

There are so many exercise options available to you now. Below is a short list of some exercise ideas to choose from.

Martial Arts	Yoga
Weight Lifting	Dance
Aerobics	Tai Chi
Bowling	Bicycling
Skiing	Baseball/Softball
Tennis	Power Walking
Swimming	Jogging
Gym Machines	Kickboxing
Racquetball	Volleyball
Basketball	Hockey
Skating	Horseback Riding
Belly Dancing	Ballet

Pick something that sounds fun and start doing it. Try to find a business that doesn't require you to go on contract, or will give you a short trial period to see if you like it. Then, if you find out you don't like it, quit and try something else. Keep trying new things until you find something that holds your interest and enjoyment.

Chapter Thirty Eight Exercise #1
Start to become conscious of when you're eating energy depleting foods. Begin adding more energy food to your diet. Start a new grocery list and include all the alkaline foods you love. Stop stocking so many energy depleting foods in your pantry and refrigerator.

Chapter Thirty Eight Exercise #2
Make the commitment to exercise your body at least three hours a week. Find a friend to join you and work as a motivational team. Ask your friend to encourage and motivate you on days you want to back out. Do the same for them when they're struggling. Try something different if you've never liked exercising before. Keep experimenting until you find something you enjoy.

Chapter 39

Pamper Yourself

*Take time to pamper yourself so you don't need to create an illness to get the extra
pampering you desire.*

Many times we create and manifest problems to *allow* ourselves to get sick. It is hard to believe that we would *choose* to make ourselves sick, isn't it? As miserable as illness and pain can be, it is a wonderful time for us to feel forced to pamper and care for ourselves at a much greater level than we normally do, or have time to do.

When you become sick or are in pain, you tend to take extra care of yourself. You begin to rest more, stay home from work or other activities, and even receive extra sympathy and care from other people. This feels good and cozy to us and can actually help the healing process. What we need to do is maintain that good, cozy feeling within ourselves all of the time so we don't have to come up with an excuse like illness to get it.

We all need a little extra attention and pampering at times, and that's okay as long as we don't feel the need to have to make ourselves ill to get it. When you feel pushed beyond your comfort zone, your body will do whatever it takes to allow yourself down time.

Pampering is food for your soul. Anytime you indulge in a pleasurable activity, you allow the Light within you to shine brighter and stronger. Pampering is another way to increase your energy and lift your spirit as well. When your energy is low it affects your physical performance. Spending time on a loving gesture toward your body increases your energy.

Pampering is an expression of love. When we take the time to pamper or care for someone else, our actions are saying 'I love you'. It is important to love ourselves and we can express that love by indulging ourselves in a pleasurable, pampering experience. Don't get pampering confused with playing or being creative. Those things require your physical participation. When you tell yourself 'I love you' by pampering, it should be totally relaxing and enjoyable. The only involvement on your part is to experience pleasure and joy. Pampering is nothing more than that. You may already be thinking of ways to pamper yourself. Each of us has our own favorites, but in case you can't think of anything I will give you a few ideas.

Bathing

Bathing is completely free of charge, you don't need to make an appointment, you can do it whenever you want and in your own home. Taking a warm, peaceful soak is good for cleansing and recharging your energy body. Add 1-3 cups of sea salt and 1-3 cups of baking soda to your bath to aid your energy body. The baking soda cleans your aura. Sea salt removes toxins and feeds your body the natural energies of the water it came from. If you can't find sea salt, you can use Epsom salts. Sea salt is preferred but Epsom salt will work.

I have learned that sea salt is hard on septic tanks, as it kills the good bacteria needed to break down waste. Epsom salt does not affect the bacteria. If you have a septic system and take a lot of sea salt baths, you can flush a five pound bag of sugar down your commode once a month to put the good bacteria fighters back in your system. Large quantities of sea salt may be difficult to find. In the Houston area, I can by a 50 lb. bag at a store called Whole Foods. It's much less expensive to buy bulk.

Along with your salt and baking soda, try adding some essential oils to your bath. Use an oil that supports how you feel or what your body needs that day. Sage oil is one that I use in every bath. Sage has a wonderful cleansing ability and will help clean up all negative energies you may have absorbed. I generally add two or three dif-

Chapter 39

ferent oils to every bath. You will only need to use 2 drops of each oil when using a blend of three different oils.

Lighting a candle or two is also a pleasant asset to your bath time. As you soak, look into the flame and allow your mind to calm. Realize that you have that same inner light and flame within you. Visualize your own inner light dancing, flickering, and getting brighter, stronger and bigger. See your inner light radiating out from your body and illuminating the water, then filling the entire bathroom, and then the whole house. Visualize all the worries, fears, stress and negativity in you being drawn out of your body as you soak. See those things permanently and instantly dissolving into the water. Soak for ten to twenty minutes. Try to get as much of your body under water as you can. I even do a few full body dips, allowing the oils, salt and baking soda to cover my crown and third eye chakras.

There is no need to rinse off, in fact the effects of the salt and oils will continue to work even after you're out of the tub. As you dry your body off, visualize wiping away any remaining particles of negativity from your body so that you are totally cleansed and pure once again. Contrary to how it may sound, the salt will soften and smooth your skin. It will not dry you up.

If you're not into bathing try to take *at least* one bath a week for health reasons.

Ear Candling

Ear candling is another wonderful way to pamper and cleanse your body, especially if you have sinus congestion or stuffy ears. You can purchase a pair of candles at most health food stores or buy them directly over the internet. Ear candles are made from bees wax and have a hole through the center of the candle. They do not drop wax like other candles. Most come with directions but if yours do not, follow this simple procedure.

Poke the small end of the candle through a piece of tin foil or a paper plate. This will keep a protective layer between the burning candle and your head in case there are some falling ashes. Put a small amount of oil around the narrow end of the candle or directly on the outside of the ear canal. Lie down in a comfortable position with a pillow under your head. Place the narrow end of the candle gently into your ear. It's nice to have a partner hold the candle or keep an eye on it but you don't need one. I usually put a mirror in front of me to watch the candle.

Light the candle and hold it in your ear until it is only an inch or two long. As the candle burns, it draws out wax and debris from your ear canal and sinus cavities. It feels warm and soothing and you will be surprised at how much junk comes out of each ear. Once the candle burns down, take it out of the ear and drop it in a cup of water.

Children love ear candling too and it is a great way to keep them free of ear infections and hearing restrictions due to excessive wax build up. There's no harm in doing ear candling as much as you like but it's probably not needed more than every three to six months. The more ear wax you have, the more often you will need to candle.

Massage
Massage is a marvelous way to connect body, mind and soul, and center your self. We all need and love to be touched, but if you feel uncomfortable about being naked under a sheet, be honest with your massage therapist. They are sensitive to your needs and can easily adjust their therapy to make you feel safe, comfortable and relaxed.

Massage is an experience that allows you to feel, rather than think. It stimulates and cleanses the physical body while helping to release at an emotional level. Although the only thing you are engaged in is feeling pleasure from touch, the massage breaks up and moves negative energies. It stimulates your lymphatic, immune and circulatory systems. It also breaks up knots caused from stress, tension, cellulite or overexertion. It gives movement and flexibility back to your muscles and soft tissues. If you work out three or more hours a week, you should be getting massages every month or two to help break up the lactic acid buildup it creates.

Many Massage Therapists will use aromatherapy and essential oils applied directly to your skin to help heal and rejuvenate you. I have a Massage Therapist that channels pertinent information regarding my physical body as she works on me. She has picked up past life information that explains certain physical restrictions, pains and sensitive areas. This is extremely beneficial in helping my body

Chapter 39

release cell memories that can be instigators of my current pain and discomfort.

Manicures/Pedicures and Facials

These things are purely pampering activities. Although they don't have as many therapeutic qualities as the previous methods, they are purely pleasurable and allow you to sit back and become beautiful. I have a tendency to not place much emphasis on my hands, feet or face, but when I push myself to get a manicure, pedicure or facial I feel prettier and develop an overall better self image. They aren't just for women anymore either. I see at least one man enjoying these luxuries every time I go to the salon. Men should take care of their hands and feet as much, if not more, than women. The more you use, or abuse, your hands and feet, the more you should take care of them.

Pedicures are my favorites. I didn't get my first manicure or pedicure until I was forty six years old. A student gave me a gift certificate for Christmas that year. At first I thought it sounded disgusting to have someone cleaning, clipping and fussing over my feet, but I wanted to use my certificate. Oh my gosh, was I wrong. After my first pedicure I was hooked. I try to use them as pampering time every now and then. If you've never had one, you must try it at least one time. Allow someone else to pamper you and make you more beautiful.

Reflexology

Reflexology is an extremely therapeutic, energetically based way to get pampered, feel relaxed, and recharge. It involves rubbing and applying pressure to the feet and hands as a way to heal the body. All the parts of your body, head, arms, torso, legs, organs and glands, have corresponding nerve pressure points and meridians on your hands and feet. As these points are stimulated, the nerves send messages to the body that activate healing, repair, or simply wake up stagnant energy. Although you can perform reflexology on yourself, it is much more enjoyable sitting back and letting someone else do it for you.

My Reflexologist, Sherry Gay, has a chair that vibrates to the sound and rhythm of the music she plays. You can use the headphone to block out the world and become completely enveloped in the music and touch, or you can chat with her while she works. To begin, she rubs oils on my hands and then puts them into a warm bean bag pouch. She will occasionally place warm rocks on various parts of my body to help stimulate the area.

Sherry starts massaging and rubbing my feet, then works a little on my legs. Sometimes I don't want to have the headphones on because she will tell me about my health issues as she works. She can tell me what areas have a decreased energy flow and which body parts may be malfunctioning, such as bladder, liver, lungs, hearts, etc. As she works on my feet, she also picks up on emotional, mental or physical disorders. When she finishes with my feet, she wraps them up to keep them warm and moves to my hands. She massages my hands and fingers and works with the energy flow throughout my arms. To finish, she gently stimulates and massages my scalp, head, ears, face, neck and back.

Reflexology is something I highly recommend as not only a pampering device, but a preventative health care method. You can feel energy shifting and moving throughout your body as the therapist works on you. It's wonderfully refreshing and relaxing.

These are a few of my favorites but there are many ways to pamper your self. The important thing is to make the time, schedule it in, and do it. Your body, mind, soul and general health will benefit immensely.

Pampering places you in the moment and allows you to feel and connect to your body, the earth, and the universe. It services and enhances all that is human and spiritual about you.

Chapter 39 Exercise #1
Make time to pamper yourself as soon as possible. Don't put it off.

Chapter 40

Energy Healers

    I think of Energy Workers and Alternative Health Care Providers as preventative maintenance. Most of the time people seek medical care after they already show symptoms of a problem with their health or body. If you regularly use energy healers as maintenance check ups, they will be able to diagnose a potential problem before it manifests into something serious and often before symptoms occur. This is because they address our health at not only the physical level but the mental, emotional and spiritual levels as well. Since our illnesses and pain stem from a combination of these aspects of our self, it is important, and mandatory, that our health care also addresses each of these areas. When a potential problem is diagnosed and treated, we eliminate the need to create illness, pain and serious health problems of any kind in order to deal with it physically.
    While western medicine has its place in providing us with certain health and healing issues, their approach is often at a more suppressive or symptomatic relief level. Broken bones or conditions that have manifested to such an extent that the need for more drastic measures is already warranted, still benefit greatly from the addition of energy work.
    Energy work can help the body prepare for surgery or recover from illness and surgery. For instance, if you break a bone you need to have it set and put in a cast. No energy worker can do this, however the body's healing ability can be intensified at a deeper level by the addition of energy work. Perhaps you need open heart surgery in order to get well. After the surgery it is still important to address the underlying cause of that illness in order to have complete healing at all levels.

Energy workers address underlying causes so that the physical healing can be permanent and complete. Their healing methods can be used alone or in combination with western medicine, but I strongly urge you to include them in your health care. When you support, maintain and maximize your health at the spiritual, mental, emotional, and energetic level, the need for western medicine diminishes. Your body won't have to create illness, pain and disease as a result, because you have diagnosed and treated yourself of the underlying cause.

For my own health care, I choose to use only natural and energetic approaches. I haven't been to a western medicine doctor in years. This doesn't mean I wouldn't go to a doctor if I felt it was needed. I will always be open to western medicine, but only as a last resort. I have found that if I continuously maintain my energy body, I don't have a need to see those doctors.

There are many types of energy healers. I suggest you try what feels right for you. Use your intuition, inner guidance, pendulum, yellow pages or the internet to decide which method is best for you. You will, and should, have your *own* personal favorites. The following is a list of the alternative healing methods I am familiar with. You may find others that I have not included and that does not mean they are not just as good or effective as those listed. While some of the following practitioners use a combination of different modalities, I will list them separately.

Acupressure	Acupuncture
Aromatherapy	Body Talk
Chiropractors	Craniosacral Therapy
Energy Workers	Flower Essence Therapy
Healing Touch	Herbalists
Homeopathy	Hyrdotherapy
Hypnotherapy	Kinesiology
Magnet Therapy	Massage Therapy
Myofascial Therapy	Naturopathy
Nutritionists	Qigong
Reflexology	Reiki
Shamanic Medicine	Shiatsu
Spiritual Healers	Therapeutic Touch

Chapter 40

If you are nervous about trying these types of healing methods, some more closely related to western medicine are the Holistic Physicians (M.D.) and the Osteopathic Doctors (D.O.). There are even many Holistic veterinary clinics available now for your animals.

Remember that your life is supposed to be as exciting, fulfilling and healthy as possible. This book has taught you a variety of things you can personally work on, but there's nothing wrong with getting additional help from others. We are all here to learn from each other and work with each other. Do not hesitate to ask someone else to help you if you are having difficulty handling a situation on your own. Be thankful that there are so many wonderful Earth Angels out there to do so.

The existence of mankind extends beyond the perceptions of our conscious mind and the matter of our physical world. Life's purpose unravels ever more as we become aware of the connection between body, mind and soul. We are but a tiny fragment of the universe in which we live, yet all the gifts of the universe are ours to explore, enjoy, and utilize.

Draw yourself out of your physical body and mind. Connect to the vastness of the universe and look down upon your life to see the truth within your soul, for it is your soul that will guide you to abundance, health and happiness. You have already chosen your destiny and path for this lifetime. Understanding your spiritual truth will unveil it for you. You are very special and your life is extremely important.

May God hold you in the palm of his hand and bless you as you take each step along the path of your life.

Suggested Reading Material

Although there are many wonderful books and talented authors to choose from, I have listed only a few of my favorites. You will feel drawn to books and authors as your own needs require. Do your own shopping and let your inner voice guide you to the books best suited to you. I truly believe the books you are meant to read will end up in your hands one way or another. You will be guided.

Staying in the Present Moment
The Power of Now, by Eckhart Tolle
Stillness Speaks, by Eckhart Tolle

Spirituality
Discover Your Spiritual Destiny, by Kim O'Neill
The Four Agreements, by Don Miguel Ruiz
Seat of the Soul, by Gary Zukav, Ph.D.
Pathways to the Soul, by Carlos Warter, MD. Ph.D.
The Seven Spiritual Laws of Success, by Deepak Chopra
Divine Prescriptions, by Doreen Virtue, Ph.D.

Developing your Psychic Abilities and Channeling
How to Talk With Your Angels, by Kim O'Neill
Discover Your Spiritual Destiny, by Kim O'Neill
Divine Guidance, by Doreen Virtue, Ph.D.
The Lightworker's Way, by Doreen Virtue, Ph.D.
Messages From Your Angels, by Doreen Virtue, Ph.D.

Angel Therapy, by Doreen Virtue, Ph.D.
The Book of Angels, by Sylvia Browne

Past Lives and Cell Memory
Past Lives Future Healing, by Sylvia Browne
How to Uncover Your Past Lives, by Ted Andrews

Self Healing
Spontaneous Healing, by Andrew Weil, M.D.
Sacred Contracts by Carolyn Myss
Why People Don't Heal and How They Can, by Carolyn Myss
You Can Heal Your Life, by Louise Hay
Heal Your Body, by Louise Hay
The Power Is Within You, by Louise Hay
I Can Do It, by Louise Hay
Peace, Love and Healing, by Bernie Segel, M.D.
Prescriptions for Living, by Bernie Segel, M.D.
The Power of Intention, by Dr. Wayne Dyer
Your Sacred Self, by Dr. Wayne Dyer

Energy Medicine
Energy Medicine, by Donna Eden
Light Emerging, by Barbara Ann Brennan
Hands of Light, by Barbara Ann Brennan
Instant Reflexology, by Rosalind Oxenford
Anatomy of the Spirit, by Carolyn Myss

Physical Healing
Spontaneous Healing, by Andrew Weil, M.D.
Natural Health, Natural Medicine, by Andrew Weil, M.D.

Rocks/Crystals
The Crystal Bible, by Judy Hall
Crystal Therapy, by Doreen Virtue, Ph.D.
Crystals and Gemstones, by Daya Sarai Chocron

Suggested Reading Material

Herbs and Homeopathy
Encyclopedia of Natural Medicine, by Michael Murray,
    N.D, and Joseph Pizzorno, N.D.
Earl Mindell's Herb Bible, by Earl Mindell, R.Ph., Ph.D.

Flower Essences
Heal Thyself, by Edward Bach, M.D.
Heal Yourself With Flowers, by Nikki Bradford
The Encyclopedia of Bach Flower Therapy,
    By Mechtild Scheffer

Essential Oils
Aromatherapy 101, by Karen Downes
Complete Book of Essential Oils and Aromatherapy,
    by Valerie Ann Worwood
Aromatherapy for Healing the Spirit, by Gabriel Mojay

Dowsing/Pendulums
Energy Therapy, by Sheila Hollingshead

Animal Totems
Animal Speak, by Ted Andrews
Animal Wisdom, by Susie Green

*If you would like to contact Jody Howard,
Please visit her website:*

www.InnerLightAwareness.homestead.com

or email her at

InnerLightAware@aol.com

Made in the USA
Lexington, KY
08 October 2018